POWERFUL TIMES

Praise for *Powerful Times*

"Eamonn Kelly's imagination is grave, prehensile, and informed by a splendid breadth of context. This is an absolutely fascinating book, and one I look forward to re-reading at the earliest opportunity."

—William Gibson, science fiction writer, author of
Neuromancer and *Pattern Recognition*

"The world is changing fast in ways we dimly comprehend. Eamonn Kelly provides us with the ideas to better understand what is going on. He lays out the dilemmas we face and hints at ways in which the global agenda might evolve. He is a master of the 'big picture.' This is must reading for those who need to know about the future of planet Earth."

—Ged Davis, managing director and head,
Centre for Strategic Insight, World Economic Forum

"This book is a wake-up call for all who may not recognize the powerful uncertainties that are shaping our future. Those of us in business will need to upgrade our skills to learn how to balance market and moral wisdom, and to move from our narrow focus on competition to embracing adaptiveness as well."

—Crawford Beveridge, senior vice president of people and places,
Sun Microsystems

"The world around us is a very confusing and complex place; making sense of where we are, let alone where we are headed, is fraught with uncertainty. In *Powerful Times*, Eamonn Kelly has given us a something far better than predictions that can be proven wrong. He has crafted an insightful map of the plausible landscapes unfolding in front of us, a map that enables us to navigate these surprising times. Kelly helps us to understand and prepare for the often contradictory and paradoxical cross currents shaping our future so that we are equipped to make better decisions today that will stand up to an uncertain tomorrow."

—Peter Schwartz, co-founder, Global Business Network;
author, *Inevitable Surprises*

"History is unleashed, the future is unwritten, and this is the best assessment of today's highly turbulent driving forces that you are likely to find anywhere. Reading Eamonn Kelly's book is like watching him break a kaleidoscope and number the bits."

—Bruce Sterling, science fiction writer (*Holy Fire, The Hacker Crackdown*);
Viridian design activist; *Wired* blogger

"I love this book; it is an easy and thought-provoking read. In a world seemingly torn by multiple uncertainties and tensions, *Powerful Times* sorts them out for us into a clear map of outcomes and consequences. And rather than dispense formulas—like so many business books—Kelly challenges us to think for ourselves about strategies we might not have otherwise imagined."

—Luis Jimenez, senior vice president and chief strategy officer, Pitney Bowes

"Eamonn Kelly's *Powerful Times* could as well have been called *The Art of the Wide View*. In times of great upheaval, he demonstrates, the critical skill for decision makers is to avoid being prisoner of one's expectations. Kelly shows us how to array our forces so as to be prepared not just for rose petals being strewn at our feet, but also road bombs. Kelly's profound lesson is that 'both/and' thinking is the only way to make hard decisions in the face of ambiguity and uncertainty."

—Joel Garreau, author of *Radical Evolution: The Promise and Peril of Enhancing Our Minds, Our Bodies—and What It Means to Be Human*

"Any company that bets on a single future is likely to be blindsided by events that fall outside their peripheral vision. Eamonn Kelly's insights will help organizations tune their peripheral vision, perhaps even see out the back of their heads, so they can anticipate the most lethal threats or take advantage of a currently hidden opportunity."

—Daniel Rasmus, director of information work vision, Microsoft; IT industry observer; former vice president of Forrester Research

"Kelly carries on the rich tradition of Global Business Network in raising the important questions that society, business, and government will be facing in the future. *Powerful Times* does a masterful job of framing these questions with a richly illustrated story of how the future is unfolding right before us."

—Andrew Hines, executive director, Association of Professional Futurists; lecturer in future studies, University of Houston

"In *Powerful Times*, the practical realities of scenario thinking instruct the reader from start to finish. Kelly's storytelling makes easy reading of the otherwise daunting realities of future challenges and proposes frameworks for the decisions we must make as individuals and corporations in a changing and interdependent world."

—Nancy Ramsey, author, *The Futures of Women*

"Anyone trying to anticipate the future—to seize the great investment opportunities or to dodge potentially enterprise-ending risks—should pay attention to Eamonn Kelly's insights, honed from years of scenario thinking on the world business stage. A distinguished futurist, Kelly has filled his canvas so richly that any perspective will gain from his explication of the global forces that envelop all human enterprise— from the impacts of India, China, and AIDS to the range of energy or meteorologic futures that could unfold from this moment forward. Kelly argues cogently that while continued wealth and prosperity are plausible, they are no one country's or region's manifest destiny."

—Eric Best, global scenario strategist, Morgan Stanley

POWERFUL TIMES

RISING TO THE CHALLENGE OF OUR UNCERTAIN WORLD

Eamonn Kelly

Ideas. Action. Impact.

Upper Saddle River, NJ • Boston• Indianapolis • San Francisco
New York • Toronto • Montreal • London • Munich • Paris • Madrid
Capetown • Sydney • Tokyo • Singapore • Mexico City

Kelly, Eamonn.
    Powerful times : rising to the challenge of our uncertain world / Eamonn Kelly
    p. cm.
    Includes bibliographical references.
    ISBN 0-13-36624-6 (hardback : alk. paper)
    1. Civilization, Modern--1950-   .   I. Title.
    CB428.K44 2005
    909.08--dc22
2005015071

Vice President, Editor-in-Chief: Tim Moore
Wharton Editor: Yoram (Jerry) Wind
Editorial Assistant: Susie Abraham
Marketing Manager: John Pierce
International Marketing Manager: Tim Galligan
Cover Designer: Chuti Prasertsith
Managing Editor: Gina Kanouse
Project Editor: Kayla Dugger
Copy Editor: Elise Walter
Indexer: Lisa Stumpf
Interior Designer: Michael Thurston
Senior Compositor: Specialized Composition, Inc.
Manufacturing Buyer: Dan Uhrig

©2006 by Pearson Education, Inc.
Publishing as Wharton School Publishing
Upper Saddle River, New Jersey 07458

Wharton School Publishing offers excellent discounts on this book when ordered in quantity for bulk purchases or special sales. For more information, please contact U.S. Corporate and Government Sales, 1-800-382-3419, corpsales@pearson-techgroup.com. For sales outside the U.S., please contact International Sales at international@pearsoned.com.

Company and product names mentioned herein are the trademarks or registered trademarks of their respective owners.

This product is printed digitally on demand.

First Printing

ISBN 0-131-36624-6

Pearson Education LTD.
Pearson Education Australia PTY, Limited.
Pearson Education Singapore, Pte. Ltd.
Pearson Education North Asia, Ltd.
Pearson Education Canada, Ltd.
Pearson Educatión de Mexico, S.A. de C.V.
Pearson Education—Japan
Pearson Education Malaysia, Pte. Ltd.

WHARTON SCHOOL PUBLISHING
Editorial Board

UNIVERSITY *of* PENNSYLVANIA

The Editorial Board of Wharton School Publishing is comprised of the following members from the senior faculty of the Wharton School. The Editorial Board ensures all manuscripts and materials meet Wharton's standard by addressing important topics with ideas and insights that are

- Relevant
- Timely
- Implementable in real decision settings
- Empirically based
- Conceptually sound

■ Dr. David C. Schmittlein
Ira A. Lipman Professor
Professor of Marketing
Deputy Dean, The Wharton School
Chair of the Editorial Board

■ Dr. Yoram (Jerry) Wind
The Lauder Professor, Professor of Marketing
Director, The Wharton Fellows
Director, SEI Center for Advanced Studies in Management

■ Dr. Franklin Allen
Nippon Life Professor of Finance
Professor of Economics
Co-Director, Financial Institutions Center

■ Dr. Peter Cappelli
George W. Taylor Professor of Management
Director, Center for Human Resources

■ Dr. Thomas Donaldson
Mark O. Winkelman Professor

■ Dr. Richard J. Herring
Jacob Safra Professor of International Banking
Professor of Finance
Co-Director, Financial Institutions Center

■ Dr. John C. Hershey
Daniel H. Silberberg Professor
Professor of Operations and Information Management

■ Dr. Paul R. Kleindorfer
Anheuser-Busch Professor of Management Science
Professor of Business and Public Policy
Co-Director, Risk Management and Decision Processes Center

■ Dr. Ian C. MacMillan
Fred R. Sullivan Professor
Professor of Management
Director, Sol C. Snider Entrepreneurial Research Center

■ Dr. Andrew Metrick
Associate Professor of Finance

■ Dr. Olivia S. Mitchell
International Foundation of Employee Benefit Plans Professor
Professor of Insurance and Risk Management and Business and Public Policy
Executive Director, Pension Research Council
Director, Boettner Center for Pensions and Retirement Research

■ Dr. David J. Reibstein
William Stewart Woodside Professor
Professor of Marketing

■ Kenneth L. Shropshire
David W. Hauck Professor
Professor of Legal Studies

■ Dr. Harbir Singh
Edward H. Bowman Professor of Management
Co-Director, Mack Center for Technological Innovation

■ Dr. Michael Useem
The William and Jacalyn Egan Professor
Professor of Management
Director, Center for Leadership and Change Management

Management Committee

■ Barbara Gydé
Managing Director, Wharton School Publishing
Director of Advertising Strategy, The Wharton School

■ Mukul Pandya
Contributing Editor, Wharton School Publishing
Editor and Director, Knowledge@Wharton

■ John Pierce
Vice President, Director of Marketing
Wharton School Publishing, Financial Times Prentice Hall, and Prentice Hall Business

■ Timothy C. Moore
Vice President, Editor-in-Chief
Wharton School Publishing, Financial Times Prentice Hall, and Prentice Hall Business

■ Dr. Yoram (Jerry) Wind
Wharton Editor

With love and gratitude to my wife, Rita;
my children, Adam, Sam, and Leona;
and my parents, Anne and Edward

Contents

Acknowledgments

This book draws heavily upon much that I have learned from the remarkable community that is Global Business Network, a consultancy dedicated to helping organizations of all sorts master the uncertainty of our complicated era. To all of our members, clients, and staff, I am deeply indebted. Special thanks go to the founders and key members of this intellectual explorers club: Peter Schwartz, Napier Collyns, Stewart Brand, Jay Ogilvy, Lawrence Wilkinson, Kees van der Heijden, Steve Weber, Kevin Kelly, Hardin Tibbs, Eric Best, Katherine Fulton, Joel Garreau, Chris Ertel, Doug Randall, Erik Smith, Jesse Goldhammer, Rebecca Wayland, Andrew Blau, Pete Leyden, Lisa Solomon, Don Derosby, Lynn Carruthers, Diana Scearce, Gerald Harris, Susan Stickley, Art Kleiner, Jaron Lanier, and Chris Riley. Since 2001, when GBN became part of the Monitor Group, I have been blessed with new conversation partners who have also been influential, including Jim Cutler, Alan Kantrow, Mark Fuller, and a host of extraordinary new colleagues from whom I learn every day.

To several friends and thought partners I am particularly grateful. Jonathan Star helped me greatly as I started to wrestle with the concept and sheer scope of the "both/and" dynamic tensions and the hard task of getting focus on what matters most. Jonathan's help in developing the frameworks for this book and organizing my research was invaluable. Graham Leicester helped me at the critical stage of turning too many frameworks and ideas into a single book, challenged me to articulate half-baked thoughts into useful ones, and supported my efforts to flesh these out better than I alone could have achieved. Jamais Cascio helped me iterate and craft the scenarios; he is a gifted writer without whose help the scenario vignettes would lack their art. (Jamais is also a founder of one of the best blogs you could hope to read, worldchanging.com—please visit it.)

Acknowledgements

Assistance with research and editing at various stages was provided with outstanding professionalism by a variety of people: development editor Russ Hall, my colleagues Jenny Collins and Laura Likely, the brilliant researchers Courtney Gomez, Joe McCrossen, Tina Estes, Chris Coldewey, Victor Chang, and Erica Bjornsson. Kelly Kauffman brought facts to life through her visual skills. Julia Cashin lent her considerable organizational talents to various stages of the project. And Jeanne Scheppach secured a startling array of permissions faster and more efficiently than I dared hope. Thank you all!

Three other people stand alone. Tim Moore, editor-in-chief, Wharton School Publishing, FT Prentice Hall, saw the potential in this book and supported it with an energy, confidence, and humor that I will always remember and appreciate—and in the process moved swiftly from editor to adviser to friend. Jenny Johnston is an editor without parallel in my experience, who improved this book in so many ways—helping me to find my voice, forcing me to address structural weaknesses, removing my superfluous words, improving the illuminating examples, checking facts and finding better ones. Nancy Murphy, the connector who holds so much of Global Business Network together, wanted more than anyone to see this book become a reality. It is largely because of her tireless commitment, involvement, professionalism, and support that it has.

Finally, if it is possible to hold down a demanding job, write a fairly complex book, and be fully present for one's family—then this is a trick that I have as yet failed to master. Love and thanks to my wife Rita and children Adam, Sam, and Leona, and apologies for my too frequent absences (even when I was at home). It is your presence in my life that fuels and sustains my passion for the better future I am convinced we can and will forge.

About the Author

Eamonn Kelly is the CEO of Global Business Network (GBN), the renowned futures network and scenario strategy consultancy, and a partner of the Monitor Group. For over a decade, he has been at the forefront of exploring the emergence of a new economic, social, and geopolitical order and its far-reaching consequences for organizations and individuals. Kelly has developed insights, tools, and methodologies for mastering uncertainty and has consulted at senior levels to dozens of the world's leading corporations, governmental agencies, and major philanthropic organizations. Kelly co-authored *What's Next: Exploring the New Terrain for Business* (2002) and *The Future of the Knowledge Economy* (1999).

Preface

We humans are truly remarkable. We have, so quickly, taken such commanding control of our planet, developed such powerful sciences and technologies, and assumed such profound and audacious responsibility for our own destiny. Yet for all our ambitious and aspiring ways, we have not, in our essence, moved so very far from our ancestry. While capable of incredible sophistication of thought and discovery, we still desire clear, compelling stories to make sense of our world. We still crave certainty and simplicity and shy away from complexity and ambiguity. We still tend to default, whenever we can, to black-and-white, "either/or" logics that allow us to discern neat patterns and construct comfortable worldviews. We still appear to be motivated primarily by the primitive dual forces of love and fear, and we still, for the most part, fear "the other"—the unknown, the strange, the distant.

Today, there is growing dissonance between the dynamic and uncertain world that we have created for ourselves and our instinctive preferred postures toward that world. We lack a shared story of our times. Instead, we live with many critical but disconnected storylines (globalization, war, materialism, fundamentalism, dotcom bubbles, terrorism, decline of multilateralism, economic growth, rise of China, agony of Africa, climate change, and so on) that are incoherent at best and hazy, flickering, and out of focus at worst. Our world is increasingly complex and confusing, a crazy kaleidoscope of important but ambiguous dynamics from the worlds of politics, technology, economics, and culture—all amplified, but not necessarily clarified, by a ubiquitous yet partial global media. As incorrigible meaning-makers, we are compelled to identify patterns in the messiness. But the signals we extract from the white noise of daily events often appear mutually incompatible and even paradoxical. And yet our world is so transparently interdependent, our economies so integrated, our boundaries so permeable, distance so diminished, that increasingly there is no "other" to fear, reject, or hold at arm's length. There is only an emergent "we" that we have yet to come to know and understand, let alone trust and love.

The world, then, is increasingly messy, complex, and interconnected—and it is also increasingly volatile. It has been obvious for more than a decade that we live in an age of change; today, it appears that we are also living through a *change of age*. In the decade ahead, the collective choices and actions of people, businesses, organizations, and governments everywhere will likely define and shape global civilization for the next generation and beyond.

These are indeed powerful times, and they will demand an openness of mind and of heart that does not come readily. Our times demand that we adopt a powerful orientation toward learning, experimentation, and discovery that will require us to acknowledge uncertainty and embrace ambiguity—even as our impulse is to seek comfort in certainty and adhere to a set of familiar convictions, assumptions, and beliefs that provide us with a reassuring true north. Our times demand that we make diversity and multiplicity a virtue, that we bridge divides, make connections, and find alignments and points of commonality—even as our differences frighten us, our ideologies polarize us, and our enemies enrage us (and this is as true within countries and regions as it is between them). Our times demand that we think long term, imagine the futures that we may be creating today, and prepare for the challenges and opportunities of tomorrow. Yet how can we possibly try to make sense of the future when the present is so profoundly perplexing?

Can we, then, really rise to the demands of our powerful times? I am deeply hopeful that we can. Since the late 1990s, I have enjoyed the privilege of leading a unique organization that is dedicated to exploring our changing world and anticipating the futures that may await us—and that we can collectively act to create. Global Business Network, a Monitor Group company, was founded close to 20 years ago as an unique new networked business. Part consulting firm, part think tank, it is a pragmatic learning community that includes future-oriented strategists, business leaders, public servants from the world of governance and intelligence, educators, and executives from nonprofit and philanthropic organizations, combined with a network of deep, wise, independent thinkers and visionaries from the sciences, the arts, and academia. Believers in the necessity of diverse perspectives, we have deliberately chosen to work with a fantastic array of organizations—from global corporations to community colleges, from large government agencies to small nonprofit organizations, from philanthropic foundations to global institutions. Our work with them all is exploratory yet practical. It is aimed at helping our clients make better sense of the world they inhabit; think afresh about the multiple possible futures they might face (and are also helping to shape); gain new insight into what they must track, observe, and understand better over time; and, above all, make wiser decisions and take better actions to ensure their own success while contributing to a better future for us all.

My colleagues and I are repeatedly humbled by the people, teams, and organizations that we support. We have learned, again and again, that in every organization, every community, and every network there are people with the passion, energy, talent, and humanity to make a true difference. They are people who seek out the big picture, imagine the future, create meaning, and figure out ways to both succeed and contribute over the long term. They are able to acknowledge, explore, and understand uncertainty without being forced into denial or overwhelmed by paralysis. They are open to alternative perspectives, opinions, and beliefs, however uncomfortable that sometimes can be. Sometimes they are senior leaders with the power to make decisions and set directions. Sometimes they are acknowledged thought leaders—designated explorers with voice and credibility. Sometimes they are regarded as idealists, even heretics. Yet they all share three characteristics: a belief that the world is changing in critically important ways, a conviction that there are ways of making better sense of those changes, and the confidence to embark upon a difficult journey with no clear destination or endpoint.

It is this group of people—this type of person—who inspired this book. They are, to borrow a nature metaphor, the "scout bees" among us. In every hive, there are scouts whose job it is to discover new sources of pollen. They set out for new pastures, and when they discover a promising area, they return to the hive and perform an intricate dance that signals to others the direction and distance to the new harvest. These scouts play a critical role as explorers and providers of new knowledge and new direction; without their constant searching and steady perseverance, the hive could not live, let alone thrive. There are always a small number of scouts who, sadly, cannot dance well, and end up sending their fellows on an unknown path—until they, too, eventually and inevitably find new pollen. Even these inaccurate explorers, then, serve as a source of hope, renewal, and new discovery.

This book is for all of the "scout bees" of the human world—those explorers who find it their calling to seek, on behalf of us all, a better future. I hope it makes a modest contribution to strengthening your wings, animating your dance, refreshing your optimism, framing your insights, and, above all, helping you make a difference in the world.

Using This Book in Your Life and Work

In *Powerful Times*, I have set out some frameworks that have proved extremely useful for my own thinking and learning about our volatile world. I have populated these frameworks with information and ideas that I consider highly important. But learning only becomes embedded and useful when it is made immediately relevant and specific to your own context.

Therefore, I hope that you will find it helpful to reflect on how the content of this book relates to you and your organization. To facilitate your thinking about this, the Afterword provided at the end of the book poses a series of questions about each of the main chapters, which might help structure your ideas and insights. You can turn to these pages as you read *Powerful Times* to make notes, or simply review the questions after you have finished reading the book. I hope that you might also be interested in using this book as a catalyst for strategic conversation within your team or organization. And I hope that many of you will share your ideas on the *Powerful Times* website—**http://www.powerfultimes.net**—a place where we can explore the future together over time. I look forward to meeting you there.

Chapter 1

History Unleashed

And the end of all our exploring will be to arrive where we
started and know the place for the first time.
—T. S. Eliot

Five hundred years ago, Niccolo Machiavelli, the Second Chancellor of
Florence, was asked by the city's ruling council to investigate why
Pandolfo Petrucci, the Lord of neighboring Siena, was so inconstant in his
behavior and so prone to intrigue. Machiavelli was deeply impressed by
Petrucci's explanation: "Wishing to make as few mistakes as possible, I
conduct my government day by day and arrange my affairs hour by hour,
because the times are more powerful than our brains."

"The times are more powerful than our brains." The phrase is remarkably resonant today, in these early years of the third millennium. We find
ourselves in a period of unprecedented complexity. The world is changing
at an astonishing rate. The entire planet is interconnected in ways that it
has never been before. It is hard to make sense of what happens in our
world in a single day, let alone what it means for tomorrow. Individually
and collectively, our uncertainty about the future—indeed, even the
present—is mounting. History is truly in motion, unfolding before us at
a pace we can barely keep up with, leaving us to wonder and worry about
what will come next.

Each month brings new drama and fresh ambiguity. Are we descend-
ing down a path toward geopolitical instability and fractured alliances
or are we stamping out an era of terror before it takes root? Is the
United States fulfilling its role as the lone superpower with humility and

judgment that will be applauded in the years ahead, or is it becoming a rogue superpower, increasingly resented across the world? Does the United Nations have a meaningful future in global affairs, or is it slipping into irrelevance? Can China maintain its extraordinary growth as a major global power, or will internal political, social, and economic tensions derail its progress? Is the global economy robust or fragile? Will technology standards globalize and converge or regionalize and fragment? Will global protection of intellectual property rights tighten or loosen? Can free trade prevail over protectionist instincts? Can developed nations continue to generate jobs for their populations as waves of economic progress and success wash over the developing world? Is declining trust and confidence in corporations a passing phase occasioned by disparate scandals or evidence of mounting pushback against the growing power of the global marketplace? Was SARS an isolated incident or a harbinger of new plagues to come? Is global warming "much ado about nothing" or our dreadful legacy to future generations? These are difficult questions because they force us to identify and challenge some of our most basic and embedded assumptions about how the world works and how it will continue to work in the future. But *not* challenging these assumptions is dangerous business. Why? Because how the world has worked in the past will not carry over into the future. Much of what we take for granted today, based on centuries of experience and history, might be in the process of unraveling.

Five Centuries of History Coming Undone

The roots of the future are buried deep in the past; so are our assumptions about the way the world is meant to be. Perhaps the greatest cognitive barrier we face in making sense of the world is that we have come to view certain realities as part of a "natural order" that will remain unchallenged. In fact, many "fundamental truths" that we take for granted are simply the fragile constructs of history and could shift radically in the decade ahead. We are at a critical threshold in which much that has been established during the last five centuries may significantly change, and with remarkable speed. A quick tour through these centuries reveals just how much is poised to change.

At the dawn of the sixteenth century, when Petrucci so presciently spoke of powerful times, there were 300 million people on the planet (less than 5 percent of our current population) and Europe's "scientific revolution" was well underway. Led by figures like Leonardo da Vinci and Nicolaus Copernicus, this revolution drew heavily upon Chinese and, particularly, Islamic knowledge in mathematics, medicine, astronomy, and experimental scientific methods, fields that these ancient civilizations had pioneered and refined. But the breakthroughs of this period shifted the center of gravity, establishing the West as supreme in the understanding and innovation of science and technology, a status it continues to maintain. This created an unconscious sense of entitlement that Western models and approaches—even its civilization—should prevail over the rest of the world. Such expectations are in for a harsh reality check as China, India, and other non-Western nations emerge as true powers in their own right, poised to develop and export innovations back to the West.

In the seventeenth century, following decades of wrenching religious war, much of central Europe lay devastated. The cost in blood and treasury had been staggering; some regions lost almost half their populations and saw their economies crippled. Exhausted, the great powers sued for peace. In 1648, they forged the Treaty of Westphalia, heralding a new order of European nations. The importance of the nation-state has underpinned all subsequent centuries of European and world history, creating modern states committed to achieving peace (not always successfully) and prosperity for their citizens and willing to accept shared accords as a means of moderating their behavior toward one another. We have come to think of the nation state as the natural level and form of governance.

Yet in our connected and interdependent modern world, it is time to question whether that should still be true. Economies are no longer "national" in character. Growth in global trade has been outstripping growth in global GDP for many decades. Likewise, most major businesses and institutions have a distinctly international character. Our greatest challenges—terrorism, environmental problems, infectious diseases—observe no borders. Nongovernmental organizations are increasingly important and are often either very local or transcend national boundaries. Given these changing circumstances, can and should the concept of the nation state remain as central to our identities and governance systems as it has in the past? In the coming decade, the concept and importance of the nation state will be challenged as new entities and experiments emerge.

By the latter half of the eighteenth century, the Enlightenment had arrived—a remarkable period that invigorated science and reason and led to new understandings and attitudes about society, human nature, governance, and commerce. The enlightenment revolutions in the U.S. and France challenged the right of old monarchies and aristocracies to rule and helped establish the modernist principles of freedom, justice, and democracy that became the ideals of Western civilization. With the explicit separation of church and state and the assumed dominion of man over nature, a new, secular, and materialist modernity was forged—and has largely prevailed ever since.

For 200 years, it appeared that as education and prosperity increased, the "sacred" worldview—one that goes beyond the material and embraces the spiritual—would inevitably decline. That is no longer the case; the sacred is clearly back, and in many forms. Witness the resurgent evangelical and fundamentalist Christian movements in the U.S., the astonishing growth in Pentecostalism globally, the widespread resurrection of religious practice in many parts of the former Soviet Union, the rise of radical fundamentalism within Islam, the spread of Eastern religious traditions throughout the West, the growing tendency for indigenous people to reconnect with their own traditional spirit-based cultures, and the mushrooming of "New Age" spirituality practices among the world's affluent. Secular modernity now has sacred company, adding to the complexity of our times.

In the mid-nineteenth century, at the opening of the first Great Exhibition in London, Britain's Prince Albert gushed, "We are living in a period of most wonderful transitions, which tend rapidly to accomplish that great end to which indeed all history points—the realization of the unity of mankind." Hyperbolic, certainly, but his sentiment was not entirely ridiculous. This was the century in which, for the first time in human history, a single powerful empire was setting many of the global rules, especially the rules of economics and trade by which others had to learn to play. By the latter part of the century, the U.S. was limbering up for its turn as the defining global superpower. Since then, with the economic triumph of the Western capitalist model over the communist experiment, it is reasonable to argue that Great Britain and the U.S. together have largely established the rules that almost every nation in the world must follow today.

But that is now changing. New powers are emerging—powers that may refuse to play by rules that were set to the advantage of others. In particular, the West has more highly evolved notions of ownership and property rights than much of the rest of the world, and it has aggressively transferred these concepts, created in the physical world, into the intangible world of ideas and intellectual property. Several of the largest countries—notably China and Brazil—may change these rules. Already, they are challenging Western notions of intellectual property rights and embracing open source approaches in their efforts to generate new knowledge and technologies. Some of our most basic assumptions about the rules of the global economic game will increasingly come under attack in the coming decade.

Fast forward to the twentieth century, arguably the most remarkable to date, during which we became accustomed to astonishing economic growth and rising prosperity. The population increased sixfold to 6 billion people; per capita GDP climbed from a few hundred dollars to $8,000. Indeed, any developed economy that was not enjoying around 3 percent annual growth in GDP was considered "weak," and any business that could not confidently predict double-digit annual growth rates was a poor investment. The concept of accelerating and compounded growth became ingrained in our expectations as we witnessed the economic output of this single century surpass that of all prior human history combined. Yet with prosperity also came greater polarization. The "haves" became increasingly separated from the "have nots" of the world. The very economic and technological dynamism that spurred prosperity also brought industrial restructuring and adjustments that were experienced unequally across regions and occupations; even in the most developed countries, many suffered from the friction burns associated with rapid change. Probably more challenging still, our prosperity was achieved at an environmental cost that we are only now beginning to appreciate. The evidence is clear that our human economy has triggered profound changes in climate, created a voracious appetite for scarce resources, and despoiled the natural environment. While we can expect to witness the continued rapid spread of prosperity in the decade ahead, we should also be prepared for much deeper concern about and attention to the critical issues of equity, transition, and sustainability. Different parts of the world will adopt different perspectives on these challenges, which will become a growing source of geopolitical tension.

In our fledgling twenty-first century, we can already see unique challenges on the horizon. Underpinning progress throughout the last five centuries has been a deep and widely shared confidence that the power of science and technology can be harnessed for human benefit. The fact that there are now about 15 times more humans alive than there were in 1500 and that there has been a 50-fold increase in GDP per capita is primarily a function of our remarkable and accelerating technological progress. But already in the twenty-first century we can observe a level of anxiety and concern about the potential downsides of technology that far exceeds the pushback and caution witnessed during previous eras. With its capacity to re-create nature and even change what it means to be human—steroids and stem cells are barely the tip of the iceberg—science is now confronting us with moral dilemmas and profound choices that will require deeper global dialogue and greater systemic thinking than we have ever achieved.

As we move into the future, not only will we see history being made—we will see it unmade as well. Five hundred years ago, Pandolfo Petrucci recognized that history was speeding up toward an unfathomable new complexity and bemoaned that "the times are more powerful than our brains." Today, as the "natural order" that evolved over the last five centuries starts to unravel, the times are more powerful than ever. So should we, like Petrucci, adopt a reactive strategy of taking things as they come, adapting as we go, arranging things day by day? I am convinced that we should not. The stakes are too high: our era is too complex, its challenges too significant, its promises too great, and its velocity too fast for us simply to react. Rather, we must amplify the power of our brains, individually and collectively, to match our new circumstances.

It is this challenge—the challenge of learning how to think proactively about our present world, to make sense of its intricacies and interconnections, to see the "big picture" rather than a thousand smaller unconnected images flickering in and out of view—that inspired this book. I wrote *Powerful Times* in direct response to the growing need of ever more people to understand the present and better anticipate the future—a need that I encounter every day in my work with organizations and governments around the world. My aim is to help us all to see patterns where before we saw chaos and to give us the tools and imagination to think for ourselves about how the future might play itself out.

The lucky news is that we have never, as a planet, been more equipped to make sense out of utter complexity. We have greater access to data and information about both our challenges and opportunities than ever before. We have new means of sharing our knowledge, our ideas, our insights, our perspectives. Above all, we have a thirst for knowledge and understanding—a desire to make sense of the world and anticipate where it is headed. But before we can dive into the task of seeing the "big picture" in fresh light, we must first consider why we haven't seen it already.

Gobbledygook and the Gorilla

Humans are sense-making creatures. We love patterns and are remarkably adept at recognizing them, even unconsciously. Consider the following gobbledygook. This series of sentences recently made the rounds through the world's email inboxes:

> Aoccdrnig to a rscheearch at Cambrigde Uinervtisy, it deosn't mttaer in waht oredr the ltteers in a wrod are, the olny iprmoetnt tihng is that the frist and lsat ltteer be at the rghit pclae.

> The rset can be a total mses and you can sitll raed it wouthit porbelm.

> Tihs is bcuseae the huamn mnid deos not raed ervey lteter by istlef, but the wrod as a wlohe.

> Amzanig huh?

Our powers of perception manifest themselves in myriad ways. Many people have outstanding instincts. They are able, for example, to sense imminent dangers, read the moods of crowds, or detect when others are lying or telling the truth, all from very subtle clues. Most people can quickly construct coherent narratives that link and explain seemingly disparate facts. We are typically good at spotting anomalies—things that don't fit our understood patterns and structures—and figuring out what they might mean. These are fundamental human skills, and for millennia they have been applied effectively to increasingly complex systems and phenomena, enabling the incredible development of human knowledge and understanding.

Yet we are also capable of spectacular misinterpretation of what is happening around us. We are often victims of severe cognitive challenges that inhibit the power of our perceptions. One of the greatest of these has to do with focus: we miss important changes simply by focusing our attention too narrowly. An example from my own experience illustrates this nicely. For several years, I have commenced many speeches and workshops by showing a 30-second video in which six people are playing with two basketballs. Three are wearing white t-shirts; the other three are wearing black. Each "team" has its own basketball, which it passes only among its members.

Before starting the video, I tell the audience that their task is to count how many successful passes the white team completes. I make a fuss about defining what constitutes a "successful pass"—a ball moving from the hands of one player to the hands of another, either through the air or off the floor. Often I introduce an element of competition, instructing participants to share their answers with others at their table and agree on a number, and telling them that the table that comes closest to the right answer will be rewarded.

After running the video and hearing their answers, I ask if anyone noticed anything strange on the screen. Typically, a very small number of people (seldom more than 10 percent and never more than 20 percent) observed something unusual. What they saw, halfway through, was that someone dressed in a gorilla suit entered the frame, walked center stage, stopped, faced front, and dramatically beat his chest several times before sauntering off-screen again. It is so startlingly obvious when you watch the video the second time (without the distraction of counting passes) that no one can believe they missed it. On one occasion, I ran the exercise with 40 senior corporate executives and *none* of them saw the gorilla. Indeed, they emphatically accused me of playing a different video the second time.

The point of this story is that we often see only what we are looking for and are readily distracted from observing what should be fairly obvious. If we keep our focus narrow, we will probably not notice the big picture. But in a world of unexpected and radical changes, we will need to widen our lenses in order to make sense of our unfolding, and often surprising, reality.

Mental Maps and Paradoxical Certainties

There are numerous other constraints on our sense-making capabilities— indeed, there are close to 100 known forms of cognitive bias that can severely skew our perceptions and understanding of the world around us. Some of these become deeply embedded. My colleague Peter Schwartz, a renowned futurist and one of the founders of Global Business Network, has in his office an original map of North America, made by Dutch cartographer Herman Moll in 1701. Based on reports from Spanish explorers, Moll, like other mapmakers of the seventeenth and eighteenth centuries, depicted California as an island, with a wide gulf separating it from the remainder of the continent. These erroneous maps are now collectors' items, but otherwise they are mere historical curiosities. Yet they confirm two important points about the power of maps.

The first is that faulty maps lead to faulty actions. The maps showing California as an island were carried by missionaries on their journeys to the New World. When they landed near today's Monterey, they disassembled their boats, packed them on mules, and hauled them across California and up and over the Sierra Nevada mountains. It was only then, looking out upon the vast "beach" before them, that they realized their plight: there was no sea, the maps were wrong, their boats were useless, and their labors had been for naught. The second point is that it takes considerable force of will to change maps after they have been created. Reports from missionaries that California was not, in fact, an island came back to Europe for decades, yet many mapmakers refused to change their maps until compelled to do so by an edict from the king of Spain in 1747.

This story holds important insight for us today as we wrestle with an uncertain and accelerating world. Every decision we make—in business, in government, in our personal lives—plays out over time and is influenced by knowledge (based primarily on our known facts and experience) and judgment (based primarily on our perceptions, or "mental maps"). If our maps are wrong, our judgment will be wrong. Worse, even our knowledge is heavily influenced by our mental maps. These maps not only reflect how we see things, but also profoundly influence what things we see, the facts we choose to gather. Our mental maps, then, act as powerful filters. They can help us make sense and meaning but can also serve to inhibit our ability to perceive and understand what is happening in the world. And they are extremely resistant to change. Indeed, by framing what we observe and then how we interpret what we observe, they so influence our perceptions as to become tacitly self-reinforcing devices.

It is therefore essential that we learn how to put our mental maps under pressure, make our assumptions more explicit, test them assiduously, and open our minds to additional, different, and challenging possibilities. Few of us would argue with that. Yet as the world around us becomes increasingly ambiguous and uncertain, we often lean in the opposite direction, defaulting toward firmly held and quite polarized convictions about the shape and fate of the world. The "either/or" logic that works so well for politicians, media pundits, and even some academics results all too often in heated but uninformative "either/or" debates: globalization is good or bad; the Middle East is hungry and ripe for change or it is a dangerous and backward-looking threat; the U.S. has a sacred duty to promote and enable democracy globally or it is a nation on a collision course with history; genetic engineering will feed and cure us or it will inadvertently destroy us.

While such debates provide good theatre and may even be comforting in their simplistic certainties, they are unhelpful and, I believe, increasingly dangerous. They generate noise and heat from which it is hard to extract signals and light. They encourage overly simplistic and formulaic thinking. They distract us from understanding the deep patterns of the recent past and present—an understanding that can help us anticipate what lies ahead. They appeal to our laziest instincts, not our aspirational capacities. Simplicity, clarity, and certainty are undoubtedly virtues, but they are hard won. "I would not give a fig for the simplicity this side of complexity," Oliver Wendell Holmes once remarked, "but I would give my life for the simplicity on the other side of complexity."

Simplicity on the wrong side of complexity appears to be running rife in public discourse today, especially in the sphere of popular politics. Enter any bookstore in the U.S. and observe the remarkable array of shrill and partial books that appear to decry all liberals "traitors" and all conservatives "liars." In truth, few of us are entirely immune from knee-jerk, biased, and overly simplistic framing of the world; we all have our mental maps. Consider how you react to the following two competing stories of our world today, and what your reactions reveal about your own biases.

THE BEST OF TIMES...

We are blessed to live in an era of unprecedented opportunity and potential. Prosperity is growing and flowing around the globe, with literally billions of the hitherto impoverished achieving decent income levels.

China, India, Indonesia, much of Eastern Europe—the list goes on—are enjoying staggering levels of economic growth and becoming fully integrated into the global economic mainstream. Educational opportunities are reaching more and more children with each new generation; adult literacy has risen to 74 percent globally, while in most of the developed world tertiary education has become the norm.

The end of the Cold War enabled the rise of many new democracies, while the number of totalitarian states has declined dramatically over the last 20 years. The collapse of rigid, centrally planned economies has brought wealth and opportunity to many countries previously hampered by allegiance to a defunct ideology. The dismantling of the former Soviet Union has led dynamic countries to emerge and to participate in the remarkable new European experiment in governance. Moreover, the end of the defining ideological tussle of the twentieth century has allowed many nations to cash in a sizable "peace dividend." For the most part, the world has continued to enjoy an era of relative peace; outside of Africa, there are fewer victims of war per head of population than at any other time in the last thousand years. The U.S. has by far the greatest military strength in the world and, while not yet fully grown into its role as lone superpower, has an established record of responsibility and fairness in its deployment of strength and power.

People are living longer; the average life span is now 67 years. Infant mortality has declined to 5.6 percent globally. With birth rates falling in more and more countries, we can now anticipate the imminent end of the "population explosion." Breakthroughs in the production and distribution of food are making a serious dent in world hunger. Meanwhile, many diseases are falling to the power of science; even AIDS, so recently a formidable and fearsome killer, can now be tamed by a potent drug cocktail. And the mapping of the human genome and innovations in biotechnology hold enormous promise for the future health—even enhancement—of much of humanity.

New information and communication technologies are connecting people, places, markets, capital, ideas, and cultures as never before, creating a new economic platform along with truly global opportunities for human well-being and wealth creation. More broadly, our global knowledge base continues to grow and integrate, drawing upon evolving scientific knowledge and unprecedented discovery processes informed by spectacular new technologies and tools. These expanding knowledge assets provide us with a reliable source for the transformative technologies of the future. In particular, with wise investment in alternative energy technologies, we stand to reduce significantly the world's dependence on fossil fuels, with all their corollary pollution challenges.

If we can hold our course for the next decade or so, the longer-term future looks bright indeed…

THE WORST OF TIMES…

Our tragic species, doomed by its own arrogance and constant dissatisfied striving, stands ready to reap the catastrophic harvest it has been mindlessly sowing for centuries. In our hunger to consume and "prosper," we have wrought economic havoc on our environment and our communities. The market-based values that we embraced have empowered amoral corporations to set the agenda of our times. We have been driven by simplistic metrics of progress that overemphasize the material and deny the spiritual and the human.

And what have we gained? A third of the world's population subsists on less than a dollar a day; this is less than the public subsidy for every head of cattle in Europe. We have failed to support deteriorating and disorderly states around the world whose people suffer disproportionately from disease, starvation, and premature death. We have allowed the gap between rich and poor, between the "haves" and the "have nots," to increase apace—even in that promised land of plenty, the U.S. We have permitted the once robust infrastructure of the developed world to begin to crumble, from the railways of Britain to the electric grid of the U.S. And we have failed to invest adequately in the essential life-supporting infrastructures for the emergent world. We have allowed squalid conditions to breed virulent versions of once controlled diseases, leading to fear of a "post-antibiotic" world. We have enforced intellectual property rights that protect the interests of drug manufacturers over the needs of the poor, including too many of the many millions afflicted by, and still dying of, AIDS.

We play with the fire of new technologies, especially those relating to the redesign of nature through biotechnology—a tinkering with the essence of life that carries risks we cannot calculate because we do not understand them. We espouse secular governance while observing—and too often pandering to—fundamentalism in every major religion. The lone superpower of our era, the U.S., has abandoned multilateralism and alienated its friends, and its attempts to strike down its enemies have instead multiplied and energized them. Terrorist outrages, including the more apocalyptic threats of bioterrorism and dirty bombs, not to mention full nuclear threats, seem more imminent every day. Meanwhile, we despoil and take for granted the planet that is our only home and watch in denial as changes in the climate, many of which we prompted, threaten its stability.

Perhaps worst of all, we are disabled in our capacity to understand and address these matters. We can no longer readily separate truth from fiction, reality from spin, substance from presentation. The World Wide Web is proving to be a source of as much confusion, distortion, and conspiracy as insight and understanding.

In this foolish age, incredulity is the only rational stance—other than anger, frustration, and despair…

I suspect that both of these versions of our current reality would find plenty of supporters if put to a vote. Indeed, even more extreme versions of both stories are being told every day around the world. Both are essentially true sketches of our times—which, of course, is exactly the point. The world we live in does not follow a single, easy storyline, and neither will our future. This ambiguity may be deeply uncomfortable, but it is nonetheless real. The more strongly we hold our own particular beliefs in an attempt to make coherent sense of the world, the less sense, paradoxically, we are able to make. Above all, neither blind optimism nor defeatist pessimism will prove an effective posture for any of us in the complex future ahead.

Making Sense of a Transformative Era

This book, then, is intended to be a useful resource for those seeking to make better sense of our powerful times. Its premises are based on several convictions.

First, the world has never been certain. Humanity has experienced great shifts and rifts, profound anxieties, and deep confusion many times throughout its history, as Petrucci's observation confirms. Yet the world—the entire world—has surely never been more uncertain. As our systems—technological, financial, social, economic, cultural, and political—become more complex, more global, more interdependent, and develop at an accelerating pace, increasing (and increasingly widespread) uncertainty is an inevitable and ongoing consequence.

Second, much of this uncertainty is clearly visible—the stuff of the daily news, the issues and questions we wrestle with constantly in our personal and professional lives. But there are also less apparent but deep and fundamental dynamics at work, and we may currently be witnessing nothing less than the significant unraveling of much that we have come to take for granted over the last five centuries. If so, we are not at all well prepared for the transformations ahead.

Third, the changes that are currently underway are not only complex and systemic—they are also paradoxical and contradictory, which makes them much harder to perceive and interpret. This is greatly compounded by the fact that individuals and organizations have strong cognitive biases (including a tendency to oversimplify) that seriously impede our ability to observe and make sense of change.

Fourth, we are at a threshold. Profound challenges and opportunities for our emergent global civilization lie ahead—and in the relatively near future. How well we acknowledge, understand, and address these in the coming decade will have a very significant impact on the remainder of this century and beyond.

Fifth, no single actor—no person, institution, ideology, marketplace, religion, region, or nation—can come close to controlling the future in isolation, to solving our problems or fulfilling our dreams. In a tightly interconnected world, increased distribution of responsibility—and the opportunity to contribute—is inevitable. This will require people in many walks of life, in all sorts of organizations, in every sector, in all parts of the world, to learn and understand better and faster the nature of our changing world and to imagine what could and should lie ahead. Every decision and every action taken everywhere has consequences, and in accumulation, they will come to shape our future. The wiser our separate choices, the better our shared future will be.

This book aims to contribute to that better future. It is organized into four sections.

WHAT'S HAPPENING?: PREDICTING THE PRESENT

This section cuts through much of the complexity we see in the world right now by laying out seven "dynamic tensions"—multiple, confusing, and often contradictory forces that are largely fueling the transition from our present to our future. These call attention to some fundamental paradoxes and contradictions that are in play today and that require us to adopt a "both/and" rather than an "either/or" logic.

WHAT IF?: CHALLENGES AND CHANGES AHEAD

Given these dynamic tensions, I then explore two of the most important areas in which we will experience major challenges and changes in the coming decade—governance and innovation—and suggest that in both we appear poised for radical and important shifts.

WHAT'S NEXT?: SCENARIOS FOR THE NEXT DECADE

Having laid out these tensions and challenges, I then consider how we might expect a new global order to evolve, offering three very different scenarios that we might see unfold in the coming decade. While we must prepare for all three of these futures, each holds profoundly different implications.

SO WHAT?: ACTING IN AN AGE OF TRANSFORMATION

Finally, I consider some of the critical implications of this transformative era, and explain how and why three important sets of actors—businesses, leaders, and global citizens—will be largely responsible for shaping a better future.

There can be no "completeness proof" for the long term; I cannot hope to cover in this book everything that might matter in the coming decade as we create the foundation for a new century. But I believe that this is a very useful primer to the future, one that lays out powerful frameworks for making sense of an uncertain world and inspires us to turn our collective power and passions to the challenges and opportunities ahead.

Section 1

What's Happening?: Predicting the Present

> The opposite of a false statement is a correct statement.
> The opposite of a profound truth may well be another
> profound truth.
> —Niels Bohr, Nobel Prize-winning physicist

We cannot anticipate the future without first reflecting upon and deepening our understanding of the current dynamics that will shape things to come. This is particularly true during turbulent times, when our past experiences may be a poor guide and our embedded assumptions may be outmoded and irrelevant. I think it was Marshall McLuhan who observed that if we drove our cars the way we live our lives there would be wrecks on every street corner. When we navigate through the present with our eyes half-trained on the rearview mirror, we filter a great deal of what's ahead of us through the lens of the past—a habit that's both distracting and distorting. It is no real surprise, then, that we sometimes don't understand the present very well at all.

"Predicting the present" requires that we challenge our own deep assumptions, look beyond the easy certainties and the "right way of thinking" offered by so many pundits, and examine multiple facets of important issues, covering broad terrain while hopefully avoiding the pitfalls of "paralysis by analysis." It is no small challenge, but one that I think is vital if we are, as individuals and collectively, to understand not just the events and trends that keep us gripped yet confounded as we read our morning papers, but the deep currents that underlie those events and trends—as well as others yet to reveal themselves. The ability to put the world in context will be one of our greatest challenges in the coming decade. It is the intention of this book to equip you for that challenge.

From "Either/Or" to "Both/And" Thinking

Throughout my childhood in Paisley, Scotland, I regularly encountered a man named Cuthbert. He seemed always to be out on the street, and he was exuberantly, wonderfully mad. He had a shock of white hair, always wore a bowtie and a tartan vest, and he swung a stick like Charlie Chaplin. He struck up conversations with everyone who crossed his path. Adults may have avoided him, but we children often drew toward him, listening with fascination to his untamed talk and theorizing. He used words so skillfully, I thought. He was obviously wildly off balance and disturbed, but he was also poetic and strangely insightful.

Cuthbert, the story went, had been a brilliant student at the local grammar school, and was considered a boy of great promise. But as he was preparing to go to university, his mind came unhinged, and he never recovered. What caused Cuthbert to lose his mind was a matter of much speculation, and competing theories abounded. But the town's favored explanation was elegant and simple. Cuthbert had fallen victim to his own brilliance: one day, while studying for school examinations, he had "thought two thoughts at once." And it had driven him permanently mad.

"The test of a first-rate intelligence is the ability to hold two opposing ideas in mind at the same time and still retain the ability to function," F. Scott Fitzgerald famously wrote. Cuthbert failed the latter part of the test. Most of us, though, don't even pass the former part: holding opposing ideas in our minds in the first place. But it is an ability that I am convinced we will all need to work hard to acquire and improve as we try to make sense of an increasingly complex and paradoxical world.

This is not to say, of course, that the classic Western thought processes of debate and separation, the dialectic of thesis and antithesis, are without merit. Far from it. The "either/or" model is an extremely powerful way to generate insight, deepen knowledge, strengthen understanding, and arrive at syntheses that are much richer than the starting points. The approach is also quite essential in the many circumstances where there is indeed one single correct perspective, one right answer to be discovered—or, to borrow Bohr's terms, when we must distinguish between "false statements" and "correct statements."

But an "either/or" mindset can be futile at best and catastrophic at worst when it culminates in the strict choice of one "profound truth" over another. Consider, for example, the decades of heated yet often sterile debate (not to mention parental confusion and guilt) between the competing advocates of nature and nurture as the defining causes of personality and intelligence. The influential theories of Hans Eysenck and Benjamin Spock, for example, were built almost exclusively upon nature and nurture respectively. In retrospect, it seems blindingly obvious that both genetic and environmental factors play a role—and indeed interact—in our development, and that the "nature/nurture" debate was a false and unhelpful dichotomy.

The truth is that we live in a world in which multiple contradictory forces, all of great strength and relevance, are exerting themselves at the same time. The ability to think in terms of "both/and" is an extraordinarily valuable and effective enabler of learning about what is happening around us. It opens up our vision to a complex and multi-faceted world that "either/or" thinking does not, by its nature, allow us to see.

Dynamic Tensions

I started this book by contemplating the critical uncertainties that are shaping our present and driving our future and then looking within and between them for recurring themes and patterns. I eventually identified seven matching pairs of forces that most effectively captured and clarified the multiple, confusing, and contradictory forces at work in the world today. I termed them "dynamic tensions"—profound but competing truths that appear to contradict or challenge each other, but both of which will increase in significance in the decade ahead. The world is moving toward both sides of these tensions simultaneously; that is our complex reality. Thinking only "one thought at once"—choosing sides, or acknowledging one profound truth while denying the other—teaches us very little about the world that we live in and the one we can expect.

Much of the importance of these competing dynamics seemed to lie in the very fact that they coexist in the present and will co-evolve in the future. By simply making explicit the existence of these paradoxical forces, our powerful times become less confusing and more comprehensible. In the following chapters, I set out and explore each of these dynamic tensions in turn.

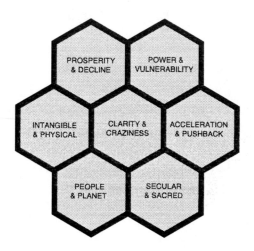

Chapter 2

Clarity and Craziness

In the coming decade, our world will grow more transparent. Our ability to collect, integrate, interpret, and distribute data will increase exponentially; sensors and connective and surveillance technologies will converge; and access to a staggering array of words, images, and sounds will spread globally. The results will be profoundly contradictory. On the one hand, our insight into the workings of corporations and governments, our knowledge of science, and our understanding of systemic global issues will be greatly enhanced. On the other hand, we will also experience an explosion of fear and confusion, fueled by our ubiquitous access to immense amounts of information. We will see competing interpretations of major world events, driven by ideology and informed by selective "evidence." A growing abundance of conspiracy theories and falsehoods will travel the world instantaneously, and the very tools of connectivity that will enable so much transparency will also serve to enable ever-more sophisticated means of theft and fraud.

Clarity

> When the world and the mind are both transparent, this is true vision.
> —Bodhidharma, Indian Zen Buddhist monk who brought Zen from India to China (c. 520 A.D.)

The world is becoming increasingly transparent, precipitating a rapid and extraordinary transformation that will change our lives for better and for worse. This trend toward transparency was not intentional, and because we have so far experienced it only in piecemeal fashion, it has attracted little attention. Yet it is difficult to imagine (let alone describe, detail, and assess) the remarkable systemic changes it is bringing about. We are entering new and uncharted territory for the future of global society—a future for which we have no map and few points of reference.

Factors Enabling a See-through Society

Several factors are coming together to create this world of transparency. The first involves the mind-boggling quantities of data and information that are now being created, captured, and made widely accessible. In 2002 alone, the amount of stored information produced globally was equivalent to 37,000 new Library of Congress book collections. It would take about 30 feet of books to store the amount of recorded information produced *per person* in the world each year. Indeed, we are often unconscious producers of new data. Every time we use a credit card at the grocery store or pay a highway toll with an electronic pass, information about our habits, patterns, and preferences is instantaneously uploaded, ready to be analyzed.

Thanks to the continuing acceleration of computing power and the spread of broadband connectivity, we are able to access, scrutinize, and interpret all this information with extraordinary new precision. Much is made instantly available on the Internet, where search engines have opened the doors to a storehouse of information that would otherwise have remained hidden. We can now uncover, with just a few keystrokes, in just a few seconds, highly targeted information that 10 years ago could have only been unearthed after weeks of steady searching. Having such wide access to so much information at once is also enabling new correlations and cross-connections to be made, thus creating even more knowledge and information.

This ability to access and connect is moving beyond the written word to include other forms of information as well. An array of new data visualization tools are making complex relationships and linkages more accessible and understandable. Filtering technologies, such as TiVo, now allow us to control and edit what we watch on television. Soon we will be able to accurately search the Internet not just for words, but for images and video. Google and Yahoo! have already launched these types of services.

Do You Know Where Your Child Is? Keeping Kids Safe with New "Clarity" Technology

- A Texas school district sparked controversy among privacy advocates when it equipped 28,000 students with ID badges containing Radio Frequency Identification (RFID) tags that can be "read" when they get on and off school buses. The information is then fed by wireless phone to the police and school administrators.

- In some parts of Japan, GPS-enabled blazers are now part of the school uniform. The jackets allow parents to track their kids and also feature a panic button that, when pushed, summons a security guard to their location. Backpacks with built-in GPS have also become popular.

- The Legoland amusement park in Billund, Denmark, offers wireless- and RFID-enabled wristbands that parents can place on their kids and track (to within 5 feet) via cellphone.

Sources: *The New York Times*, CNET News.com, *CIO Magazine*.

Another important factor underpinning transparency is the increased surveillance of almost everything. In the UK alone, more than 4 million closed-circuit TV cameras are trained on public spaces; a shopper in London can expect to be captured on video several hundred times a day. Overhead, an expanding number of satellites are recording and relaying detailed visual images and "listening" to a great deal of terrestrial communication. Governments are leading the charge in deploying these satellites; China alone has announced plans to launch more than 100 surveillance satellites by 2020. But commercial satellites are also heading skyward, fulfilling a broad range of functions for farmers, civil engineers, geologists, city planners, and others.

Satellites also play a key role in enabling ever-more sophisticated (yet ever-more inexpensive) tracking and sensing technologies. Twenty-nine U.S. navigation satellites form the backbone of the GPS technology already found in vehicles all over the world and increasingly embedded in cellphones and other devices. Europe is planning a potentially more powerful GPS system of its own, known as Galileo, involving 30 much newer satellites with higher functionality. Meanwhile, wireless sensors that can identify torque, heat, vibration, and strain are also being deployed, monitoring the behavior of such complex systems as traffic flows and weather patterns.

Sensors, Sensors, Everywhere

"By 2008, there could be 100 million wireless sensors in use, up from about 200,000 today, market-research company Harbor Research says. The worldwide market for wireless sensors, it says, will grow from $100 million this year to more than $1 billion by 2009."
—Information Week, January 24, 2005

- Science Applications International Corp. is developing tiny wireless sensors that the U.S.'s defense and homeland security departments can deploy in batches of hundreds in order to "sniff out" dangerous cargo and suspicious movements on U.S. borders, ships, and bridges.

- Gentag Inc. has patented a "smart" removable cellphone sensor module that can be used to detect dangerous levels of carbon monoxide; the company is also developing a "smart" skin patch that will allow parents to distantly monitor a child's temperature via cellphone.

- Yale applied physics professor Robert D. Grober has developed a golf club with motion-detecting sensors embedded in its shaft. The sensors read the speed of the club and then convert it into audio feedback that can be heard by the golfer through wireless headphones and can be used to greatly improve his or her swing.

- Researchers at Connection One, a National Science Foundation research center in Arizona, are developing wireless sensors that help amputees control artificial limbs more easily.

- Researchers at the University of California, Berkeley, have designed and launched a wireless sensor network to monitor and record the behaviors of nesting birds on an island off the coast of Maine. The network allows scientists to collect field data without human impact or disturbance.

Sources: *Information Week,* SecureIDNews, AZCentral.com, *CIO Magazine,* U.C. Berkeley Department of Electrical Engineering and Computer Sciences.

All these examples are, without doubt, merely the early indicators of a much larger and more pervasive phenomenon. The next wave of transparency will be powered by the further radical development of new technologies, especially in the fields of biotechnology and nanotechnology. In the last decade, we have seen the growing power of biotechnology to produce clarity—for example, the use of DNA testing to solve crimes often many years after they occur or diagnose illnesses years before they present themselves. In the coming decade, genetic science will also help anticipate with ever-increasing accuracy our individual propensity for certain diseases.This will create interesting dilemmas regarding who should have access to this information, which could seriously affect, for example, insurance premiums and employment opportunities. The field of nanotechnology (the science of the very small) holds even more startling prospects. By designing circuitry on the infinitesimal level, our ability to gather and decode information on the tiniest plane is growing in ways that are reminiscent of science fiction.

The Promise of Clarity

It is hard to overstate the potential benefits we can expect will flow from our migration toward a more transparent world. On the micro level, we are already seeing innovations like the Poseidon, a drowning detection system that uses computer vision technology to serve as a "third eye" for lifeguards and parents at swimming pools; the system uses its cameras to sense and report abnormal activity in the water. Or consider the VeriChip, an RFID device roughly the size of a grain of rice and designed to be implanted just under the skin of humans. Approved by the FDA in October 2004, it had already been implanted in more than a thousand people—including, interestingly, Mexico's attorney general and about 160 of his staff, in order to control access to their office building and facilitate tracking in the event of a kidnapping.

Toward a Transparent Ocean

California's Monterey Bay Aquarium Research Institute is launching the first-ever underwater lab capable of continuously monitoring and collecting data about activity on the ocean floor. The laboratory, dubbed MARS, will be located 20 miles off the coast on the upper edges of a 4,000-foot-deep canyon. It will feature a host of new technologies, including:

- The Benthic Rover, a small roving tank-like device that will collect the first-ever long-term data on seabed sediment, communicated back to scientists via an acoustic modem

- Autonomous underwater vehicles that will use sonar to create high-resolution maps of the ocean floor, and can "stalk" and study various forms of aquatic life

- Three 1,000-foot-deep "bore holes," filled with advanced gauges and sensors that will study the movement of fluid through sediment; one will be equipped with a seismometer, the first ever to be placed west of the San Andreas fault

- A central "node," connected by cable to a lab on land, that will serve as an underwater power strip and transfer data back to land at the speed of DSL

Source: *Outside Magazine,* February 2005.

At the macro level, growing transparency offers the prospect of a greater and more coherent understanding of our global society and our physical world—including better comprehension of the changing environment of our planet. In 2002, the NEC Corporation delivered what was then the most powerful ultra-high-speed vector parallel computing system in the world to Japan's Earth Simulator Centre. This massive computer is capable of a staggering 35 trillion calculations per second (the world's fastest supercomputer, Blue Gene/L, run by IBM and the Department of Energy, can now run an exponentially staggering 270 trillion calculations per second). Right now it is being used to forecast global climate changes, but it is capable of modeling Earth's environment for the next thousand years. Such forecasts are possible because of the increasing availability of micro-detailed data about the planet. The proliferation of cheap sensing devices is making once-opaque processes of the natural world, from weather systems to glacial flows, more and more transparent.

As our ability to interpret and model the data increases, so too will our understanding of Earth.

Corporations Creating (and Exploiting) Clarity

Not surprisingly, businesses and governments everywhere are alert to the remarkable possibilities of a world of growing clarity and transparency—and they are beginning to take advantage of those possibilities. Information is the lifeblood of business; increasingly, the ability to collect, track, integrate, interpret, and utilize data is a key success factor in every industry. Companies spend vast sums on information technology each year; Gartner forecasts that global IT spending will reach $1.75 trillion in 2005. Such investment has spurred remarkable productivity gains and significant changes in business models and practices over the last few decades, and the trend will only continue. Much of the data generated and exploited by information technology relates to basics, such as inventory, logistics, competitors, and market conditions. But much of it also relates to customers, current and potential.

Businesses have been gathering, using, and even selling information about their customers for years, with or without the customers' knowledge or permission. Consumer transactions generate great volumes of data about buying habits, financial positions, and lifestyle choices. When analyzed, this data is extremely valuable, and the market for it is substantial. Corporations are accessing and exploiting more and more data through the use of sophisticated and powerful "data mining" technologies, which comb large databases for hidden and complex patterns and can help companies increase revenues by tailoring their offerings based on customers' discovered buying patterns. Though the technology that fuels modern-day data mining has only been around since the mid-1990s, the worldwide market for such tools is expected to reach $1.85 billion in 2006—a 343 percent increase over spending in 2001, according to IDC research.

One of the most effective adopters of the technologies of transparency is Wal-Mart, which was an early user of bar codes and electronic data interchange and has been so aggressive in promoting the use of RFID tags that it has already attracted the wrath of privacy groups. Wal-Mart accumulates and interprets more data about customers and products than any other retailer—and to great effect. At the beginning of the 2004 hurricane season, for example, the company mined its giant databases to help anticipate what people in storm regions would want to buy before a hurricane.

The answers, based on past buying habits, were surprising—who would have guessed that strawberry Pop-Tart sales increased sevenfold during a hurricane? The results enabled Wal-Mart to stock up appropriately, increasing its profits by making sure its stores had the products that customers wanted.

Government Intelligence and Surveillance

Governments are also making effective use of transparency technologies. Many are using a combination of surveillance and data mining to learn more about their citizens, as well as citizens of other countries. Sometimes referred to as "dataveillance," the main objective of such efforts is to enhance security and minimize risk and vulnerability. Not surprisingly, since September 11, 2001, this has become a much higher priority in many parts of the world. This coincides with an explosion in the power of the technologies that enable such scrutiny, setting the stage for a mutually reinforcing interaction of increased capacity for information gathering, analysis, and dissemination on the one hand and a growing sense of the need for such activity on the other hand.

One controversial feature of dataveillance is the growing tendency for information to be captured for one apparent purpose and then redeployed for another. Recently, in London, a "congestion tax" was levied on cars entering the city center, and video surveillance of traffic was established to enforce compliance. Hundreds of new cameras were installed to read license plates and check them against registered drivers. However, it was quickly discovered that the cameras had an additional purpose. The images they captured would be passed through military and law enforcement databases capable of deploying facial recognition technology to seek out known terrorists and criminals. In the U.S., the passing of the controversial Patriot Act, which greatly empowers the government to collect and analyze data for whatever purpose, clearly signals a trajectory for dataveillance on a wide scale.

Biometrics

Successfully passing yourself off as another person is becoming a thing of the past:

- By the end of 2005, all new U.S. passports will be "intelligent documents." They will include a "smart chip" that contains a full-face image of the passport-bearer. EU passports are also going biometric and will feature both retinal and fingerprint recognition biometrics on their chips. Thailand is planning to issue national biometric ID cards to all of its approximately 64 million citizens.

- Caesars Palace, one of the largest hotel-casinos in Las Vegas, is building a new tower in which guests will open the doors to their suites with fingerprint biometrics, not keys.

- More than 4 million biometric fingerprint sensors are already in use in cellphones, PCs, and access control devices throughout Asia. Hand vein pattern recognition is also gaining popularity in that region, particularly among banks.

- A 2005 survey found that 56 percent of firms in Saudi Arabia plan to introduce iris scanning and fingerprint recognition for security in their office buildings. Half expect to implement these plans within the next two years.

Sources: *The Christian Science Monitor, The Register* (UK), Precision Biometrics AB, silicon.com, AuthenTec, SecureIDNews, AME Info.

Meanwhile, the U.S. intelligence and defense communities have been actively exploring the potential for increased clarity and transparency in the "war on terror." In the coming decade, we will see considerable additional focus on implementing the recommendations of the 9-11 Commission, which identified two primary intelligence challenges for the U.S. in the future: gaining access to information and knowing what sense to make of it—in other words, how to connect the dots. In response to the Commission's findings, new focus has been placed on stepping up intelligence collaboration and information sharing, as well as making highly centralized attempts to "mine" that information for the nuggets it might contain.

Now and in the future, it is not likely that such activities will escape the attention of privacy rights advocates. Consider, for example, the ill-fated Total Information Awareness (TIA) project—launched in 2002 by the Defense Advanced Research Projects Agency (DARPA), quickly renamed the Terrorist Information Awareness project, and then shut down in fall of 2003 in the face of heavy criticism. The scope and ambition of this project was remarkable and indicative of the potential capabilities that lie ahead of us. One task of the project was to develop the ability to more effectively identify critical bits of intelligence within the overall global flood of information by "enabling heterogeneous databases to be queried as if they were one logical 'virtually' centralized database." In short, TIA was an unprecedented attempt to develop the capacity for incredibly sophisticated cross-referencing of public, private, and government databases that would highlight potential terrorist activity within the vast volumes of personal data trails that we all leave in our everyday lives. But the idea of the U.S. government having privileged access to vast amounts of private information about its citizens proved too controversial for the project to survive. As California Senator Dianne Feinstein put it, "This is a panoply, which isn't carefully conscribed and controlled, for a George Orwell America. And I don't think the American people are ready for that by a long shot."

The U.S. defense community is also actively exploring the military possibilities opened up by technologies of transparency. Two examples are worth considering. The first is the development of what has been termed a "second Internet" for the exclusive use of the U.S. military. It is a system of surveillance and analysis, based on satellites, sensors, computers, and secure broadband connectivity, that will enable military planners to observe, track, and respond to movements of even very small forces and arms; observe and assess battlefields in real time; and track suspicious sites all over the world for signs of everything from terrorist training to nuclear weapons production.

On a more micro level, experiments in gaining "total awareness" of particular locales are being conducted through the use of "smart dust"—in this case, thousands of tiny microphones, cameras, and heat and vibration sensors deposited in a specific geographic zone, all wirelessly connected to one another and able to relay real-time information. While such a technological edge would be extremely helpful in conventional battlefield scenarios, it could also prove invaluable in less-conventional scenarios, including operations in populated urban areas, which seem likely to consume much military effort in the decades ahead.

Does Privacy Have a Future?

The unprecedented availability, collection, and integration of data, images, and other information is steering us toward a future in which our actions will be more readily tracked and observed. Despite outcries over privacy rights and civil liberties, surveillance of regions, civic spaces, and people will continue to expand. It seems reasonable to suspect that no one will fall outside the boundaries of such scrutiny and that information about our private behavior will be spread and assessed in ways we have not sanctioned. These developments, in both the corporate and public spheres, will no doubt pose serious ethical and privacy issues in the coming decade. For example, while companies may be free to mine data to better serve their customers—to mutual advantage—should they be allowed to sell or make that data available to others? When Google launched its free email service Gmail, it did so with a contingency: in exchange for the free service, users would be shown targeted ads based on the content of their messages, which would be "read" by a computer and then matched to appropriate advertisements. Soon after Google announced the service, 31 privacy and civil liberties organizations wrote an open letter calling for the company to terminate Gmail, saying that the act of scanning personal emails and inserting related ads was a violation of users' "implicit trust" and that the information gathered through this process could be used in other unauthorized ways.

Such debates are becoming more common, and they are often directly linked to security issues. For example, in 2003, JetBlue Airways was forced to make a public apology after word leaked out that it had shared 5 million passenger records with a defense contractor at the behest of the Department of Defense. The contractor had matched JetBlue's information with Social Security numbers, income levels, vehicle ownership, and other personal data in order to investigate the viability of developing an airline passenger profiling system, which would assign a risk level, from green to red, to every passenger and screen out suspected terrorists and felons. JetBlue endured considerable backlash for its actions.

Yet it seems unlikely that we will witness any meaningful retreat from the drive toward clarity and transparency in all areas of our lives and society. We will place some constraints on unwelcome intrusions, to be sure, but in the coming decade, our sense and expectations of privacy will inevitably be challenged and changed as technology is able to discern and track more and more of our individual actions. As a *Washington Times* editorial put it: "It was only for a brief period after industrialization, when masses were pushed into sprawling cities, that the experience of being literally one among millions provided a sense of privacy through anonymity. The electronic revolution is merely ending a temporary phenomenon created by industrialization." Or, as Sun Microsystems CEO Scott McNealy has said, "You have zero privacy anyway. Get over it!"

Avoiding a "Panoptican" Society

In the late eighteenth century, the English social reformer Jeremy Bentham, alarmed by the often inhumane conditions and behaviors prevalent in penal institutions of the time, designed a novel prison. It was a circular structure several stories high; each story was a ring of cells, all open toward the center of the ring, and each cell had a window on the external wall. In the middle of the ring stood a watchtower in which guards, concealed from the prisoners, could have full view of every cell, all of them backlit by their external windows. Prisoners could never know when they were being watched, but knew they could be watched at any time. Bentham reasoned that every inmate would always assume they were being watched, and therefore would conform to prison regulations. As the French philosopher Michel Foucault described it in his 1975 work *Discipline & Punish: The Birth of the Prison*, the major effect of this prison design was "to induce in the inmate a state of conscious and permanent visibility that assures the automatic functioning of power."

Bentham called his design the Panoptican ("all seeing"). Today, some fear that what he envisaged for the inmates might be an appropriate way of thinking about the fate of all consumers and citizens—being seen, but unable to see back. Some evidence supports this fear. For example, in 2003, the Bush Administration protected some 14 million documents from being declassified—an increase of 39 percent since 2001. While requests to access federal material under the Freedom of Information Act tripled between 1997 and 2003 to more than 3.2 million, the federal resources to handle those requests have not increased. While we may have to recast our thinking about privacy and transparency in the decade ahead, the idea of a society based primarily on one-way, top-down surveillance and scrutiny is deeply offensive to most. It is inconsistent, surely, with the basic human desire for freedom, autonomy, dignity, and respect.

To some extent, we may be able to reduce the sense of invasion and continuous oversight through regulation and limitation of the transparency trends. For example, the European Union has strict rules for how companies can use and disseminate the information they gather, and similar regulations are cropping up in other parts of the world. But a much more promising prospect is that access to information and scrutiny of behavior will work as much from the bottom up as from the top down—in other words, that transparency will be democratized.

The Two-Way Solution

There is cause for both optimism and concern in the breadth of transparency technologies now available to the public—and our tendency to use them. A 2003 U.S. nationwide survey found that 14 percent of Americans would sign up for a service that allowed them to surveil their own homes through Internet-connected cameras. The use of "nanny cams" to check on babysitters has proliferated, and parents in many countries watch their children play at their nursery over the Internet. With GPS becoming an increasingly common feature of simple cellphones, some parents are even tracking their teenage children's movements. In Cincinnati, surveillance cameras have been installed in certain known crime areas—and it is not Big Brother who is watching them but local residents, registered as part of neighborhood anti-crime units and logged on to a special website. Amateur astronomers, using powerful yet affordable telescopes, have created a website, HeavensAbove, that shows satellite paths and sightings for your town at the click of a button. Google now offers satellite photos of buildings and neighborhoods as part of its map service; type in your address, click a button, and a bird's eye view of your house appears.

As citizens become more accustomed to working with the tools of transparency, they will become increasingly adept at enforcing more transparency on corporations and governments. Indeed, there is early evidence that the trend is beginning to go both ways. Companies in many parts of the world are now required to reveal more about their activities, and what is not submitted voluntarily is often uncovered by the systematic scrutiny of highly trusted nongovernmental organizations (NGOs).

A growing number of independent organizations are tracking multinational corporations and governments and publicizing their behaviors for all to see. Scorecard.org, for example, offers a searchable database of local companies known to pollute, complete with zip code searches and hotlinks to send protest notes to those companies and to local politicians. Fundrace.org, a site that takes publicly available data about political donations and then codes them geographically, can identify donations by locale and even by building—revealing, for example, that New York City's top Republican donor is 85 Broad Street, home of Goldman Sachs. Some examples of transparency emerging from and contributing to "people power" are actually promoted by businesses themselves. A growing number of online retail sites are including product feedback and reviews as part of their service (Shopping.com's "epinions" network, for example), which is shifting the balance of power between corporate advertisers and consumers.

There are other obvious ways in which transparency will increasingly apply as much to institutions as to citizens. The video recording of Rodney King being beaten by police sent a very clear early message regarding the age old question "who will watch the watchmen"—the answer is, we will. WITNESS, a nonprofit championed by the musician Peter Gabriel, uses "video and technology to fight for human rights" by giving camcorders to activists around the world so that they can document human rights abuses; the organization's website now hosts an enormous archive of videos. Even the horrible images of prisoner abuse from Abu Ghraib are informative. Though the images were taken by the perpetrators themselves, the ease and speed with which they spread around the world was remarkable—and the damage they have done to the reputation and standing of the United States in many Muslim countries is incalculable.

A positive outcome of a more "bottom-up" transparency will be corporations and public bodies, knowing their actions are watched and documented, taking pains to preempt criticism through social and civic responsibility. For example, when Merck decided in the fall of 2004 to withdraw its blockbuster painkiller drug Vioxx from the market in light of growing but not yet conclusive evidence that it might increase the risks of heart disease, it was getting ahead of regulatory requirements and public pressure; it was "doing the right thing" in a world in which failing to do the right thing is becoming increasingly easy to discover and punish.

Yet it also seems inevitable that this trend toward clarity will become a matter of growing concern in the decade ahead. The signs are already here. The fact that more and more cellphones now have digital or video cameras built into them challenges our privacy in new ways. Websites dedicated to displaying salacious shots taken by camera phones have sprung up; it is not just celebrities who can be "caught" out in public and not just professional paparazzi who are behind the lens. We are on the verge of having access to amazingly cheap and tiny cameras, about the size of a postage stamp, that can be stuck anywhere and can send images wirelessly to a computer—and will surely spark another round of privacy challenges.

Looking forward, it seems unlikely that current constraints will solve the problems associated with having ubiquitous lenses on our lives. The more data and images that are captured, and the more accessible they are to others, the more we will find ourselves contending with the curious new realities of our world of crystal clarity, where we know so much more, can solve so many problems, and can seize so many new opportunities—and where our technology leaves us with nowhere to hide.

Craziness

> A lie gets halfway around the world before the truth has a
> chance to get its coat on.
> —Winston Churchill

And yet everything that creates clarity also creates the conditions for craziness—for deep and profound misinterpretation and misjudgment. In other words, our increased access to information and to new tools for gathering it will confuse as much as it will clarify.

We are, everyday and in myriad ways, bombarded with information not just from the news media but from entertainers, from advertisers, from our own experience, and from one another. "Information overload" makes it difficult to find the signal within the noise. Much of the information we consume turns out to be of little value, while what is "useful" overwhelms us by its sheer volume. This endless flow of information exposes us to more important data and issues than we can reasonably handle; as a result, we are forced to undertake a kind of "cognitive triage" to select what seems important and discard whatever remains. In this we are enabled by the emergence of "narrowcast" media, in which we as consumers can choose and select our filters and our sources with increasing precision. This in turn can present us with an equal and opposite problem from information overload—too much of the same sort of information, supporting our existing biases and prejudices.

While more data can indeed create increased clarity, it can also generate compelling evidence for very different, even opposing, perspectives. In our attempts to make sense of the world, we are forced to make more choices about meaning than ever before. No matter the quantity or the quality of data we assess, or how many tools and angles we use to understand it, ultimately we will impose meaning based on subjective factors, including our own worldview. Even the most well informed and well intentioned of us can and will make mistakes of interpretation and judgment.

Moreover, as more "evidence" is generated for and from many perspectives, it will be subjected to a variety of interpretations in support of multiple agendas and belief systems. In our multifaceted world, there is no single "truth," no one interpretation. Ask a poor citizen of South Africa what a weapon of mass destruction is and she might say it's the patents that protect the intellectual property of pharmaceutical firms. "Bioterror" to a South Pacific Islander may soon come to mean the death of species due to global climate change. In much of Colombia, the drug trade is "valid commerce" and the leading edge of the global economy. In the twenty-first century, the spinning of alternative versions of reality in support of very different perspectives will be endless, dizzying, and powerful—and increasingly well "informed" by supporting "proof."

Conspiracy Theories Everywhere

G.K. Chesterton once said, "When people stop believing in God, they don't believe in nothing. They believe in anything." Indeed, a growing climate of distrust can paradoxically lead to ever-greater credulity. So too can a global environment in which events seem to occur with little rhyme or reason. Conspiracy theories can, ironically, provide an ordered framework with which to understand chaotic and random events. Within that context, the very availability and flow of data and ideas that enable new transparency and clarity will therefore also empower alternative—and often quite crazy—interpretations of reality. This is being fueled especially by the connectivity and access offered by the Internet. Philip Plait, an astronomer at California State University at Sonoma, is a leading debunker of moon landing conspiracy theories. In an interview with the *Houston Chronicle*, he explained why such speculation continues to run rampant. "I've known about this moon hoax stuff for years, but it was such a ridiculous, tiny thing that I didn't worry about it. But conspiracy theories fester on the Web, and for this particular conspiracy theory, which relies very heavily on the misinterpretation of pictures, the Web is a Petri dish."

His analysis certainly appears to be correct—and not just for lunar conspiracy theories. For example, layer upon layer of theory and counter-theory are still being developed about September 11, and most are "supported" by multimedia data—documents, photographs, video, and audiotapes. Most of these theories implicate the U.S. and/or the Israeli government for either executing the attack or knowingly failing to prevent it. Some claim there were no planes involved at all and that the images seen around the world by billions of people were sophisticated holograms. Others claim that the planes were not scheduled flights but special aircraft with "pods" fitted and filled with explosives and guided by remote control. Others claim that explosive devices deep in the foundations of the Twin Towers and other fallen buildings were responsible for their collapse. Still others claim that all these theories are preposterous and unbelievable disinformation spread by government agents to discredit those trying to raise awareness of the "true" story—that the U.S. government enabled or allowed the attacks in order to align public opinion around a radical interventionist policy agenda in the Middle East to secure future oil supplies. These might sound like ridiculous theories that would garner little support, but each have vociferous advocates. So do numerous other conspiracy theories about September 11. In a Gallup poll taken months after the attacks, 86 percent of Pakistanis, 74 percent of Indonesians, and 43 percent of Turks said they did not believe Arabs were responsible for the attacks.

Even natural disasters can provoke an almost immediate outbreak of conspiracy theories. Many speculated that the Indian Ocean tsunami in December 2004 was triggered by U.S. underwater nuclear testing—a theory that gained ground on numerous websites and blogs. Others raised pointed questions about the fact that the tsunami failed to damage the U.S. military base on the island of Diego Garcia; the matter was even raised as a talking point by the BBC on its website.

Another conspiracy theory gathering some speed involves RFID tags—a technology of transparency. Taking their cue from the Book of Revelations, some theorists claim that RFID tags are part of a sinister plot to barcode or otherwise mark people on their right hand or their forehead in fulfillment of the prophecy that Satan would so identify all those entitled to "buy or sell" in his kingdom with "the mark of the beast." The theory might be farfetched, but companies involved in the manufacture of RFID technology have had to respond to these allegations. Businesses will have to become increasingly aware of the power of rumor to become socialized as truth—to harden into urban legend. Conspiracy theories and rumors can be devastating and difficult to stamp out.

Top Six Urban Legends

Snopes.com, a website dedicated to tracking and substantiating or debunking urban legends, posts a running list of the "25 hottest urban legends," updated regularly and ranked according to the frequency of their circulation over email, on the Web, and by the media. Snopes defines an urban legend as a tale that "circulates widely, is told and retold with differing details (or exists in multiple versions), and is *said* to be true. Whether or not the events described in the tale ever *actually* occurred is completely irrelevant to its classification as an urban legend."

The top six urban legends of the week of April 22, 2005:

1. You must sign up with the national Do Not Call list to prevent telemarketers from calling your cellphone. (false)

2. Boycotting gasoline produced by companies that import oil from the Middle East will cut off the funding of terrorists. (false)

3. A woman evaded a rapist posing as a policeman by calling #77 (or *677) on her cellphone. (rape tale—undetermined; #77 dialing—true in some states)

4. Bill Gates, Microsoft, and AOL are giving away cash and merchandise to those who forward an email message. (false)

5. Parking lot thieves are rendering their victims unconscious with ether-laced perfume. (false)

6. Starbucks refused to send free coffee to G.I.s serving in Iraq. (false)

Source: http://www.snopes.com/info/top25uls.asp.

Big global brands are conspiracy's most common targets. For example, the Colombian trade union has accused Coca-Cola and its bottling partners of supporting right-wing death squads that harassed and attacked union members. Coke quickly dismissed the accusation as "outrageous." And yet the rumor became a heated topic at Coke's annual shareholders meeting, resulting in the ejection of one shareholder from the room. Even small, and therefore more vulnerable, businesses can find themselves at risk. Consider, for example, the story of Caribou Coffee. At the time of writing, if you do a Google search on "Caribou Coffee," among the top-listed sites are several addressing the rumor that the coffee chain is funding Islamic terrorists. The spread of this conspiracy theory has caused Caribou's business in communities with significant Jewish populations to fall sharply. The problem is that, as with most effective rumors, there is the sliver of a single and rather meaningless fact around which the falsehood is fabricated. Caribou is 88-percent owned by Atlanta-based Crescent Capital, the investment arm of the First Islamic Bank of Bahrain. That makes the story all the more difficult to challenge and, as company CEO Michael Coles has found, "Things on the Internet don't go away."

Disinformation in the Business of Politics and the Politics of Business

Some conspiracy theorists are sincere—if badly misguided or even deluded—in their beliefs. But others are engaged in deliberate manipulation of the beliefs and perceptions of others to their advantage. In the field of political advertising, sophisticated techniques for influencing opinion in an age of information overload are being honed to a very fine edge. Regular polling surveys find that people dislike negative advertising and, given the choice, would prefer positive messages and communication. The same preference is revealed in focus groups; when shown a positive advertisement for a political candidate and a negative attack ad, they overwhelmingly prefer the positive one. But four days later, when asked what they can remember, they have much greater recall of the negative ad. Abundant research confirms that negative images and messages are easier to recall—in other words, they stick.

The Social Role of Conspiracy Theories

Marcus LiBrizzi, an assistant professor of English at the University of Maine, explained in *The Christian Science Monitor* why he encourages his students to discuss conspiracy theories: "Even far-out conspiracy theories reveal how people make sense of the world. These theories have social functions; they reflect responses to alienation, the feeling of being disconnected. With conspiracies there are no accidents—everything is linked together. The individual who can figure things out also feels empowered. 'They may have gotten to the rest of you,' this individual reasons, 'but at least I know the truth.'"

Source: Marcus LiBrizzi, "Students Are Highly Motivated in Class? It Must Be a Conspiracy," *The Christian Science Monitor*, April 9, 2002. Reprinted by kind permission of the author.

It is not just in political campaigns that governments and their agencies walk a thin line. Consider the story of the dramatic rescue of Private Jessica Lynch during the Iraq war. The original story, accompanied by dramatic nighttime footage of a daring raid, was that she had been captured after engaging in a firefight, assaulted by her captors, and rescued from a heavily guarded hospital. Later, it appeared that the story had been substantially elaborated and stage-managed by the U.S. Army and the media. Lynch had been injured and knocked unconscious when her vehicle crashed; she had not participated in a firefight. She had, by her own account, been well treated. The "raid" was on a hospital that had been long abandoned by enemy soldiers. NBC showed a two-hour film version of her story—with glaring inaccuracies. Lynch herself wrote a book recounting a rather different version of her story, but nonetheless timed to capitalize on the publicity generated by the NBC film. While the truth about the incident remains murky, it is clear that aspects of her experience were deliberately manipulated and distorted.

The Power of False Facts

"What we remember depends on what we believe.... 'People build mental models,' explains Stephan Lewandowsky, a psychology professor at the University of Western Australia, Crawley. 'By the time they receive a retraction, the original misinformation has already become an integral part of that mental model, or worldview, and disregarding it would leave the worldview a shambles.' Therefore, he and his colleagues conclude in their paper, 'People continue to rely on misinformation even if they demonstrably remember and understand a subsequent retraction.'.... Even many of those who remembered a retraction still rated the original claim as true."

Source: Sharon Begley, "People Believe a 'Fact' That Fits Their Views Even if It's Clearly False," *The Wall Street Journal*, February 4, 2005. Reprinted by permission of *The Wall Street Journal*. Copyright © 2005 Dow Jones & Co., Inc.

Corporations sometimes knowingly help to legitimize the spread of misinformation. Recognizing the power of viral marketing, some corporate marketing departments and lobby groups orchestrate "astroturf" campaigns that revolve around a fictitious grassroots organization, coalition, or event, invented by the corporation or public relations firm to further a specific agenda. These efforts frequently involve letter writing from the nonexistent groups to politicians, postings on do-it-yourself websites, and the creation of shell organizations with no real members. Astroturf campaigns are now estimated to be a $1 billion a year industry. They often originate as "guerilla marketing" attempts to counter the comments by unhappy (or mischievous) customers but can spiral into attempts to shut down public criticism, no matter how legitimate.

NGOs are also learning how to control and package information in order to shape opinions, taking cues from the once "hidden persuaders" in the world of politics and business. For example, campaign groups have learned how to subvert the "official" version of events with their own interpretation. In 2003, Citigroup ran a global advertising campaign on the theme "This Is Citigroup," which featured pictures of smiling people around the world. The Rainforest Action Network, an environmental group, countered with its own campaign, aping the original but with photos of projects (funded by Citigroup) that it claims are damaging the ecosystem.

Today, many people and organizations are falling afoul of a much more sinister trend: the exploitation of our inability to distinguish authentic communication from sophisticated fraud. Again, the Internet has proved a potent breeding ground for con-artistry in this area. "Phishing," the use of spoof emails and official-looking websites to fool people into handing over personal financial data, is on the rise; in a recent study by the International Data Group, 96 percent of the 459 corporate IT security officers surveyed agreed that phishing scams will only proliferate. Indeed, they are difficult to stop. Banks have been especially targeted, with official-looking emails directing customers to highly convincing fake websites and compelling them to enter their account details for some spurious administrative purpose. Users of the popular auction site eBay have also been misled by hoax emails into revealing their account details, passwords, and other private information. This new category of "identity theft" is on the rise: 7 million adults in the U.S. fell victim to it during the 12 months leading up to June 2003, according to Gartner—a rise of 79 percent from the previous year.

The Imperative of Trust

In the coming decade, we will without a doubt witness a radical increase in suspicion, misinformation, disinformation, misinterpretation, conspiracy theories, and fraud. A critical consequence of this will be the growing importance of reputation and trust—for people, organizations, and governments.

One of the most extraordinary achievements of eBay is that it has created a sophisticated way for strangers separated by continents to trust one another by aggregating feedback from those they have already done business with. Increasingly, all companies will have to pay much greater attention to the issue of trust. For most, this will mean ensuring that customers continue to have confidence in them. The concept of "brand" is becoming a proxy for reputation and integrity, and that trend will surely continue in the decade ahead.

Governments will face similar pressures—even the democratic process in the U.S. is coming under increased scrutiny—and we should expect this to continue as well. The 2000 presidential election results spawned a host of conspiracy theories, as well as a new research industry that examines the mechanics of voter registration, paper trails (or the lack of them), and electronic voting machines. The 2004 presidential election sparked even more conspiracy theories, some of them the identical twins of theories that had circulated four years earlier, others brand new. As Paul Krugman predicted, with some accuracy, in *The New York Times* three months before the 2004 presidential election: "When I say that the result will be suspect, I don't mean that the election will, in fact, have been stolen. (We may never know.) I mean that there will be sufficient uncertainty about the honesty of the vote count that much of the world and many Americans will have serious doubts."

Trust has never been more critical than it is right now—and it has never been more threatened. Treating reputations and truth as strategic resources to be protected and grown will no doubt become an increasing collective obsession.

The tension between growing clarity and transparency in the world and spreading craziness and disinformation is strongly related to the interplay between reason and belief, between information and conviction. This interplay is powerfully mirrored in the next dynamic tension— between the competing perspectives of the secular and the sacred.

Chapter 3

Secular and Sacred

In the coming decade, we will witness a growing tension between the secular models of society, governance, business, and economics that have characterized Western modernity and the increasingly sacred worldviews of billions of people on every part of the planet. The secular lies at the heart of Western notions of civilization, with reason, science, and logic trumping religion and belief in the management of civic affairs and the public domain. Secular principles are so embedded in our laws and our institutions that, for the most part, we no longer notice them. Yet the power of the sacred as a mobilizing force is making itself felt with increasing strength. Fundamentalist movements (themselves a direct response to secularization) have emerged in every major religion and are gaining muscle on most continents—and by no means exclusively in the Islamic nations. Meanwhile, an almost opposite—and certainly gentler and more inclusive—"sacred" reaction against the strictly secular can be seen in the rise of spirituality, which also seems poised to play a role in defining our future values, customs, and behaviors.

Secular

> **God, protect me from your followers.**
> **—Anonymous**

The Enlightenment laid the deep and strong foundation upon which modern Western civilization was built. Enlightenment principles and values, such as reason, tolerance, respect for science, and belief in the virtue of human nature—quite radical in their day—profoundly shaped the Constitution and the character of the United States (the first true democracy), and have continued to spread in influence and deepen in impact for more than two centuries. Sitting at the core of enlightenment values is secularism, derived from the Latin word *saeculum*, meaning "the present world." Secularism is generally understood as the explicit separation of the religious and church-based from the functioning of the state and the regulation of civic society.

By the mid-nineteenth century, this separation had spread across the Western world, while the role of established religion as an ordering principle for political, economic, and social life waned significantly. Developments—such as the rise of industrialization, migration to urban areas, remarkable economic growth, and the rise in the value of the material over the spiritual—all served to further undermine established religion after it had ceased to be influential in political life. George Holyoake, a friend of the British socialist industrial reformer Robert Owen, coined the term "secularism" in the mid-nineteenth century to refer to a set of beliefs rooted in daily experience and intended to improve the lot of workers in this life rather than reward them in the next. "Secularism is a code of duty pertaining to this life founded on considerations purely human, and intended mainly for those who find theology indefinite or inadequate, unreliable or unbelievable," he explained. Secularism, social reform, and materialism became entwined as complementary factors in adapting to and shaping the modern world.

The Secular Mindset

The secular mindset, while not essentially or necessarily anti-religious, is about more than restricting the influence of religion on civic governance. It is the outcome of a deeper philosophical shift in which reason supplanted belief as the central maker and organizer of meaning, and in which mankind was understood to have the power to shape and change the world to serve human needs and wants without reliance upon God. This shift enabled new modes of enlightened thought and reasoning that came to define secular modernity—they are now so embedded in Western worldviews that they have become invisible and unremarkable.

In particular, the rise of secularism was powerfully linked to a human-centric view of the world that placed the desires of people in a separate category from the needs of other species; the physical environment was but an endless catalogue of resources to be exploited and manipulated to serve human interests. This, in turn, was linked to a powerful belief in science and scientific methods as the means through which incontrovertible truths and single "right answers" about the natural world could be discovered that could then be used to further man's dominion over nature. Above all, secularism fostered a potent and optimistic pragmatism that placed the highest value on knowledge, insights, and ideas that could address and solve the problems that mattered most to mankind.

The Secular Unleashed

The Enlightenment rationality underpinned the development of economics and Western theories of how business should work. Especially in the developed West, it became the guidebook for how to think and perceive the world, as well as how to value and measure success and progress. It also underpins many of our social theories and the ways in which civic society and political systems have been constructed.

The payoffs have been tremendous. Principles and ideals that people in the developed world tend to take for granted today (and sometimes assume to be timeless) owe their origins and their power to the relatively recent Enlightenment perspective. Democracy, freedom, individual liberty, and tolerance of differing belief systems are all offspring of secular modernity. The remarkable march of economic and material progress and growth of the

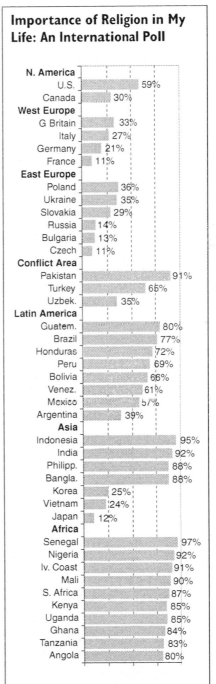

Importance of Religion in My Life: An International Poll

N. America	
U.S.	59%
Canada	30%
West Europe	
G Britain	33%
Italy	27%
Germany	21%
France	11%
East Europe	
Poland	36%
Ukraine	35%
Slovakia	29%
Russia	14%
Bulgaria	13%
Czech	11%
Conflict Area	
Pakistan	91%
Turkey	65%
Uzbek.	35%
Latin America	
Guatem.	80%
Brazil	77%
Honduras	72%
Peru	69%
Bolivia	66%
Venez.	61%
Mexico	57%
Argentina	39%
Asia	
Indonesia	95%
India	92%
Philipp.	88%
Bangla.	88%
Korea	25%
Vietnam	24%
Japan	12%
Africa	
Senegal	97%
Nigeria	92%
Iv. Coast	91%
Mali	90%
S. Africa	87%
Kenya	85%
Uganda	85%
Ghana	84%
Tanzania	83%
Angola	80%

Source: "Among Wealthy Nations…U.S. Stands Alone in Its Embrace of Religion," The Pew Research Center for the People and the Press, December 19, 2002. Reprinted by permission of The Pew Global Attitudes Project.

last two centuries has been fueled in many ways by Enlightenment-inspired scientific and technological innovations. Evolving corporate, legal, regulatory, infrastructural, financial, and governance systems were all influenced enormously by the economic theories that flowed directly from the insights of Adam Smith and his contemporaries. The ongoing spread of wealth and opportunity across much of the world, increase in life expectancy, and growth in literacy rates are a testament to the power and effectiveness of the secular mindset.

Meanwhile, societies that have eschewed Enlightenment principles are generally less wealthy, less equitable, less democratic, and far less innovative. *New York Times* columnist Thomas Friedman's patent statistics exemplify this fact: "Between 1980 and 1999 the nine leading Arab economies registered 370 patents [in the U.S.] for new inventions," Friedman wrote in 2003. "Patents are a good measure of a society's education quality, entrepreneurship, rule of law, and innovation. During that same 20-year period, South Korea registered 16,328 patents for inventions."

It is not surprising, then, that the secular perspective has taken such firm root. By the mid-twentieth century, the rise of modernity and a shift to the secular had become apparently inseparable. Anthropologist Anthony Wallace captured the prevailing wisdom well when he predicted in the 1960s that "the evolutionary future of religion is extinction." A clear self-reinforcing cycle had begun: as the authority of religion diminishes in social and political affairs, its attractiveness, endurance, and cultural reach falls into decline.

This cycle has been most visible in Europe. In his book *God Is Dead: Secularization in the West*, respected sociologist of religion Steve Bruce takes data from Britain as typical of the trends in the liberal, democratic, economically developed modern world. Whether it is involvement in religious organizations, church attendance, training for the priesthood, commitment to religious ideals, or just simple belief, Bruce concludes that religion has long been in steady decline. He describes modern secular Britain in unambiguous terms: "Christian ideas are not taught in schools, are not promoted by social elites, are not reinforced by rites of passage, and are not taken for granted in the mass media. Given those changes it would indeed be a miracle if Christian ideas were as popular as they were in the 1950s."

A Secular Britain

Percentage of Brits who claimed no religious affiliation in 2000: 44

That percentage in 1983: 31

Percentage drop in the number of people who said they were members of Britain's state religion, from 1983 to 2000: 40

Percentage of 18-to 24-year-olds in the UK who say they have no religious affiliation: 66

Percentage of Brits who claimed to belong to a religion in 2000: 48

Percentage in the U.S.: 86

Percentage in Italy: 92

Percentage of the British population that Peter Bierley, the leading expert on church attendance in Britain, believes will be attending church services in 2040: 0.5

Percentage by which seminary enrollment dropped from 1970 to 1995, according to the Center for Applied Research in the Apostolate at Georgetown University: 50

Sources: BBC News, *The New Criterion*, Associated Press.

Moreover, the dominant powers of today's world—nation-states, multinational corporations, and international organizations—are overwhelmingly secular. This has become the norm in modern global governance and commerce: we expect a separation of church and state, religious tolerance, an absence of religious persecution, and a breaking up of religion's hegemonic or monopolistic power in society. In the West, we have come to expect secularization as a precondition of good governance, so much so that our state-based institutions have difficulty accommodating state-sponsored religion. For example, the European Union has hesitated to welcome Turkey as a member in large measure because of lingering suspicion that its secular constitution may not be truly genuine and that it will revert to operating like an Islamic state.

In the coming decade, secularism will be further reinforced by several factors. The first is the continuing spread of proven business-based practices and approaches across the world and across every sector of activity. The dominant Western model of business is resolutely secular: reason and rationality consistently trump intuition and instinct; data and evidence overwhelm belief and faith; the quantitative is more trusted than the qualitative. These values continue to spread across the world. Moreover, as the stability of fragile states becomes a matter of growing concern, we can expect global institutions, international lenders, and nongovernmental organizations to place more emphasis on encouraging and enabling "good" local governance arrangements around the world. The core principles of such arrangements will flow directly from the secular paradigm. Finally, the mounting issues of the modern world—large populations to be fed, important security concerns, climatic change, burgeoning energy needs—call for more and better rational, scientific solutions.

Jacques Chirac Bans Head Scarves in French Schools

"The Islamic veil—whatever name we give it—the kippa, and a cross that is of plainly excessive dimensions: these have no place in the precincts of state schools. State schools will remain secular. For that a law is necessary.... Secularism is one of the great conquests of the republic. It is an element crucial to our social peace and national cohesion. We cannot let it weaken. We must work to reinforce it."

Source: The president's address to the nation of France, December 17, 2003.

Today's organizations and institutions came to life during a profoundly secular era and are predominantly ingrained with a secular outlook and values. Looking forward, our sensibilities regarding global politics, economic development, technology change, social and cultural matters, and environmental issues are equally imbued with a strongly secular perspective. However, the very success of secular modernity has generated its own profound challenges, and these will become more pressing in the coming decade.

Weaknesses of the Secular Model

The complexity, connectedness, and volatility of the world today require us to amplify our comfort with ambiguity, tolerance of difference, and openness to alternative interpretations. Yet our embedded forms of secular reasoning sometimes stand in the way of this. The secular worldview is built upon reason and "truth" discovered through scientific methods and debate. This rationalist model has little tolerance for ambiguity or doubt; indeed, it tends to be structured around a crisp "either/or" logic through which ambiguities can be conclusively resolved one way or another. This black and white perspective, which increasingly informs civic and political discourse around the world, often leads to polarization and false certainty built around ideological models that are too firmly held as fact rather than opinion. (The greatest such schism is now behind us: the twentieth-century clash between two competing forms of secular modernity, capitalism and communism, both of which were zealously promoted as the "only way" by their advocates.)

Moreover, science and reason are driven largely by evidence, quantification, and measurement, placing significant emphasis on numbers and giving the knowable supremacy over the unknowable. Yet, as Einstein observed: "Not everything that counts can be counted, and not everything that can be counted counts." Today we tend toward an almost obsessive fascination with metrics—measurable indicators that can be tracked and used to judge success and failure, progress and decline. In business, the metrics we choose often drive rather than measure performance, and not always for the better or in the ways intended. The field of education has also developed increased reliance on metrics and measurement in an effort to raise standards and accountability—with the inevitable consequence that an increasing amount of student time is being spent preparing for and taking tests rather than learning. As the old saying goes, "You don't make the hog any heavier by weighing it repeatedly." The strengths of secular approaches become weaknesses when they pull us too far away from our own judgment and provoke unintended consequences.

The secular perspective starts and ends with the needs and desires of mankind; everything else—and crucially, all of nature—is too often regarded as a resource pool to be drawn upon, consumed, and manipulated for human purpose. There is no place in this worldview for the more ancient notion that man "must tread lightly upon the Earth." In the secular scheme, mankind has dominion over the planet, and with science as its key tool, it can and should shape the natural world to human advantage. Luckily, after more than two centuries of rapid economic growth unconstrained by consideration of the impact it might have on the planet and its other species, we are becoming more aware of the profound negative environmental consequences of this perspective. Yet even as we struggle to make real the concept of sustainability, we are in part constrained by our deep-seated, unconscious secular sense of human entitlement.

American "Happiness"

"No society in the history of the world has ever enjoyed the standard of living Americans know today....Yet since 1960, the divorce rate has doubled, teen suicide tripled, violent crime quadrupled, the prison population has quintupled, and some estimates put the incidence of depression in the year 2000 at 10 times what it was in the year 1900. Americans are less happy today than they were 40 years ago, despite the fact that they make 2.5 times as much money."

Source: Barry Schwartz, Ph. D., "Waking Up From the American Dream," *Psychology Today*, July/August 2000. Reprinted by permission of *Psychology Today*. Copyright © 2000 Sussex Publishers, Inc.

By definition, secularism is about improving material conditions in the here and now and worrying less about the spiritual or the "afterlife." This way of thinking has significantly, if invisibly, influenced the science of economics and the practice of business and commerce—sometimes adversely. Materialism and high levels of consumption have become widespread characteristics of developed societies. Yet they do not appear to be making us any happier. Surveys in most developed countries, including the U.S. and Japan, reveal that there has been no increase in happiness over the last several decades despite substantial economic growth. Depression is on the rise; each year, as many as 14 million American adults experience an episode of major depression, 10 times more than in 1945. According to the World Health Organization, suicide rates have increased by 60 percent worldwide in the last 45 years. WHO now ranks depression as the leading cause of disability globally and projects that depression will be the second leading health problem in the world by 2020.

Complaints about the "soulless" nature of organizations, designed to harness human reason rather than honor human spirit, are also on the rise. Early economists' focus on the production of material and measurable goods led to accounting methodologies that failed to value a great deal of the work that holds families and communities together—particularly work typically undertaken by women, including child-rearing, housework, and relationship nurturing. Businesses and financial markets have little obvious means of connecting with higher moral purpose and are typically obliged to conform to short-term thinking and a desire for immediate returns. These are issues of growing concern today, and are deeply connected to the secular origins of the modern economy.

Above all, the secular mindset, reinforced by two centuries of unrivalled achievement, has perhaps become far too confident about the supremacy of its role in shaping the future. Even as secular civilization mobilizes to address challenges generated by its own embedded philosophy, another worldview—less prominent and less of a defining force in recent centuries—is reemerging to take its place at the table. The "sacred" perspective has returned, and the secular world is going to have to learn how to accommodate it.

Sacred

> **I've read the last page of the Bible. It's all going to turn out alright.**
> **—Billy Graham**

To the bewilderment of many Europeans and even many Americans, the 2004 U.S. presidential election highlighted the fundamental yet rising significance of religious conviction in the U.S. today. Perhaps it is not surprising that a country founded and regularly refreshed by immigrants seeking freedom from religious persecution should not only be the first modern secular state but also the one that has sustained the highest levels of religious participation. In the U.S., the epitome of modernity, churches and organized religion have endured as a potent popular and political force. Church attendance remains stable. Sixty percent of Americans say that religion plays an important role in their lives, according to a 2002 Pew Research Center survey. This is so unusual in the developed world that Pew titled its survey report "Among Wealthy Nations…U.S. Stands Alone in Its Embrace of Religion." Pew's conclusion: "Americans' views are closer to people in developing nations than to the publics of developed nations."

Not only have the practice and influence of religion remained strong in the U.S.—they are also growing. Driven by the continued rise of evangelical Christianity in the U.S. since the 1970s, religion has been moving back into the everyday discourse of American civic and political life. In 1984, 22 percent of voters believed that presidential candidates should discuss the role of religion in their lives; 75 percent said that it should not be part of a presidential campaign. The same survey taken by *The New York Times* during the 2004 presidential campaign showed a dramatic change in those figures: 42 percent wanted to hear about candidates' religious beliefs, while just 53 percent thought that religion should be kept out of the campaign.

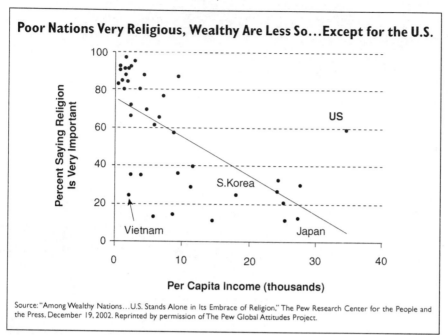

Poor Nations Very Religious, Wealthy Are Less So…Except for the U.S.

Per Capita Income (thousands)

Source: "Among Wealthy Nations…U.S. Stands Alone in Its Embrace of Religion," The Pew Research Center for the People and the Press, December 19, 2002. Reprinted by permission of The Pew Global Attitudes Project.

This is a considerable shift in 20 years and confirms the wider fact that the secularization trend is reversing itself in the U.S. It should not be surprising, then, that during his visit to the Vatican in June 2004, President George W. Bush, leader of the world's first constitutionally secular nation, actively sought the intervention of Pope John Paul II in the U.S. election campaign, asking the Pope to acknowledge his anti-abortion credentials. Meanwhile, Bush's campaign team targeted membership lists from Christian churches.

Is the U.S. a curious anomaly—or leading evidence of the broader durability and permanence of the sacred perspective? Secularists have long assumed that with increased prosperity, better education, and the advance of scientific understanding, societies would inevitably turn away from religion. However, this appears to have occurred as expected only in Europe, and emphatically not in the U.S. The evidence elsewhere remains ambiguous and to some extent contradictory. In Muslim countries, for example, opinion appears to embrace both the promise of modern governance and adherence to strict religious rule. A 2003 Pew Global Attitudes Project survey revealed that this dissonance still persists. "People in Muslim countries place a high value on freedom of expression, freedom of the press, multi-party systems, and equal treatment under the law," the survey found. At the same time, most Muslims "favor a prominent—in many cases expanded—role for Islam and religious leaders in the political life of their countries."

Meanwhile, around much of the world, we are witnessing the phenomenal growth of Pentecostalism, a Christian movement born in the U.S. in the early twentieth century now believed to have more than 20 million adherents in the U.S. and more than 400 million adherents worldwide, as well as the world's largest church—the Yoido Full Gospel Church in South Korea, which in 2003 had 780,000 members. It is interesting to observe that this is a new strand within Christianity—one that places emphasis on the spirit and that is energetic and engaging for its participants, providing grace plus community and belonging. In fact, much of the current growth in religious conviction involves novel forms of the monotheistic religions (perhaps because the moderate establishments of each were largely acquiescent in the move toward secularism). Worryingly, they include a powerful rise in new forms of fundamentalism.

New Fundamentalism

The rise of fundamentalism around the world has been a subject of commentary since the September 11 terrorist attacks. But it was the object of quieter (and generally wiser and more balanced) review long before that. Fundamentalist belief systems are less filled with love and hope than Pentecostalism. They are characterized by exclusivity, certainty, and separateness; they create the potential for increased tribalism and violence, as well as profound assaults on the prevailing secular worldview.

The rise in Islamic fundamentalism continues to be widely regarded as a threat to the Western world, and the U.S. in particular. Less acknowledged is the fact that fundamentalism was on the march during the twentieth century in all three of the monotheistic religions of Abraham and has also been spreading into other religious systems wherever the modern world is making new inroads. In India, there has been a resurgence of Hindu fundamentalism, with reported violence against Christian and Muslim minorities. In South Korea and Taiwan, a "neotraditionalist" Confucianism has emerged. Japan has experienced growth in radical Buddhism, and the Sikh religion has become progressively more fundamentalist, spurred by threats of Hindu and Muslim violence in Northern India. As Phillip Longman says in his book *The Empty Cradle,* if the birthrate in the developed world continues to decline, it is fundamental-ism that will benefit. "In a world of falling human population only fun-damentalists would draw new strength," Longman writes. "For the deep messages of the Bible and the Koran...are relentlessly pro-natal."

Religious fundamentalism is not, as is sometimes assumed, a return to old established ways. It is an innovative new phenomenon. The term was first used by American Protestants in the early twentieth century. Indeed, Christianity (in the U.S.) was the first major religion to give birth to a fundamentalist movement. Given the U.S.'s place at the vanguard of sec-ular modernity, this may seem surprising. But fundamentalism is always associated with a sense of threat against the survival of a religious belief system; primarily, it is a fear-driven response to the encroachment of modernity and a coercive secularism. Acclaimed religious historian Karen Armstrong is unequivocal on this: "Fundamentalism is an essential part of the modern scene. Wherever modernity takes root, a fundamentalist movement is likely to rise up alongside it in conscious reaction." As the encroachment of modernity becomes stronger, so the fundamentalist reaction becomes more extreme and entrenched.

This may represent a collective, almost instinctive reaction to increasing complexity and tempestuous change. In a highly unstable world, some will inevitably search for a firm and steady anchor, an absence of ambiguity, and a clear, simple, and authorized set of rules. But fundamentalism can also be viewed as a subset of another, broader reaction to globalization and increased interdependence and interaction: a desire for separateness. Fundamentalist beliefs are by nature exclusive and divisive. A single set of absolute truths can tolerate no competing set of perspectives.

Religious fundamentalism often also holds the promise of a better life in the next world to compensate for earthly suffering or reward commit-ted sacrifice. This is a potent promise—and is one reason that funda-mentalism can foster conditions for extremism and violence among many faiths and in many forms. Timothy McVeigh's bombing in Oklahoma City and the 1995 assassination of Israeli President Yitzak Rabin demon-strate that Christianity and Judaism are not immune from spawning their own forms of violence and should also remain causes of concern. However, there is no doubt that the tendency toward violence within fundamentalist movements is significantly increased by a societal conflict of lingering tensions, conflict, or even war, and that such conditions exist today in many parts of the Islamic world in particular. Islamic fundamentalism (and the extremist violence it can foster) is, without doubt, one of the most significant challenges of the next several decades. It is all too easy to imagine it getting worse before it gets better.

What's Driving Islamic Fundamentalism?

In all the monotheistic religions, fundamentalism builds upon a return to Holy Scripture as the literal foundation for a belief system. Mainstream moderate religious followers tend to embrace a fluid and evolving faith, one in which scripture is considered as much a product of iterative development as the origin of the belief system and is subject to reinterpretation over time. Fundamentalism rejects this openness, seeking to lock down the religion according to the most literal and inflexible interpretation.

The earliest seeds of this reaction in Islam were arguably sown in the eighteenth century with the emergence of the reform movement known as Wahabbism, which, while not itself a fundamentalist movement, sought to eradicate all the characteristics and forms of the religion that had been added since the time of Mohammad. Saudi Arabia, home of Osama bin Laden and most of the September 11 hijackers, is a Wahabbist kingdom.

The teachings of the Sunni Egyptian Sayyid Qutb are a more direct and powerful source of today's Islamic fundamentalism. A member of the Muslim Brotherhood, Qutb served more than a decade in prison in the 1950s and 1960s before being executed by Egyptian president Gamal Abdel Nasser in 1966. He wrote extensively during his imprisonment, producing an enormous multivolume work called *In the Shade of the Qu'ran.* Qutb's writings laid the foundation for today's Islamic extremism and violence and provide the philosophical underpinnings for Al Qaeda. The core of his philosophy is simple: for centuries, the Christian West has been driving a wedge between the godly and the scientific, between reason and belief. The result is a "hideous dichotomy" that has led to great and growing human misery and despair that is now being exported steadily all over the world.

Qutb: The Philosopher of Islamic Terror

The core of Qutb's argument was neatly summarized by Paul Berman in an article in *The New York Times Magazine* in March 2003 titled, "The Philosopher of Islamic Terror." According to Berman, Qutb wrote that God had provided Moses and the Jews with the guidance, instruction, and behaviors that were required for man to live in harmony with both the spiritual and the physical world, without tension between the two. Over time, Judaism ossified and turned lifeless. God chose another prophet, Jesus, to introduce new reforms and a revival of spirituality. But Christ's followers and the traditional Jews clashed and argued, and as a result his messages became distorted. Most tragically, the early Christians had embraced the Greek notion of separating the physical world from the spiritual world—a separation of the secular and the sacred. This created, according to Qutb, a "hideous dichotomy," one that later led humanity to disaster.

In the seventh century, God again chose a new prophet—Mohammad—and provided a new set of instructions and codes that enabled religion to sit in harmonious ease within the physical world. In particular, he stressed that man should freely take charge of the physical world and not regard it as separate from his spiritual existence. This led to the emergence of the great early science of Islam during the Middle Ages, including the creation of the inductive method, which underpins all modern scientific inquiry and discovery. For several centuries Islam enjoyed leadership in the world until, beleaguered by conflict with Christians and other attackers and weakened by failure to faithfully follow the teachings of Mohammad, Islam could not take full advantage of what it had started. The powerful scientific methods it had initiated passed instead to Christian Europe.

Therefore, science and technology developed and flourished within a growing dichotomy between the sacred and the physical, with science on one side of a divide and religion and God on the other side—reason and belief pulled apart. This cleavage split humanity in two, dividing our need for God and the divine from our appetite for knowledge of our physical world. Thus, the "hideous dichotomy" introduced by Christianity led to a modern-world crisis in which material success resulted not in happiness but in despair, and anxiety and skepticism prevailed. The human race had become separated from human nature. Through their technological and economic dominance, Europeans then exported this misery across the globe.

continues

Qutb spread the blame widely. He blamed Jews, early Christians, European empires, America's support of Zionism, secularism, and Muslims who had accepted Christian errors. Only Islam offered a way of living in accordance with God's intentions; only Islam acknowledged the unity of the sacred and the secular and provided a path for mankind. Yet Islam was under sustained attack from other religions and even from within its own ranks; these enemies sought nothing less than to exterminate it. To prevail, Islam had to respond. Qutb set out a program, derived primarily from the experiences of Mohammad, which included a phase of with-drawal from the world, a period of preparation, and then an offensive phase attacking the enemies of Islam. "To the end...Qutb himself remained an ideologue rather than an agitator," Karen Armstrong wrote in *The Battle for God*. But Al Qaeda is in some important measure a direct legacy of his philosophy.

Islamic fundamentalism has developed upon a core philosophy not fully understood by those it challenges. But, crucially, it is the broader context of many Islamic nations that has fueled its growth: five centuries of rela-tive economic, scientific, and technological decline; a recent history of occupation and subjugation by the empires of Europe; in some states, the imposition of alien, secular approaches to governance by elites that have not shared power and have often not shared the benefits of modernity; a demographic swell of young men in Middle Eastern countries, with stag-nant economies providing few opportunities; unresolved tension and con-flict between Israel and its Arab neighbors and between Pakistan and India; an infrastructure of education, especially the madrasas of Pakistan and Afghanistan, that promotes fundamentalist beliefs; the prolonged and much resented Soviet occupation of Afghanistan; and a growing mistrust of the U.S., widely regarded as a nation attempting to impose an insidious and profoundly unwelcome form of imperialism. Hence, the combustible combination of inflammatory ideas and people eager to adopt them that emerged in the last two decades of the last century and that will undoubt-edly help shape the first decades of this new one.

Christian Missionaries Heading to Europe

Christian missionaries from South America and Asia are at work in the United Kingdom, attempting to spread the gospel and convert secular Europeans to forms of evangelical Christianity. In 2001, about 1,500 missionaries from 50 countries were believed to be operating in churches in Britain, attempting to reinvigorate fading parishes.

Source: "Missionaries Flock to Britain to Revive Passion for Church," *The Daily Telegraph*, January 18, 2001.

The challenges posed by a rise in this tension between secular and sacred are complex and perplexing. To be sure, the heaviest burden must be carried by the majority of people in the Islamic world—people who seek harmonious and mutually beneficial relationships with the rest of the world while promoting the essence of their great religion. But they must be helped by the West, especially by the U.S. Frankly, this will require a greater sophistication of thought, word, and deed in the West than has so far been in evidence in the years following September 2001. The responses to date have included a "hearts and minds" campaign in the Islamic world, run like a corporate marketing program, to "re-brand" America in the Islamic world. Unfortunately, the authenticity of this campaign was undermined by other key signals from the U.S., including the unhelpful rhetoric of "good versus evil" and the repeated assertions that the U.S. has embarked upon a divinely ordained mission.

When Jerry Falwell proclaimed that September 11, 2001, was "God's punishment" of the U.S. for its secular ways, he was inadvertently speaking in the language of the hijackers. When President Bush talked of a "crusade" (a comment he later withdrew), he clearly did not realize the inflammatory nature of that phrase. The continued use of terms such as "evil-doers," coupled with attempts to push the margins of legality in the detention and treatment of prisoners, have created a dangerous atmosphere. This arguably helped create the conditions for the events at Abu Ghraib, which shook even the U.S.'s champions. The United States has never had a greater need to learn and demonstrate cultural competence in a fraught world. In dealing with Islamic fundamentalism's threats and violence, it must learn to step carefully back from its own tendencies in that direction.

U.S. Fundamentalism

- 59 percent of Americans believe the events in the Book of Revelations will come true.

- 17 percent believe the end of the world will happen in their lifetime.

- 45 percent of Americans believe in strict creationism and only 35 percent in evolution.

- Americans are twice as likely to believe in the devil (70 percent) than in evolution.

Source: Gallup polls conducted in May 2004 and November 2004.

Christian Fundamentalism

Indeed, while confronting the challenges of religious extremism, attention should not be focused solely on Islam. Though they have garnered much less attention, much stricter forms of Christianity are emerging, particularly in the developing world. A survey by Philip Jenkins in the *Atlantic Monthly* in October 2002 reported that the rising popularity of Christian faiths in the poorer regions of the world is likely to transform their relationship with the developed world in the next quarter century. In Africa, Latin America, and Asia, Pentecostalism is growing rapidly; so are stricter forms of Protestantism and less-tolerant forms of Catholicism. In his survey, Jenkins notes that "African and Latin American churches tend to be very conservative on issues such as homosexuality and abortion," in contrast to the far more liberal attitudes in many "northern" churches. The stage is set for significant schisms within the Christian faith, the largest faith in the world.

The drift toward fundamentalism in Christianity is not confined to the developing world, however. A similar dynamic is underway in the U.S., perhaps most dramatically illustrated by the spectacular popularity of the Left Behind book series—11 novels about the lives of people "left behind" after the sudden, apocalyptic disappearance of millions of Christians. Described by Salon.com as "a Tom Clancy-meets-Revelation saga of the Rapture, the Tribulation, and presumably, the eventual return of Jesus," more than 60 million copies of the Left Behind books have been sold. *Time* magazine estimates that only half of Left Behind readers are evangelical Christians.

Mel Gibson's "The Passion of the Christ"

- Earned more than $370 million at the North American box office, making it the top-grossing R-rated movie of all time

- Made $239 million in overseas theaters, so that worldwide gross in theaters = $609 million

- DVD sales of the film topped $4.1 million in a single day; the editor in chief of *DVD Exclusive* predicted that sales of the "Passion" DVD would ultimately reach between 15 million and 18 million copies, generating as much as $400 million

Source: Box Office Mojo, CNN Money.

Another Path to the Sacred—The Rise of Spirituality

There is another, quite different "sacred" response to global modernity on the rise today: neo-spirituality. Known for its embrace of inclusiveness, holism, and tolerance, neo-spirituality most commonly manifests itself in New Age world-affirming philosophies, the revival of Eastern religious practices and traditions, and the growth in psychotherapy and human potential that has emerged since the 1960s, especially in Europe and the U.S. These various forms of spirituality are often referred to as "self-religions" because, as Steve Bruce argues, "New Agers believe that the self is divine or, if it is not yet, then it can become so with the right therapy, ritual, or training." In *Holistic Revolution*, William Bloom, one of Britain's leading holistic teachers and practitioners, argues that the rise of this phenomenon is in part a consequence of an increasingly modern, secular world. "A planetary culture of free-flowing information is absolutely bound to manifest new ways of enquiring into meaning. This is to be applauded. It is liberating and deeply democratic," Bloom writes. "It encourages and empowers people to taste around until they find those pieces of the jigsaw that fit their character and temperament."

Spirituality is born of the same impulse that fuels more traditional religion and fundamentalism: a belief that a deeper level of reality can be perceived and a more profound wisdom discovered. But spirituality resides at the opposite end of the cultural spectrum from fundamentalism, attracting those who are drawn to a journey of discovery and growth, to a postmodern perspective of multiple truths, to finding new questions rather than more certain answers, and to learning and experimenting rather than subscribing to a rigid set of infallible and static givens.

These amorphous, fluid, and increasingly democratic characteristics make it difficult to pinpoint and analyze neo-spirituality as a "movement." As pointed out by U.S. social researchers Paul Ray and Sherry Ruth Anderson, who have studied at length this modern turn toward living a more spiritual and ethical life, the many millions of people pursuing this path are largely hidden from mainstream political or religious analysis because their beliefs are multifaceted and difficult to categorize. But even if neo-spirituality is not an easily defined movement, it is certainly a powerful trend. In the U.S. today, one of the fastest growing religious groups comprises people who classify themselves in census returns as "nones"—those who do not subscribe to any particular branch of religious belief yet are not atheistic. Their ranks in the U.S. have doubled in the last decade, to around 30 million. In the UK (where *Cosmopolitan* magazine has recently appointed a "spirituality editor"), a 2000 survey by David Hay and Kate Hunt found that 76 percent of people acknowledged having had a religious or spiritual experience—far more than belong to and participate in churches. In China, Falun Gong, an integrative practice that incorporates Buddhist and Taoist principles with body and mind exercise and healing techniques, claims 100 million members; that is 40 million more people than belong to the Chinese Communist Party. Threatened, the Chinese government has denounced Falun Gong as a dangerous "cult" that "under the pretense of religion, kindness, and being nonpolitical, participates in political activities," and has declared it illegal.

Looking forward, we can anticipate two likely neo-spiritual dynamics in the coming decade. First, neo-spirituality will likely continue to integrate and align Western and Eastern philosophies and practices and draw heavily from self-improvement methodologies. The popularity of yoga, meditation, holistic medicine, and alternative therapies continues to rise. Roughly 16.5 million Americans now practice yoga regularly, an increase of 43 percent since 2002, according to research by *Yoga Journal* magazine. Americans spend $27 billion annually on alternative medicine, and 88 percent believe in its efficacy. One study in the early 1990s found that New Agers represent 20 percent of the population, and are the third largest religious group in the U.S.

The second dynamic we are likely to see is the integration of spiritual and religious belief with deep concern for the physical environment. Groups within mainstream Christian and Jewish religions are already moving in this direction, as seen in such nascent movements as "What Would Jesus Drive?" and "Rabbis for the Redwoods." And there is growing evidence that evangelical are "going green"; in October 2004, leaders of the National Association of Evangelicals, which has 30 million members, adopted an "Evangelical Call to Civic Responsibility," proclaiming that it is every Christian's duty to preserve and protect the planet. This convergence might even fuel a resurgence of Gaia-like concepts and belief systems. The Gaia theory, developed by James Lovelock, suggests that the Earth be viewed as a coherent system of life, self-regulating and behaving as if it were a super-organism made up from all living things and their material environment. "We now see that the air, the ocean, and the soil are much more than a mere environment for life; they are a part of life itself," Lovelock writes.

Fundamentalism and spirituality, then, represent two extremes of the re-emerging sacred: one a reversion from modernity to traditionalism, the other a struggling journey into postmodernity. The more established conventional religions will find themselves increasingly squeezed and threatened by these two flanks. Meanwhile, the assumptions of a dominant secular worldview may be seriously undermined. It is likely indeed that the tension between the sacred and the secular will play out in several interesting and different ways. The West will need to learn how to combat Islamic extremism without fueling it. Muslim nations like Saudi Arabia, Pakistan, Iran, and Iraq will struggle to find a balance between Islam and the secular structures of the modern world in order to define their own futures. The environmentalist movement will struggle to express its spiritual intuitions about the nature of nature and our place in the world within a secular worldview. And our organizations and institutions, born and matured in an era of deep secularism, will need to learn how to align with the growing desire—indeed, insistence—of the sacred world, in its many manifestations, to reintegrate with and help shape modern society.

The tension between the secular and scared worldviews—and, in particular, between different sacred belief systems—seems set to be an important source of political and social strife in the coming decade. Therefore, it will contribute to the growing dilemmas about the optimal projection of power in a volatile world, as well as to the growing sense of threat and vulnerability. The next dynamic tension explores these issues.

Chapter 4

Power and Vulnerability

In the coming decade, the accumulation and exercise of power will rise in strategic importance as a new global order begins to take shape. The U.S. will be obliged to confront and resolve the challenges sparked by its global military supremacy, and it will continue to wrestle with the delicate interplay between "hard" and "soft" power as both are deployed to achieve complex foreign policy objectives. In the shadow of the U.S., many other nations will be required to review their military policies and expenditures; all over the world, nations will have to distinguish more clearly between the metaphoric and literal meanings of the "war on terror." As they do so, the paradoxical relationship between power and vulnerability will come into sharper relief. The U.S. and the rest of the world will continue to experience the trauma of terrorism, both real and imagined. Other vulnerabilities will be felt more acutely as well. The growing tentacles of organized crime, the fragility of our increasingly vital connectivity technologies, new and rapidly spreading diseases—these and others will contribute to a rising, global sense of threat.

Power

> You can get more with a kind word and a gun than with a
> kind word alone.
> —Al Capone

In the years following the end of the Cold War, optimism flourished that a new global order was emerging. Not imposed by any single actor, it was evolving through the convergence of invisible yet historic forces related to the power of the market, the supremacy of democracy, and the innate human urge for freedom and autonomy. Above all, it seemed that the future was being shaped primarily by economic factors, or market power. The spread of wealth and opportunity was the vanguard, and political and social change was bound to follow. Adam Smith's "invisible hand" was quietly recasting the globe in a Western image. As Frank Fukuyama has said, a new order based on the triumph of liberal democracy and market economics seemed inevitable.

Conflict and wars continued to erupt in the more disorderly parts of the world, and world peace remained a distant dream. Yet there were strong reasons to believe that the long-term, large-scale violence that had recurred throughout history and had so scarred the twentieth century might be behind us, replaced by a new economic order based on competitive, open trade. With this came the hope that traditional power—the capacity for the enforcement of will through political strength underpinned by military might—may fade in priority. Bolstered by this notion, Europe reduced its military from 3 percent of its GDP in 1990 to 2 percent by 2000. The U.S. cashed in a substantial "peace dividend" during the same period, cutting its military spending from 5.6 percent of its GDP to 3.2 percent.

Yet in the early years of the twenty-first century, the imperative of military power has been firmly re-established. It is this form of power, not market power, that is again shaping the future. The U.S., arguably the most powerful nation in history, sits squarely at the center of this revival. How it chooses to wield its military might—and how others react—will be a defining theme in the coming decade. It will set the course of international affairs and global order for decades to come.

The Reluctant Empire

In 1776, Adam Smith observed in *The Wealth of Nations* that the founders and forgers of America were "employed in contriving a new form of government for an extensive empire which, they flatter themselves, will become, and which, indeed, seems very likely to become, one of the greatest and most formidable that ever was in the world." In 2004, another Scot, Niall Ferguson, commented upon the degree to which the U.S. had become a *de facto* empire, even if it was unwilling to accept the label: "Officially, the United States remains an empire in denial.... Freud defined denial as a primitive psychological defense mechanism against trauma. Perhaps it was therefore inevitable that, in the aftermath of the September 11 attacks, U.S. citizens would deny their country's imperial character more vehemently than ever. It may nevertheless be therapeutic to determine the precise nature of this American Empire—since empire it is, in all but name."

The U.S. achieved its central status in the world primarily through its entrepreneurial talent, innovative excellence, economic might, and cultural ubiquity. As a result, it has largely avoided the problems and resentments associated with most nineteenth-century notions of "empire"—the perils of over-reaching, the bitterness of the subjugated, the dependence of those whose ways have been destroyed, and the arrogance of its own bureaucracies. In the decade ahead, however, the U.S. will face the same tests that previous global powers have largely failed. Whether the U.S. can deploy its strength wisely, avoid the trappings and responsibilities of empire, and, above all, not sow the seeds of its own defeat is one of the greatest questions of our times.

In this, the U.S. has one considerable advantage. In past centuries, great powers deliberately sought out conquest and expansion. Today, the principal reason for projecting power across the globe is not to colonize territory but to defuse chaos. The U.S. does not want "empire" in the sense of subjugated dominions for which it assumes responsibility. But it does crave security—and reassurance that the zones of lawlessness that threaten a stable world order can be brought under control.

The impact of the September 11 terrorist attacks cannot be exaggerated in this regard, for they led to nothing less than a fundamental refocusing of foreign policy aims—a shift in strategy that is now polarizing both the U.S. and the world. While the new focus is centered on the prevention of terrorist attacks against U.S. territory and interests, the ambition is much greater—the spread of Western concepts of freedom, democracy, and economic development to every part of the globe, particularly disruptive areas capable of generating conflict, disorder, and danger.

In *The Pentagon's New Map*, Thomas Barnett neatly sums up the U.S.'s re-evaluation of its priorities in security strategy, outlining a "zone of chaos" that he argues will attract most of the U.S.'s foreign policy attention. Barnett draws a link between a nation's failure to integrate with the processes of globalization and its potential to threaten the world system and U.S. interests: "If a country is either losing out to globalization or rejecting much of the content flows associated with its advance, there is a far greater chance that the U.S. will end up sending forces at some point." The final report of the 9-11 Commission makes a similar point: "In the

twentieth century, strategists focused on the world's great industrial heart-
lands. In the twenty-first, the focus is in the opposite direction, toward
remote regions and failing states."

This changing world will pose new challenges for the lone superpower
of our times. But one of these challenges appears to be a slam dunk: establishing and sustaining true military dominance. Others—such as adapting to new enemies and new forms of conflict, securing continued domestic support for a new "Pax Americana," balancing the deployment of
"hard" and "soft" power, sustaining strong collaborative relationships with
other nations, and retaining goodwill around the world—will prove considerably tougher. Each of these challenges is briefly reviewed next.

U.S. Military Dominance

The U.S. is well positioned to maintain and even build its military dominance throughout the next decade—dominance over not just its potential enemies but the rest of the world. The U.S.'s military budget is now
more than eight times larger than that of its nearest spending rival, China.
It is more than 29 times as large as the combined spending of Cuba,
Libya, Iran, Iraq, North Korea, Syria, and Sudan—the seven "rogue"
states classified as the U.S.'s most likely adversaries. U.S. military expenditure is more than double the combined spending of its European allies,
whose role as the "European pillar of NATO" is increasingly written off
as militarily irrelevant. Global military spending has now reached just
over $905 billion per year. The U.S. accounts for 43 percent of that total.

After reducing its military and security spending in the 1990s, the U.S.
starkly reversed this trend in the early 2000s, boosting its budgets in
response to the threat of terrorism. Between fiscal year 2001 (the last
before the September 11 attacks) and fiscal year 2004, U.S. spending on
defense, homeland security, and international affairs rose 50 percent.
Spending climbed above Cold War-era levels by 2002, and it is still climbing. In 2004, U.S. military spending was $399.1 billion; the U.S. mili-
tary budget request for 2005 was $420.7 billion—an increase that does
not include the "supplemental" military spending associated with the war
on terror; the U.S. military involvement in Iraq alone is expected to cost
more than $150 billion. These numbers are consistent with President
Bush's national security strategy, which states that the U.S. will not allow
any rival to build a comparable military force and will reserve the right to
engage in pre-emptive strikes as deemed "necessary."

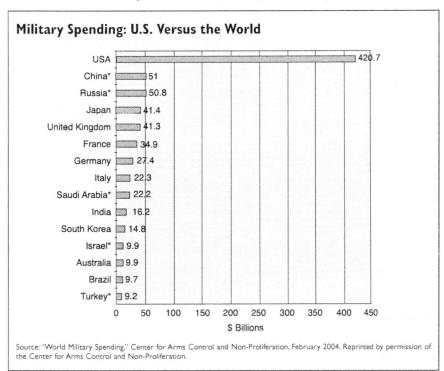

Military Spending: U.S. Versus the World

Country	$ Billions
USA	420.7
China*	51
Russia*	50.8
Japan	41.4
United Kingdom	41.3
France	34.9
Germany	27.4
Italy	22.3
Saudi Arabia*	22.2
India	16.2
South Korea	14.8
Israel*	9.9
Australia	9.9
Brazil	9.7
Turkey*	9.2

Source: "World Military Spending," Center for Arms Control and Non-Proliferation, February 2004. Reprinted by permission of the Center for Arms Control and Non-Proliferation.

But U.S. military superiority is not based on spending alone. Rather, it stems from a confluence of four factors. The first is its military's sheer scale, in terms of firepower, equipment, munitions, and people. The second is its positioning; the U.S. military is configured to project force far from home much more than to defend its home soil. While other countries find it difficult to commit their forces to distant theatres, the U.S. assumes this as its natural role, as it was for most of the twentieth century.

A third source of U.S. military strength is the continued evolution of its technological capabilities, which massively enhance the scale and success of U.S. military power. The technology of war is being revolutionized by U.S. mastery of precision strikes, information dominance, and near-real-time targeting. The motivation for these and other innovations stems from the desire to avoid casualties by delivering force with great accuracy from a safe distance and by giving ground forces as much protection as possible when they do reach the battlefield. This makes it easier for the U.S. to commit to the use of force, on the assumption of low casualties. (This also helps in recruitment, an important consideration since military superiority still requires manpower.)

"Pentagon Envisioning a Costly Internet for War"

"The Pentagon is building its own Internet, the military's world wide web for the wars of the future. The goal is to give all American commanders and troops a moving picture of all foreign enemies and threats—'a God's-eye view' of battle. This 'Internet in the sky,' Peter Teets, under secretary of the Air Force, told Congress, would allow 'marines in a Humvee, in a faraway land, in the middle of a rainstorm, to open up their laptops, request imagery' from a spy satellite, and 'get it downloaded within seconds.' The Pentagon calls the secure network the Global Information Grid, or GIG. Conceived six years ago, its first connections were laid six weeks ago. It may take two decades and hundreds of billions of dollars to build the new war net and its components."

The fourth source of U.S. advantage is intelligence: a combination of sophisticated surveillance, infiltration, monitoring, and interpretation capacities. As Lieutenant General Michael V. Hayden, director of the National Security Agency, said in the *Washington Post*, "High-quality intelligence is the American twenty-first century version of mass. We have replaced mass on the battlefield with knowledge and precision." Although U.S. intelligence has undergone severe criticism in the aftermath of September 11, it still has no rivals on the world stage for its reach, capacity, coverage, and technological sophistication, which continue to grow in new directions.

The integration of these four strengths gives the U.S. an unparalleled ability to project force in the world. This sustainable edge will not be challenged by any conventional military in the decade ahead, regardless of investments that other nations might make; keeping up with the technology alone is beyond most other economies, never mind the ramping up in scale that would be required. The question is not whether the U.S. can maintain its military dominance over others, but whether this alone will guarantee its success and security in the years ahead.

Adapting to New Enemies and Conflicts

The wars of the future will largely be unconventional conflicts, involving unconventional weapons and targets and fought against unconventional foes—not nations but networks, not geography-based but ideology-based. How quickly and well can the U.S. military adapt to this new reality? How radical will the changes have to be?

The first significant change has already been signaled. The refocusing of U.S. policy on the "new map" of chaotic and disorderly regions gives a sense of where U.S. forces will be deployed in the next decade. President Bush has already announced his intentions to reduce the U.S.'s commitment in Japan and Europe, for example, which is consistent with the changed analysis of global threats. But these shifts of U.S. resources will significantly alter the larger global military and economic system; they will have long-term consequences for the balance of power in Asia and for perceptions of the U.S. in Europe and elsewhere. And it remains to be seen how swiftly and completely such adjustments can be made.

But the challenge is greater than one of moving pieces on a chessboard. The very rules of the game are changing. The 9-11 Commission recommended wholesale changes in the way that U.S. government and military forces are configured and even conceptualized for the world that has emerged after the Cold War, stating that "Americans should not settle for incremental, ad hoc adjustments to a system designed generations ago for a world that no longer exists." There is a basic but serious question to be posed in this regard: just how useful are the U.S.'s conventional military dominance and power in tackling the new threats of a new world?

More urgent, perhaps, is the creation of effective policies, methods, and capabilities to fight in new conflicts against unconventional opponents who use non-military tactics and weapons and operate outside of the usual theatres of battle. We can already see evidence of the rising importance of this issue. The U.S. has appeared to improvise, reverse, and sometimes blunder its way through the evolution of new policies regarding the status and legal rights of its unconventional foes when they become detainees, and the use of "torture lite" in circumstances that might lead to the thwarting of terrorist attacks. This has culminated in confusion and resentment over the retention and treatment of prisoners at Guantanamo Bay and the prisoner abuses at Abu Ghraib.

It would appear that new methods and capabilities for engaging in unconventional conflicts are emerging within the U.S. military from the bottom-up—a networked response to dealing with new threats from networked foes. As Dan Baum reported in *The New Yorker* in early 2005, younger officers are finding new ways to share information and gain quick and vital battlefield knowledge, predominantly through the Web. Companycommand.com was launched by two Army commanders in 2000 as a way for soldiers of their rank to communicate intelligence and advice back and forth in real time; the following year they launched Platoonleader.org, which had similar goals. Sites like these represent an overhaul of the way information usually travels in the military—which is to say formally, through hierarchical channels. These sites—as well as the nimble, rapid-cycle thinking they promote and harness—have proved particularly useful in Iraq, where a new kind of war has required new forms of communication. We can expect the lessons from this engagement to influence U.S. tactics and behavior over the coming decade.

Another critical issue will be maintaining popular domestic support for U.S. military intervention in zones of chaos, which often seem like "far away countries of which we know little." Right now, the case for expending U.S. resources and manpower rests on an abstract and complicated view of the new world of international, intangible threats. Moreover, intervention in "zones of chaos" is more challenging than traditional military operations against a defined enemy in an ordered state. Casualties are more likely, and interventions are often long and drawn out, with ambiguous end points. The complex equation between costs (in money and lives) and benefits (in securing peace and spreading the American ideals of democracy and freedom) is being slowly and unsteadily resolved in Iraq. Over time, the experience there will help gauge public willingness to project military force elsewhere to achieve an enduring Pax Americana.

Sustaining Strong Collaborative Relationships

The U.S.'s military supremacy carries with it a certain degree of political influence. Even if the U.S. does not play a leadership role within many international political institutions, even if other nations and groups do not find all its values and ideas compelling or justifiable, it will nonetheless continue to exert significant political sway in the world, derived from its military and strategic might. When America speaks, the world will most certainly listen.

But there is a difference between compliance and collaboration, between lip service and partnership. America's military superiority and its attendant political influence may not prove sufficient to establish U.S. security in the decade ahead if it is not accompanied by a true spirit of shared purpose and determination. The U.S. cannot reshape the world alone. As the 9-11 Commission put it, "We should reach out, listen to, and work with other countries that can help."

Many nations will be strongly inclined to follow the U.S.'s lead, such as those in Eastern Europe that are establishing democracies for the first time and regard the U.S. as their most reliable ally in shaping their own futures. But the relationship with what members of the first Bush Administration described as "Old Europe" has become strained. The source of this tension lies in part with Europe's growing discomfort with the U.S.'s unchallengeable military dominance and its willingness to flex its power, as well as the U.S.'s growing frustration with Europe's reluctance to support the firm actions it believes are essential. Europe has tended to take U.S. power for granted as a benign source of order in the world; it was U.S. military strength that kept the peace during the Cold War, and it is U.S. military strength that continues to act as a deterrent to others' military adventurism.

Robert Kagan argues in *Of Paradise and Power* that Europe today is following a strategy of weakness, derived from the devastation it experienced when its military forces clashed in two world wars. Europe sees its future in quietly consolidating its economic power while seeking to extend the EU regime that has brought to its own warring continent "perpetual peace." The U.S., on the other hand, is pursuing a strategy of strength: it possesses both force of arms and the will to use it. Bringing these two positions into balance will require some subtle reorientation. But the costs of a serious schism are great for both sides. If the strain between these natural allies becomes a more serious rift, it could significantly undermine efforts to render the disorderly world more secure. We should expect to see considerable transatlantic diplomacy and dialogue in the years ahead as a result. Much of the focus will be on balancing the use of "soft power," as preferred by Europe, and "hard power," which the U.S. has deployed with increased frequency in recent years.

Balancing "Hard" and "Soft" Power

Foreign policy analyst Joseph Nye drew attention some years ago to the distinction between "hard" and "soft" power in international affairs. Hard power is the use of force; soft power is the use of diplomacy, influence, and dialogue to forge alliances and connections. Exerting soft power has been developed as a diplomatic art in Europe over decades of patient alliance-building, collaboration, and mutual interference in the European Union. Today, Europeans tend to believe that the conflicts of the future can be won only if they are fought with "weapons" other than force: ideas, aid, economic support, education, and the tools of integration. The U.S., in contrast, is convinced of the need to adopt a more muscular posture in the world and to demonstrate a willingness to back up threats with forceful action.

Worry About Potential U.S. Military Threat

■ Worried □ Not Worried

Country	Worried	Not Worried
Indonesia	26	74
Nigeria	27	72
Pakistan	23	72
Russia	26	71
Turkey	27	71
Lebanon	41	58
Jordan	44	56
Kuwait	44	53
Morocco	52	46

Source: Pew Global Attitudes, 2003. Reprinted by permission of The Pew Global Attitudes Project.

Nowhere is this distinction clearer, at the time of this writing, than in the respective European and American positions on Iran and its ambitions to develop nuclear weapons. Europe—primarily France, Germany, and Britain—has been working assiduously on this issue, negotiating with Iran to abandon its ambitions in return for trade, economic aid, and access to advanced technologies and industrial equipment. The U.S. is reluctant to engage with Europe in offering such carrots, instead threatening Iran with military intervention. Both Europe and the U.S. fear that the other is in danger of undermining the effectiveness of its approach.

The dilemma is clear. On the one hand, soft power that is unsupported by demonstrable hard power becomes rapidly devalued. For example, as Robert Kagan concludes, Europeans should be cautious in questioning the international legitimacy of U.S. actions if the net effect is to bring about "a diminution of the total amount of power that the liberal democratic world can bring to bear in its defense, and in defense of liberalism itself." On the other hand, hard power deployed overzealously can erode soft power; the ability to negotiate and influence diminishes in the face of what are seen as "bullying" tactics. Moreover, the exercise of hard power runs the risk of provoking extreme reactions and amplifying the very risks that military force is trying to alleviate. The desire of several nations, in addition to Iran, to secure nuclear weapons is in part a reaction to the U.S.'s willingness to deploy force that cannot be matched with conventional weapons and tactics.

Liberty's Champion, Rogue Superpower, or Both?

The United States finds itself in an interesting position. On the one hand, it tends to regard itself as the champion of a new order that is not simply self-interested but offers security, freedom, and opportunity for every part of the globe. While there is international support for this posture and the projection of force that it requires, there is also resentment and resistance, which threaten the U.S.'s reputation and its ability to wield soft power. In 2002, a Gallup International survey of 36 nations found that majorities in 23 of those nations believed that U.S. foreign policy has had a negative effect in their country (those 23 nations included nine in Western Europe, including Great Britain). Following the invasion of Iraq, global opinion continued to reflect a deep unease with the U.S.'s strategy for the new century.

How this resolves in the coming decade will hinge to some extent on how the U.S. and the rest of the world come to understand and execute the "war on terror." The phrase is effective for its power and simplicity; it is strong rhetoric. But in today's complex environment, it may become confusing language. We are accustomed to metaphors of combat that suggest the concentration of effort and resources on achieving a desirable goal—the war on poverty, the war on drugs, the war on disease. But at a more literal level, the phrase taps into old cognitive models of conventional warfare, sacrifice, power, and victory—all of which must be reinterpreted in today's world. "Terror" is not so much an enemy as a tactic, adopted throughout history by those with less power to challenge those with more. The complexity of terrorism, the variety of its manifestations, and the diversity of its origins suggest that an all-out "war" based on hard power may be doomed to fail. The language and rhetoric may raise expectations in the U.S. that will prove difficult to satisfy and concern in much of the rest of the world that will be difficult to assuage.

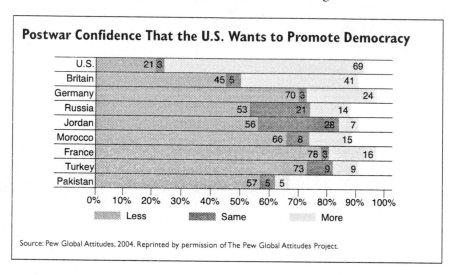

Postwar Confidence That the U.S. Wants to Promote Democracy

Country	Less	Same	More
U.S.	21	3	69
Britain	45	5	41
Germany	70	3	24
Russia	53	21	14
Jordan	56	28	7
Morocco	66	8	15
France	78	3	16
Turkey	73	9	9
Pakistan	57	5	5

Source: Pew Global Attitudes, 2004. Reprinted by permission of The Pew Global Attitudes Project.

In the coming decade, the U.S. will continue to face criticism and resistance from many parts of the world, including its natural allies, and some of it will be warranted. It will be accused of over-simplicity in its analysis of global affairs, insensitivity to cultural and other differences, and arrogance and inconsistency. Such charges are the inevitable lot of any great power that enjoys overwhelming advantages of force; if you are the biggest child in the playground, it is sometimes difficult for people to see you as anything other than a bully, especially when the circumstantial evidence fits that default perception. It also seems inevitable that there will be concrete reactions based on these perceptions, including the pursuit by some nations of non-conventional weapons to counterbalance U.S. might and networked forms of resistance to U.S. power.

The paradox of U.S. power is that it is equally a source of vulnerability. The two are intimately linked and always have been. From the story of David and Goliath to the aikido master's injunction to use the opponent's power against him, we instinctively know that big, powerful systems have their weak spots; it often takes only a little force, deftly applied, to bring them crashing down. The more technical, fast-changing, and interconnected our systems grow, the more vulnerable they become to small glitches, causing chain reactions and disastrous crashes. Some individuals and organizations devote a great deal of attention to finding these weaknesses and exploiting them. In such a world, the U.S.'s unmatched military force may not lead inevitably to security. The U.S. is in some ways very lonely in the world. With real power comes real vulnerability, and the U.S. will feel that more acutely in the decade ahead. In that, at least, it will not be alone.

Vulnerability

> All futurity seems teeming with endless destruction never to
> be repelled; desperate remorse swallows the present in a
> quenchless rage.
> —William Blake

In a world of asymmetric global power, dangerous zones of chaos, and a rise in the distributed power of often invisible networks, our individual and collective sense of vulnerability will flourish. Vulnerability is a feeling, an anticipation of danger, and as such it is difficult to remedy. This is particularly true in a world in which new forms of power, threat, and resistance are emerging among people we can't identify and in places we can't see. It is not just big power that opens us to vulnerability, but also the sorts of power that remain hard to see and imagine, hitting us in stealthy ways and taking us by surprise. In this world, the threat of terror becomes as significant as the reality.

Two powerful human pathologies serve to increase our sense of vulnerability. One is our propensity to be frightened by the perception of risk, whether that risk exists or not. Barry Glassner documents this phenomenon in his book *The Culture of Fear: Why Americans Are Afraid of the Wrong Things*. Our fear, Glassner claims, is partly the result of human nature; after we have been warned about potentially dangerous circumstances we begin to see them everywhere, and panic can set in. The media does not help since panic feeds the story and vice versa. A recent British study comparing the volume of media coverage on specific health risks with the number of deaths attributed to those risks found that reports on medical threats and diseases that carry very small or unproven risks far outweigh reports on "major killers" such as tobacco and obesity. "It takes 4,444 deaths from smoking, 846 from alcohol, and 2,538 from obesity to merit a story in a newspaper, compared with 0.375 deaths from measles…and 22.5 from AIDS." The same media "skew" also applies to non-health issues like terrorism. Roughly 2,500 deaths were attributed to terrorism globally during the 1990s; in the U.S. alone, in a single year, 15,000 people are murdered and 40,000 die in car accidents.

The second pathology might be called "closing the stable door" syndrome. The human tendency is to pay too much attention to old risks and not enough to those that are emerging. For example, the 9-11 Commission found that the Bush Administration was so focused on the supposed threat from China in its first year in office that it paid little attention to intelligence about Al Qaeda. This propensity to reinforce old patterns and habits of thought is another source of vulnerability—a failure of the imagination that more nimble minds can and will exploit. Take the world of warfare. The United States and its allies are vulnerable in unprecedented ways to enemies they cannot control—enemies who can take advantage of the falling cost of terror and the rising potential for disruption and who can access developing technologies to create new (sometimes surprising) weapons, new forms of delivery, and more effective global communication and coordination of terrorist activities. One of Tony Blair's foreign policy advisers has rightly written that the U.S. can today be described as "all powerful and all vulnerable." This extends to other parts of the world as well.

Terrorism

Among the new sources of vulnerability now in play in the world, terrorism is clearly the most prominent. We can only speculate how people in developed nations might respond to more continuous or widespread threats, like smallpox outbreaks, reports of poisoned food supplies, or suicide bombings in shopping malls. But the threat of another high-impact event is real; it may even be inevitable. For example, Harvard Professor Graham Allison's book, *Nuclear Terrorism: The Ultimate Preventable Catastrophe*, sifts through the evidence that Al Qaeda may have obtained a 10-kiloton nuclear weapon from Russia which, if let off in New York, could easily kill half a million people and paralyze the nation. Allison puts the odds at 51 to 49 that a nuclear terrorist strike will occur somewhere in the world in the next decade. But even just the belief in the threat of such an explosion could have significant psychological and economic consequences.

Governments, corporations, and others will have to become more sophisticated in how they handle and release information about such threats. As historian Philip Bobbitt has argued, in a climate of fear that can itself have damaging economic consequences, we are going to have to get smarter about how to make intelligence information available to the public. He draws the distinction between informing (placing information in the public domain), alerting (passing on specific instructions to public officials and agencies to increase their level of alertness), and warning (issuing a specific notion intended to change public activity). The default strategy of sharing everything out of fear of political embarrassment will need to become more sophisticated—both in how we calibrate the signals emerging from the noise and how we share them and their possible implications.

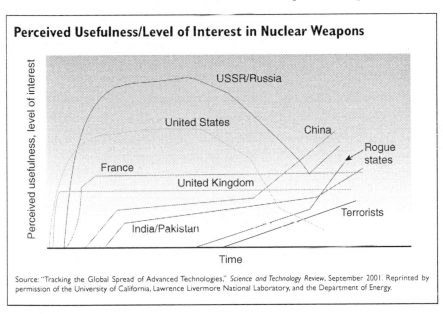

Perceived Usefulness/Level of Interest in Nuclear Weapons

Source: "Tracking the Global Spread of Advanced Technologies," Science and Technology Review, September 2001. Reprinted by permission of the University of California, Lawrence Livermore National Laboratory, and the Department of Energy.

But terrorism is only one source of unease and apprehension. Instability in the broader geopolitical context is another. The rising nuclear threat of North Korea is a source of profound concern in Northeast Asia and only one of many examples of destabilizing nuclear proliferation. Pakistan is a nuclear power in great tension with its neighbor and also internally, harboring diverse factions and enmities. Events in the Middle East—the war in Iraq, mounting anti-American sentiment, ongoing Israeli-Palestinian violence, challenged governments, and spreading disorder throughout the region—cast a dark shadow of conflict across the globe.

Lawlessness

A less visible but insidious consequence of globalization is the increasing scale and complexity of lawlessness. Moises Naim points to "five wars of globalization" that national authorities are struggling to counter: the illegal drug trade, arms trafficking, intellectual piracy, alien smuggling, and money laundering. As the world has grown more interconnected, Naim notes, criminals "have refined networking to a high science, entering into complex and improbable strategic alliances that span cultures and continents."

The Spence Money Laundering Network

"In one case, a money laundering network in New York that was not very sophisticated succeeded in laundering over $70 million for Colombian drug traffickers. The network was a fascinating mix. It included a taxi driver, an honorary consul-general for Bulgaria, a New York City police officer, two rabbis, a firefighter, and an attorney. The network was very amateurish in its methods, bringing large amounts of cash—which represented the proceeds of drug trafficking—to a Citibank branch on a regular basis and thus triggering a suspicious activity report. The deposits were transferred to a bank in Zurich where two employees forwarded the funds to the Caribbean account of a major Colombian drug trafficker. In spite of the diversity of those involved, the movement of the money across jurisdictions, the involvement of banking officials in Zurich, and the ultimate beneficiary, the network exhibited a surprising lack of sophistication."

Source: *Networks and Netwars: The Future of Terror, Crime, and Militancy*, J. Arquilla, D. Ronfeldt, eds. (Santa Monica, California: RAND Corporation, 2001), p. 84. Reprinted by permission.

The "people trade" is just one example. An estimated 4 million people are smuggled or trafficked across international borders each year. Often they are lured by promises of better jobs and better lives, and instead find themselves pressed into prostitution or other horrible situations. According to the United Nations Information Service, the people-trafficking business generates $10 billion annually, making it a core business for transnational criminal networks. In October 2004, the United Nations high commissioner for human rights called people trafficking one of the world's biggest human rights violations today. Human smuggling in the Mekong river region is so great that representatives from Cambodia, China, Laos, Myanmar, Thailand, and Vietnam recently signed an agreement—the first of its kind in the Asia-Pacific region—declaring their shared commitment to ending people trafficking through cross-border collaboration. Australia has earmarked $20 million to help stop people smuggling; in early 2004, the U.S. pledged $100 million.

These highly organized, complex, international networks also operate in the counterfeiting trade. For example, the American Apparel and Footwear Association keeps watch over something it calls "time to China"—the time it takes for a new (usually American) product to be copied in China and made available for sale on the streets of Hong Kong. In the early 1990s, "time to China" was eight months; it's now three and a half days. The problem of counterfeiting extends far beyond this, and the disservice it does to intellectual property is considerable. In 2003, transactions in counterfeit products accounted for more than 7 percent of global trade, or $500 billion, according to Interpol. The organization estimates that 10 percent of all car parts sold in Europe and 10 percent of all pharmaceuticals sold worldwide are black-market counterfeits. Ninety percent of the software running on computers in China has been pirated.

Disease

In a list of scares that could continue for the rest of this book, there is also the looming threat of new and terrifying diseases, both created and spread by increased global connections and travel. Recent fears over avian flu, the Marburg virus, SARS, and the declining effectiveness of antibiotics are all very real sources of anxiety. A recent report from the World Health Organization offers this stark warning: "In the not too distant past antibiotics could be relied upon to treat a bacterial infection. Those days are almost gone, as bacteria have emerged that are resistant to each of the antibiotics currently on the market. This trend is expected to continue."

The title of a recent book says it all: *The New Killer Diseases: How the Alarming Evolution of Mutant Germs Threatens Us All.* We are becoming victims of our own success in making sure that cheap antibiotics are available worldwide, because that success has spurred the evolution of new strains of old bacteria. For example, tuberculosis had been nearly eliminated by modern drugs. But now 2 billion people are estimated to have the disease, 60 million of them victims of fatal, drug-resistant forms. Ironically, hospitals have become breeding grounds for new bugs strengthened by the overuse of antibiotics. New strains of staphylococcus kill 20,000 patients a year in U.S. hospitals and cost the health budget $29 billion in countermeasures. In the United Kingdom, where MRSA (methicillin resistant staphylococcus aurius) now kills 1,000 hospital patients every year, health ministers have made tackling so-called hospital superbugs a top priority. The coming decade will present us with mounting evidence that we may be entering an alarming post-antibiotic world.

Avian Flu

In a world in which a host of new and old viruses with the potential to infect, if not kill, millions of people are emerging with new strength, none is of greater concern than the avian flu virus. The World Health Organization is concerned that the recent appearance and spread of the new avian flu strain H5N1—which cannot be stopped by conventional vaccines and is expected soon to evolve the ability to spread rapidly among humans—has the potential to ignite a new bird flu pandemic. The last pandemic, in 1918, killed 50 million people. WHO estimated that a new pandemic, the first of this century, would affect between 20 and 30 percent of the world's population; in its best-case scenarios of the next pandemic, up to 7 million people would die and tens of millions would get sick. Most experts believe a new flu pandemic is not an "if" but a "when." The World Health Organization has already persuaded 50 countries to draw up pandemic-preparedness plans.

Sources: Alison Abbott, "What's in the Medicine Cabinet," *Nature*, May 26, 2005; the World Health Organization.

Computer Viruses

Threatening in a different way are equivalent developments in the world of technology. Computer viruses are now released into the world at the rate of about 80 new viruses a month (2003 was a particularly virulent year, with more that 7,000 new viruses discovered). According to computer security company Symantec, there are about 80,000 computer viruses "alive" in the world today, and their ranks are growing larger every day. Of course, most viruses are merely irritating. But designed and executed well, they can be economically devastating, accomplishing terrific damage in the time it takes to open an email.

Two trends suggest that computer viruses are likely to get worse in the coming decade, causing even more widespread damage to the economy. The first trend is simply the increasing sophistication of the attacks. The Nimda virus that circulated just after September 11 was a "blended threat"—a single package that had five different ways of replicating itself and spreading across the Internet. The virus was also programmed to mutate, with the intention of keeping it one step ahead of security software. The SoBig virus, released in August 2003, was a "Trojan horse"—a form of virus that does not replicate itself but opens a back door into the host computer that allows it to be controlled from the outside. The SoBig attack cost the global economy $5.59 billion, according to mi2g Intelligence Unit estimates.

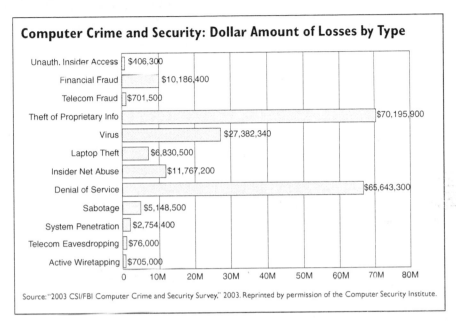

Computer Crime and Security: Dollar Amount of Losses by Type

Type	Amount
Unauth. Insider Access	$406,300
Financial Fraud	$10,186,400
Telecom Fraud	$701,500
Theft of Proprietary Info	$70,195,900
Virus	$27,382,340
Laptop Theft	$6,830,500
Insider Net Abuse	$11,767,200
Denial of Service	$65,643,300
Sabotage	$5,148,500
System Penetration	$2,754,400
Telecom Eavesdropping	$76,000
Active Wiretapping	$705,000

Source: "2003 CSI/FBI Computer Crime and Security Survey," 2003. Reprinted by permission of the Computer Security Institute.

This particular virus highlights a second trend. The SoBig virus was arguably the first to be spread as a way to make money. The virus turned every computer it infected into a magnet for spam; the virus's creators then sold the list of infected email addresses to underground bulk-emailers, who then had an easy audience for spreading their messages. Creating viruses used to be a hobby for lone hackers who later landed jobs as computer security consultants. Now it has become the domain of fast-moving, highly organized international teams that have turned it into a business in its own right. Computers taken over by Trojan horse viruses can be linked to form a massive peer-to-peer network that serves as a platform for scams that cannot otherwise be run through legitimate Internet service providers. At least a third of all spam is now sent from or relayed by personal home computers hijacked for this purpose. Now that hacking is becoming a business, we can expect it to move to another level.

Close observers of the virus trend, like Simson Garfinkel, author of *Database Nation*, draw a parallel between computer virus creation and weapons development. A new weapon first seeks a weakness to exploit, then designs a means to reach the vulnerable target, and then finally adds a powerful payload to cause maximum damage. The innovations we have seen so far in computer viruses have involved identifying weaknesses in our operating systems and designing ever more effective propagation engines, including sleeper viruses that can lie undetected in a machine, waiting for the moment to be activated. The next wave of innovation may be in payload—the damage done by the virus after it enters our computers. Viruses can do serious damage to economic, financial, trading, traffic control, emergency services, telecom, infrastructure, and other vital and powerful networks. It is the complexity, interconnectivity, and sheer scale of these networks that now makes them so vulnerable.

Perception and Response

These deep-rooted vulnerabilities, both actual and potential, are almost certain to increase the perception of new threats and security concerns. The cost of managing these threats has already been enormous for businesses and governments. But September 11 presaged a shift in the economic order at an individual level as well. For example, the U.S. government's Transport Security Agency has received a $5 million grant from Congress to test a new "registered traveler" program in which passengers pay an extra fee in order to go through fast-track security processes at U.S. airports. Security takes time, and a market will develop that trades time for money. We may also see the emergence of an alternative class system that separates those who have high levels of security clearance from those who do not.

Clearly, we are living in a growing social zeitgeist of fear and concern. In the coming decade, we can expect to see greater recognition of our vulnerabilities, as well as new ways to manage them and the risks they represent. Security is set to become a big budget item and a central concern on societal, corporate, and individual levels. While most of the efforts in this domain will focus on protection and contingency, we can also expect to witness a growing civic and corporate commitment to addressing root causes, searching for solutions to intractable global problems, and creating joint efforts to stabilize a volatile world.

The pursuit of advantages in power will continue to involve the development and deployment of increasingly sophisticated technology, while our growing sense of vulnerability will include fears about technological over-reach, contributing to serious pushback. The next dynamic tension explores the new frontiers of technology and the concerns and resistance that will be unleashed in response.

Chapter 5

Technology Acceleration and Pushback

In the coming decade, new technologies will continue to proliferate at a rapid pace, creating new opportunities and sources of value. In the next 10 years, we will witness further advances in the ways in which three technology domains in particular—computing, biotechnology, and nanotechnology—become even more "mutually catalytic," enabling and accelerating one another. This will open up startling new opportunities for sensing and connecting, for mimicking and changing nature, and for radical enhancement of human beings themselves. Not surprisingly, we will see this "progress" increasingly challenged by those who fear its ultimate, and perhaps unintended, consequences. The resulting tension between scientists and technologists and their detractors will be exacerbated by a fundamental lack of shared mental models, language systems, and knowledge bases, requiring us to develop new approaches to talking about these issues.

Technology Acceleration

> I just bought a Mac to help me design the next Cray.
> —Seymore Cray, when told that Apple had bought a Cray supercomputer to help design the next MacIntosh

Throughout human history, we have been creating and deploying new and increasingly powerful technologies at an accelerating pace. Roughly 10,000 generations ago we learned how to make tools from stone; 1,000 generations ago we learned to harness nature through primitive agriculture; 100 generations ago we learned how to extract metal from rock; 10 generations ago we learned how to harness and transport energy;

a handful of generations ago we learned how to mass produce; a couple of generations ago we learned how to automate production systems; and in the span of just one generation we have learned how to turn sand into computing power that has transformed and connected the world, opening up mind-boggling new possibilities.

Without a doubt, the greatest technological developments of the past 25 years are the direct result of the growing power of communications and computing and the exponential impact of Moore's Law (which holds that the number of transistors per square inch on an integrated circuit approximately doubles every 18 months). This increase in power and possibility has given us ever-faster computers and continually connected devices like cellphones that affect nearly every aspect of our daily lives. It has also enabled the rapid emergence of a broad array of smaller, cheaper devices designed to help us monitor and make sense of the world. Sensor and wireless networking components that would have been bulky hardware just a few years ago are now readily found in tiny, cheap, almost disposable packages—already becoming as small as a grain of sand and set to cost only pennies each. From "smart dust"—tiny wireless microelectro-mechanical sensors that can do everything from track human movement to sense minute vibrations that might otherwise be undetectable—to sensor packages meant to survive the slow-motion crush of glaciers, to RFID tags that monitor everything from Wal-Mart merchandise to oil pipelines, devices able to inform us about the conditions of the material environment are increasingly inexpensive, commonplace, and networked. As these sensing networks grow in scale and scope, they will open new possibilities for experience and knowledge.

In many ways, we are only in the beginning stages of what technology has in store for us; the momentum, the ideas, and the possibilities continue to unfold. Many scientists believe that Moore's Law will screech to a halt by 2020, primarily due to the limitations of the physical materials that have been used for decades to make chips and transistors, particularly silicon.

Moore's Law

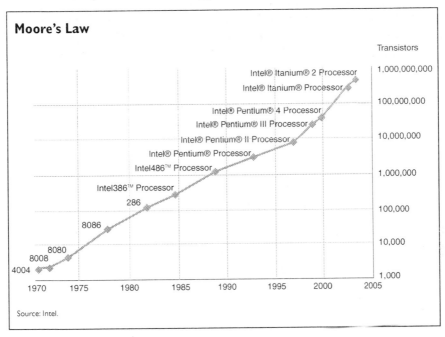

Transistors

Intel® Itanium® 2 Processor — 1,000,000,000

Intel® Itanium® Processor

— 100,000,000

Intel® Pentium® 4 Processor

Intel® Pentium® III Processor

— 10,000,000

Intel® Pentium® II Processor

Intel® Pentium® Processor

Intel486™ Processor — 1,000,000

Intel386™ Processor

286 — 100,000

8086

— 10,000

8080

8008

4004 — 1,000

1970   1975   1980   1985   1990   1995   2000   2005

Source: Intel.

But many are also confident that we will soon move beyond traditional silicon-based computing and into a whole new realm of computing platforms and architecture—and a flurry of research is underway to discover and test new alternatives. Promising progress has been made in biocomputing, for example, in which biological principles and processes are used to develop new computing technologies, from biological hardware to DNA computing. A more radical prospect is the emergence of quantum computing, initially regarded as the stuff of science fiction when it was first considered in the 1970s. By harnessing the atom's ability to form together with other atoms as quantum bits that can act as a processor and memory, a quantum computer could be many millions of times faster than today's quickest computers, opening up possibilities that defy our current imagination. While quantum computers are still in the experimental stage, the science has been shown to work, and there are literally thousands of researchers—in university and government labs and within companies—racing to push quantum computing further. As Stan Williams, Hewlett-Packard's director of quantum science research, put it, "This area has gone off like a big bang. It's breathtaking. The potential is so huge and it would be so disruptive, it could completely change the way at least some computing is done."

In the coming decade, scientists and technologists will push computing technology further and in more directions than it has previously gone.
It seems certain that a vastly different and more powerful model of computing is on its way.

Biotechnology

One of the benefits of increased computer power is that it acts as a catalyst, greatly enhancing developments in other technologies as well. This
has been particularly true for biotechnology. As the Institute for the
Future's Paul Saffo has put it, "Computers turned out to be the personal
intellectual bulldozers of biotechnologists." There is no better proof of
this than the swift completion of the Human Genome Project. Mapping
the first billion characters of the project took four years; thanks to
advances in the power of computers and software innovations, the second
billion took just four months. Researchers with Harvard Medical School's
Personal Genome Project believe we will be able to run individual
genome maps in under 90 seconds on a $1,000 computer before 2010.

The intersection of accelerated information processing power and biological research is even more critical in proteomics, the study of the structures and functions of cells' ever-shifting assortments of proteins.
Scientists are attempting to catalog all human proteins—a project considered more complex than mapping the genome—in order to better
comprehend their functions and interactions and the critical role they
play in determining biological outcomes. Distributed-computing experiments are enabling scientists to gain greater understanding of fundamental yet still mysterious behaviors of proteins, such as how some proteins
reproduce and distort themselves into deadly structures called prions,
which cause untreatable brain illnesses like chronic wasting disease and
Creutzfeldt-Jakob disease, the human version of mad cow disease.

Biotechnology is already an extremely important field in its own right.
But it is clearly poised to play a truly transformative role in shaping our
future. While much of the current focus of the biotechnology industry is
on the development of drugs, "mining" biological data, and agricultural
applications, much more revolutionary developments are rapidly
approaching. These developments will transform medical science, but
many also pose significant ethical dilemmas. Stem cell research holds
great promise as a source for cures to numerous previously incurable
afflictions; the explosion of genomic and proteomic knowledge will make

it possible to engineer children without birth defects and perhaps with "designer" characteristics; and the move of the baby boom generation toward retirement age will accelerate the already rapid work on treatments to slow the physical manifestations of aging—and perhaps even come close to stopping the aging process entirely.

Cognitive Science

Still another important technology discipline poised for breakthroughs in the coming decade is cognitive science. The field of neuroscience, for example, has been transformed in the decade since magnetic resonance imaging (MRI) came into use. An advanced system known as functional MRI now allows us to take detailed pictures of the brain as it performs specific tasks and is already being used for better diagnosis of brain disorders. Because it can literally map the workings of the mind, it is also being employed to unravel knotty conundrums such as the science of physical attraction and political preference.

Neuromarketing

Although functional magnetic resonance imaging (fMRI) has been around since the late 1980s, in the last few years it has pushed beyond the realm of medicine and into the field of advertising. The controversial new field of neuromarketing uses fMRI to uncover the unconscious attitudes that determine which products customers are most likely to buy. The machine tracks blood flow in the brain and watches how it changes as a person reacts to various stimuli, such as a brand name, a movie trailer, or a sip of Coke. Indeed, it was a "Coke vs. Pepsi" taste test conducted at Baylor College of Medicine in 2004, showing the different ways that the products lit up the brain's reward centers, that sparked considerable excitement among advertisers—but caused just as forceful pushback from consumer and privacy advocates. As one consumer activist told *The New York Times*, "What would happen in this country if corporate marketers and political consultants could literally peer inside our brains and chart the neural activity by various means, so as to modify our behavior to serve their own ends?"

Sources: Sandra Blakeslee, "If You Have a 'Buy Button' in Your Brain, What Pushes It?" *The New York Times*, October 19, 2004; Mary Carmichael, "Neuromarketing: Is It Coming to a Lab Near You?" *Frontline*, November 9, 2004.

As we learn more about the brain, our ability to enhance or repair its functioning grows more and more sophisticated. Cochlear implants are already helping a growing number of deaf people hear; artificial vision systems enabling blind people to see are currently being tested. A wide assortment of "neuro-prostheses" are also under development, from the artificial synapses currently on a silicon chip at Stanford to Infineon Technologies' Neuro-Chip, a biosensor chip that measures electrical activity in living cells and "promises both new techniques for neuroscience and the ability to develop new drugs by testing them on living neurons." In a world of complexity and information overload, imagine the power of improving how our brains process massive amounts of data. Brain science could give us insight into how to think more systematically, to make connections between disparate causes and effects.

Nanotechnology and the Molecular Convergence

Many of the breakthrough developments at the convergence of digital, biological, and cognitive sciences are happening at the smallest level imaginable—at the level of atom and molecule. At the heart of this convergence, enabling the manipulation and reshaping of the stuff of life itself, is the fourth defining technology of our future: nanotechnology, the science of the extremely small. There are myriad definitions of this emergent field, but nanotechnology generally deals with matter at the scale of one to 100 nanometers (a nanometer is one millionth of a millimeter) and involves the creation of new materials and processes through the manipulation of molecular and atomic particles.

Many of the breakthroughs in nanotechnology—like Sandia National Labs' mobile robot, with feet and a prehensile tail, which is actually a single molecule, dubbed a "motor protein"—have little practical application yet hint at startling future prospects. To date, the more practical applications are rather prosaic; nanotechnology has enabled the production of new types of sunscreen, for example, as well as "self-cleaning" clothes and other smart textiles. But the long-term promise of nanotechnology is much greater: creating food and other essentials from the atom up, mimicking the processes of nature, using hardly any energy and without negative environmental consequences. Even thinking about the prospect conjures Arthur C. Clarke's famous observation that "any sufficiently advanced technology is indistinguishable from magic."

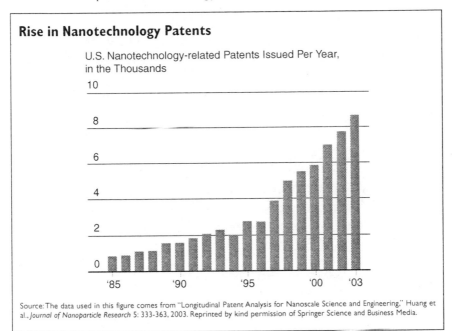

Rise in Nanotechnology Patents

U.S. Nanotechnology-related Patents Issued Per Year, in the Thousands

Source: The data used in this figure comes from "Longitudinal Patent Analysis for Nanoscale Science and Engineering," Huang et al., *Journal of Nanoparticle Research* 5: 333-363, 2003. Reprinted by kind permission of Springer Science and Business Media.

The convergence of key technologies at the nano-level will start to reorder our world in fundamental ways in the coming decade—sparking a revolution even more profound than the "digital convergence" of technologies that so shaped the last 25 years. One acronym for this new convergence points to its explosive potential: BANG, which stands for bits (information technology), atoms (nanotechnology), neurons (cognitive science), and genes (biotechnology). Importantly, these technological areas are mutually catalytic, each enabling the more rapid development of the others. For example, nanotechnology's molecular-level techniques are increasingly based on biological processes. Synthetic biology—literally programming DNA as if it were computer code—is an emerging discipline that has already been used to construct new viruses and holds great potential for targeted gene therapy. Biomimicry, the practice of developing technology that apes biological activity, also holds great promise. Biomimetic design takes advantage of organic models and can use algorithms based on natural selection to "evolve" new software and hardware.

Meanwhile, much research is underway to develop devices that take advantage of our growing understanding of molecular-scale processes in materials and biology, and our ever-cheaper, ever-smarter, ever-more-networked digital technology. In the world of medical science, for example, we can anticipate nano-scale gold pellets that accumulate in the distorted blood vessels of cancerous tissue, enabling rapid identification and even elimination via infrared laser. In the sphere of homeland security, we will see air-sniffing biosensors that can pick up the presence of chemical or biological toxins in minute quantities and provide early warning signals wherever they are required. We might even see brain implants connected wirelessly to computer networks that enable us to move real things in the physical world around us and hundreds of miles away simply through thought control. If this last example seems farfetched, consider that we have already developed such technology for monkeys, enabling them to play video games and move robotic arms in a laboratory 600 miles away by thought power alone. Experiments are underway to give similar "mind control" to paralyzed humans.

Human Enhancement

While developments in technology have largely allowed humans to manipulate and alter the physical world around us, in the near future, technology will additionally, and perhaps primarily, enable us to manipulate, alter, and powerfully enhance *ourselves*. In June 2002, the National Science Foundation issued an exhaustive yet little-noted report titled "Converging Technologies for Improving Human Performance." The report examined the implications of parallel developments across nanotechnology, biotechnology, information technology, and new human technologies based on cognitive science. "With proper attention to ethical issues and societal needs, converging technologies could determine a tremendous improvement in human abilities, societal outcomes, the nation's productivity, and the quality of life," it optimistically concluded.

So what developments in the enhancement of human beings should we expect to see in the coming years? As usual, clues to the likely frontiers of technology can be found by scanning the leading-edge work being undertaken by and for the U.S. military and defense establishments. For example, at MIT's Institute for Soldier Nanotechnologies, researchers are weaving into the fabric of soldiers' uniforms GPS guidance systems, air conditioning, wireless computers and other communication devices, biosensors to monitor the medical condition of the wearer, muscle-imitating cloth that will automatically close around a wound, and much more. It is a short step to uniforms that make physical tasks like lifting heavy items, running, and jumping easier. Indeed, there is even a U.S. military program called

Exoskeletons for Human Performance Augmentation (EHPA), which is dedicated to developing battle power suits that contain sensors to read, and machinery to amplify, every muscle movement, enabling the wearer to "handle more firepower, wear more ballistic protection, carry larger-caliber weapons and more ammunition, and carry supplies greater distances." Perhaps one day soon we will need only to put on an army uniform to perform like the fabled bionic 1970s TV character, the Six Million Dollar Man.

The DARPA Effect

Incredibly, these technological developments are at the conservative end of the spectrum of research being commissioned and undertaken by the Pentagon's Defense Advanced Research Projects Agency (DARPA). DARPA lives at the front edge of science, investing in prospects that seem impossible to many scientists. Its record of successes shows that where it leads, the future tends to follow. It was DARPA that created the forerunner of the Internet (known as Arpanet) in the 1960s; DARPA's work was also central to the invention of such transformative technologies as GPS, the cellphone, RISC computing, and advanced fuel cells. Having literally helped create the technological supremacy of the U.S. military, DARPA has since turned its focus to the biggest chink in the U.S. military armor: the human soldier. In an effort to remodel vulnerable humans into indestructible assets, DARPA has embarked upon a broad array of astonishing projects aimed squarely at helping create, in essence, "superhuman" soldiers.

My friend and *Washington Post* journalist and author Joel Garreau spent two years getting an inside feel for DARPA's latest work. I had the privilege of hearing about Joel's observations and experiences as they were unfolding. Much of what I include in this section regarding DARPA comes straight from Joel, who has now distilled what he learned into a remarkable book, *Radical Evolution: The Promise and Peril of Enhancing Our Minds, Our Bodies—and What It Means to Be Human.* The stunning projects that Joel witnessed and reported on include the development of a "pain vaccine" that remains effective for 30 days after injury, as well as radical wound-healing-acceleration technologies based on a process that uses light in the near-infrared spectrum. DARPA researchers are also developing bleeding-inhibition processes that harness the power of the brain over the body. There is even a related research effort to discover why tadpoles can re-grow amputated tails but frogs cannot—the ultimate goal being to figure out how humans might regenerate lost limbs or other body parts. Still more DARPA researchers are investigating whether humans, like dolphins, could develop the ability to never have to sleep— at least not with both sides of the brain at the same time. And they have made great progress toward developing a drug that will attack and destroy any bacterial or viral infection; they have already developed one candidate drug that works on smallpox, malaria, and even the flu and is ready for human safety trials. As if that weren't enough, DARPA researchers are also trying to improve human cells so that soldiers can live off their own fat for days at a time without tiring; attempting to rebuild customized organs within the body, avoiding the need for transplants; and working on enabling seriously wounded soldiers to go into a sort of suspended animation, capable even of surviving for a time without oxygen.

Supply Meets Demand

DARPA's research is dazzling in its scope and ambition. While many of its programs will no doubt fail, its work provides insight into a future in which radical human enhancement is not only possible, but probable. Human enhancement is a story that will unfold with remarkable speed and force over the next decade and beyond. On the supply side, we seem set for faster and more distributed innovation; we are already seeing the reduction in cost and availability of some of the necessary tools. At Target, for $39.99, you can buy a Baby DNA Kit that enables you to sample and store your child's DNA ("for future medical advances and foolproof security"); another $100 buys you a genetic blueprint of his or her DNA code and a chart comparing it to the codes of various population groups. Human genome sequencing data is freely available. In some parts of the world, the regulatory regime for fundamental genetic manipulation and research is lax to nonexistent. Even where regulations are in place, the morphing and merging of categories (drugs becoming combined in foodstuffs, for example) is making it difficult for the regulatory regimes to keep up with the market.

Already we can see a steady trend of the "medicalization" of what once were normal variances in humans into disorders that can and should be treated. Some men of a certain age used to be simply "past their prime"; now they are suffering from erectile dysfunction disorder and prescribed Viagra. Some kids used to be "fidgety" at school; now they suffer from attention deficit disorder and are prescribed Ritalin. Some people used to be destined to be short but now suffer from the treatable disorder "non-growth hormone deficient short stature" and are prescribed HGH.

Indeed, there appears to be near limitless (and remarkably risk-oblivious) demand for enhancement of one form or another. A growing number of "cognitive enhancement" drugs are entering the market, including modafinil, a drug licensed to treat narcolepsy that, when ingested by healthy people, allows them to stay awake and alert for 90 hours, with perfect concentration and no sleep deficit. Consider the endless and futile game of catch-up played by sports administrators and some sports professionals as new, more effective, less detectable means of enhancing performance emerge from scientific laboratories. The number of performance enhancers on the black market increases each year despite the proven and life-threatening dangers of many of them. Or reflect on the extraordinary sums of money spent on cosmetics to make us look better. According to *The Economist*, Americans already spend more on beauty than they do on education. The number of cosmetic surgical procedures in the U.S. has more than doubled in just a few years; in 2003, Americans spent $991 million on liposuction, $667 million on nose jobs, $54 million on chin augmentation...and the list goes on. As the baby boomers grow older, they will reinvent aging, just as they have reinvented every other phase of life—primarily by defying it through science.

Biotech and Aging

"The specter of premature death haunts everyone. There has never been a way around that. Yet the prospect of getting around that has a very powerful attraction. There is a powerful right-to-life segment, but not a powerful right-to-death one; no one is out there saying people should not live to 120. So we have an unplowed social area. And as society gets top heavy with the aged, I think this is the one area where biotech could do radical things with little pushback. If you want to market [a drug] to athletes, then first market it as a drug to help the fading grip strength of the aged. The biotech industry has tried to show how technology can save kids with golden rice. 'We will save these third-world children from blindness.' The problem is that these kids have no clout. But an old rich person will vaporize his whole fortune to eke out five more years of life. And if there was an elixir to extend life 100 years, the Pope will be the first to drink it. Of course, anything that works on elderly flesh will work much better on young people. Try on the old, then ramp up and repackage for the young."

—Bruce Sterling, science fiction and technology writer

Source: Global Business Network.

The technology-driven march to radical human enhancement, with all the unexplored promise and peril, dilemmas and tradeoffs, equalizers and inequities that it will entail, has commenced. In the coming decade, this issue will move center stage in civic debate and will generate at least as much heat as it does light.

Unpredictable Breakthroughs Ahead?

We have ahead of us a period of almost unimaginable technology-driven change, reaching into the profound territory of what it means to be human. Yet all these remarkable developments are predicated on our existing scientific paradigms. What if we also witness fundamental break-throughs in our scientific knowledge and the way we do science? The prospect has to be seriously considered. Today, we have an order of magnitude more scientists at work around the world than the cumulative total of scientists who have ever worked throughout history. More and more, they are working across the boundaries of traditional scientific domains; they are connected with one another and able to collaborate and share ideas and discoveries over time and space in ways that would be the envy of every previous scientific generation. It is through such recombination of knowledge that breakthrough innovations typically occur.

Perhaps most importantly of all, in every sphere of science today we are encountering anomalies that cannot be adequately explained by our current theories. Historically, this state of affairs has preceded remarkable new discoveries and leaps in scientific knowledge. Perhaps the question is not whether we will witness another great wave of profound scientific discoveries, but when. As my colleague Peter Schwartz wrote in his book *Inevitable Surprises,* "In 50 years' time knowledge of physics, biology, chemistry, astronomy, and maybe Earth science will be immensely different from knowledge today—far more different from today's knowledge than ours is from that of 50 years ago."

Pushback

> I don't try to describe the future. I try to prevent it.
> —Ray Bradbury

It should not be surprising that there is strong and growing pushback against today's advancing technology—nor is it audacious to predict that such resistance will continue and grow. The relationship between humans and the technologies they create has long been conflicted. The remarkable differences that new tools and capabilities have brought to lifestyles in the developed world over the last several hundred years are so profound and embedded that we can scarcely imagine their absence. Yet at each step along the way, a price has been paid for technological progress, inducing considerable resistance and fear in many. The revolt of the Luddites in eighteenth-century England signified growing apprehension over the social impact of technologies of industrialization. Mary Shelley's popular story of *Frankenstein* reflected early nineteenth-century Europe's concerns about the seemingly uncontrollable march of medical and energy technologies. The mushroom cloud was the twentieth century's iconic representation of the terrifying potential behind powerful new technologies of warfare and destruction, prompting Albert Einstein to say, "It has become appallingly obvious that our technology has exceeded our humanity." It remains to be seen what will symbolize the darker side of the technologies of the twenty-first century.

The very factors that are creating new excitement in research fields—acceleration, rising connectivity, and more convergence—also trigger new anxieties. As we learn and experiment more, fundamental concerns about our safety, our humanity, and the fate of our planet are provoked, and they serve to heighten our sense of unease. There are three distinct sources for this discomfort: moral concerns, concerns about uncertainty and unknown risks, and nervousness that new technologies might fall into irresponsible hands. All three concerns, set against the background of dauntingly complex science, together create a growing climate of fear and suspicion.

Moral Concerns

Many of the moral concerns that surround breakthrough innovations in science and technology are a reaction to the perceived offensiveness of tinkering with the very essence of what is "natural" in human beings and other forms of life. While most scientific endeavors in this area are clearly designed for human benefit, many of them appear to some people to embody a disturbing arrogance and lack of humility, along with an undervaluing of the sanctity of human life. As a result, bioethics is set to be a growth area in the next 10 years as societies, governments, and individuals grapple with the rights and wrongs of stem cell research, the genetic selection of children, and the genetic screening of individuals by insurance companies, law enforcement, or others.

Consider, for example, the international firestorm that ignited in May 2005 when South Korean scientist Hwang Woo-suk announced that he had successfully created a dozen cloned human embryos and harvested their stem cells for use in sick patients. The breakthrough was historic, but the therapeutic possibilities created by Hwang's success were over-shadowed by swift, passionate, and widespread backlash. The fear was that Hwang had taken the tampering with human life to a new and eth-ically uncomfortable level, moving science just steps away from full-blown human cloning. Hwang himself considers the creation of human clones "technically impossible" and "unethical," and reinforced that his goal was the creation of stem cells, not clones. But the pushback against his work was fierce nonetheless. U.S. President George Bush condemned Hwang's research, vowing to veto any legislation in the U.S. that would loosen federal restrictions on embryonic stem cell research. The Vatican also issued a public denouncement, even arranging a meeting between Hwang and Catholic officials to "exchange views" on science and ethics. No doubt many such meetings will continue to take place in churches, labs, and legislatures around the world.

Reproductive Versus Therapeutic Cloning: Views from Europe

Tell me if you agree or disagree with...	The reproductive cloning, meaning the identical reproduction of human beings		The therapeutic cloning, meaning the identical reproduction of human cells	
	Agree (%)	Disagree (%)	Agree	Disagree
Germany	6	94	43	57
Spain	7	87	79	18
France	4	96	57	42
Ireland	4	93	37	59
Italy	4	95	65	33
Austria	3	94	39	54
Portugal	10	85	72	22
Sweden	4	91	51	44
United Kingdom	7	92	47	46
Hungary	2	95	59	37
Romania	11	85	49	47
Slovakia	18	81	51	49
Turkey	17	73	36	54

Source: The European Omnibus Survey, EOS Gallup Europe, January 2003. Reprinted by kind permission of EOS Gallup Europe.

Particularly morally repugnant to many is science that deliberately blurs the boundaries between human and other life forms. The concept of creating "chimeras"—hybrid creatures that are part human and part animal—will no doubt become an increasingly heated issue in the decade ahead. Starting with a project in 2003 in which Chinese scientists fused human cells with rabbit eggs (they were destroyed after several days in order to extract stem cells from the embryos), we should expect to witness an explosion of experiments that create such hybrids to help test drugs, produce new medical treatments, accelerate understanding of how critical human organs (including the brain) work, and even grow spare organs for human transplants. Canada has already banned any experiments that involve placing human cells into non-human embryos and vice versa; in April 2005, the U.S. announced new federal guidelines allowing the creation of human-animal hybrids but banning their breeding. Other countries will no doubt debate similar measures in the near future.

The Fear of Unintended Consequences

Second, as we engage with technological experiments that lie at the far reaches of our understanding, there is grave and growing concern about unintended consequences and the irreversibility of our meddling with the stuff of nature itself—while the benefits may be great, the perils may prove greater still. Here we have an interesting historical point of comparison: the development of nuclear power. In the 1950s, during the optimistic era of Eisenhower's "Atoms for Peace" program, the nuclear promise of copious clean energy won significant public support. As the dangers of radiation and the long-term challenges of safely storing nuclear waste became more apparent, that support declined rapidly. Today, as the environmental damage caused by carbon fuels becomes increasingly obvious, we are beginning to see emergent support for an aggressive return to nuclear energy. Perhaps we will witness similar twists and turns in the road ahead with regard to public views on a new generation of life-altering technologies.

One focus of future debate will be the efforts underway in dozens of labs around the world to create a new organism. Well-funded teams in the U.S., Europe, and Japan have launched ambitious programs in what may well become a race to be the first to create artificial life. Some are following a "top-down" methodology that involves taking an extremely simple existing bacterium and figuring out, largely through trial and error, how to replace its natural genetic code with a much-simplified synthetic code.

Others have set their sights on something even more startling: the creation, from scratch, of a brand-new life form. It is not clear which approach will succeed, if any. But the fact that science now dares to create new, wholly manmade forms of life is sure to seep into the public consciousness in the years ahead. Some are bound to ask the question: "How might this go horribly wrong?"

An interesting early indicator of the potential nature and trajectory of such growing unease is the success of Michael Crichton's *Prey,* a bestselling thriller about nanotechnology. The book is based on a fictional future version of the technology, and the plot features tiny, swarming nanobots that spiral out of control and stalk people as prey. While serious nanotechnology researchers dismiss the plot as impossible (at least for quite a long time), the dark side of our future technologies has become lodged in our popular consciousness.

Unintended Science: From Smallpox to Superpox?

"In the January 2002 issue of *Journal of Virology,* which is the most prestigious of all the neurological journals, a group from the General Electric Labs in Australia published a study on what was supposed to have been a simple experiment with mousepix, a fairly innocuous virus. They had a problem with mice running crazy in the fields, eating all the food; they wanted a birth control method for mice. They thought that if they took a mousepox (a nonfatal and fairly benign disease, something like a cold to us), changed one gene, and then reintroduced it into the mousepox, the mice would become infertile. They didn't think it would spread much. Well, turns out they killed all the mice. Their mousepox began to spread throughout mice colonies that were not in laboratories. They had launched a fatal epidemic.

"That experiment probably cost about $50,000 to do, maybe less. And it is something that can be replicated in a thousand labs right now because they published the recipe, the whole cookbook, on the Internet. But these numbers don't matter because five minutes from now it will be more labs and it will be a lower cost. You could do exactly this to smallpox. You could do this to cowpox, or vaccinia. You could find a dead cow somewhere along the road in New Mexico that died of or with cowpox, get the vaccinia virus, make that transmutation, put it in a vial, and aerosolize it. You now have a superpox."

—Larry Brilliant, member of the World Health Organization team that eradicated smallpox back in the late 1970s

Source: Global Business Network.

Good Technology in Bad Hands

Third, some fear the potential for catastrophic *intended* consequences if new capacities get into the wrong hands. At the extreme, we may be giving ourselves and our enemies knowledge of how to nearly wipe ourselves out without necessarily knowing how to put things back together. This concern will be fueled by the democratization of new technologies as more people are able to achieve what once required enormous resources. For example, it is not farfetched to suggest that biotechnology is moving out of the academic or corporate laboratory and into the enthusiast's backyard. Sophisticated lab equipment is already accessible to the lay public. Even artists are starting to explore the new media that biotechnology is opening up—Oron Catts and Ionat Zurr, two "bioartists" at the University of Western Australia, have been growing "semi-living sculptures" as part of a Tissue Culture & Art project. As *Wired* magazine founding editor Kevin Kelly observed a few years ago: "I don't think biotech's going to make much difference in the world until it reaches the garage—the sort of street crossover point where two guys in a garage can mess with genes and biology and do something useful. When that happens, which is inevitable, then we'll see the real revolution happen." It looks as if the revolution is now under way. The question is, will everyone choose to "do something useful"?

"The twenty-first century technologies—genetics, nanotechnology, and robotics—are so powerful that they can spawn whole new classes of accidents and abuses. Most dangerously, for the first time, these accidents and abuses are widely within the reach of individuals or small groups. They will not require large facilities or rare raw materials. Knowledge alone will enable the use of them. Thus we have the possibility not just of weapons of mass destruction but of knowledge-enabled mass destruction, this destructiveness hugely amplified by the power of self-replication."

—Bill Joy, technology pioneer

Source: *What's Next?: Exploring the New Terrain for Business,* Eamonn Kelly et al.

For example, there is already growing concern over techniques used to create synthetic viruses. Scientists reported in 2002 the creation of the Ebola virus using "reverse genetics." The sequences for three out of eight segments of the influenza virus of 1918, which killed tens of millions of people worldwide, have already been published, according to the Armed Forces Institutes of Pathology in Washington, D.C., and the publication of more sequences is imminent. If this genetic knowledge falls into the wrong hands, the potential hazards are ominous. Says *New Scientist:* "All that is needed to bring [an eradicated virus] back is knowledge of its sequence and, in some cases, of what it needs to make more copies of itself."

Smallpox as a Bioweapon

The use of bioweapons is nothing new to the United States. The first recorded act of smallpox bioterrorism in the U.S. was committed back in the mid-1700s during the French and Indian Wars, when Lord Jeffrey Amherst, a British general, distributed blankets filled with smallpox scabs as "gifts" to Native Americans. Luckily, most attempts at bioterrorism through the world and throughout history have not been nearly so successful. Indeed, a strange sort of haplessness seems to kick in when a country or terrorist group tries to pull off bioterror. In 1962, the biological cocktail that the U.S. sent to Cuba to facilitate its invasion was lost in transit. In the 1980s, Saddam Hussein unleashed camelpox on Iraq's Kurdish population, only to find out later that camelpox cannot infect humans. In 1993, Aum Shinrikyo, the Japanese doomsday cult that would later release sarin gas in the Tokyo subway, sprayed copious quantities of anthrax into the air from a Tokyo rooftop. Fortunately, they accidentally chose a strain of anthrax that is harmless to humans.

By international treaty, smallpox should exist in only two places: the CDC in Atlanta, and the Russian lab Biopreparat. But in recent years, there's been much speculation that some of the former Soviet Union's stockpile may have found its way into other hands. Back in 1985, Gorbachev had signed a five-year plan allocating $1.2 billion to create a weapon out of smallpox. The five-year plan had an annual quota of 100 tons of smallpox—enough to kill every man, woman, and child in the United States. Russian scientists also conducted experiments to create a "superpox" that would be impervious to vaccine. Then the Soviet Union collapsed, funding dried up, and the scientists left. No one knows what happened to the smallpox. One of smallpox's trademarks is its swift and effortless spread: one or two cases of smallpox can become horrific epidemics. As smallpox expert Larry Brilliant put it, "A single case of smallpox would bring this country to its knees. It would stop our economic system. It would terrify everyone. In the world in which we live, which is all CNN all the time, we would fall exactly into the hands of whichever terrorists used smallpox against us."

Political and Regulatory Responses

Reactions and regulation prompted by technological advances vary markedly in different parts of the world and will likely lead to some new sources of global tension. But there will also be new hot spots of technology-driven economic growth, with China being a likely beneficiary as it assumes a leading-edge role in certain fields of biotechnology. In September 2004, a group of British scientists, under the auspices of the Department of Trade and Industry's Global Watch Stem Cell Mission, visited stem cell research facilities in China, Singapore, and South Korea. They returned extremely impressed at the world-class work being undertaken and concluded that the Chinese labs were "at or approaching the forefront of international stem cell research." They also observed that "there is much less resistance than would be met in the West to pursuing experimental therapies into clinical practice." It's also probable that some important areas of scientific investigation and discovery could become mired in "gray zones" of murky legality and moral dubiety, setting off increased tensions and diminished trust both within the scientific community and between it and the rest of society.

The global regulation of these issues will become more problematic; the research community is already global, and decisions in one political jurisdiction can have powerful effects in others. President George Bush's decision to call a halt to stem cell research, for example, gave encouragement to those countries in the European Union that have also imposed a ban (e.g., Germany, Ireland, Austria) and emboldened those that have more permissive policies and see an opportunity to move ahead of the U.S. in a vital area of new technology (e.g., United Kingdom, Sweden, Finland). The EU debate has been particularly fierce as a result, and its resolution is not imminent.

Moreover, different choices and emphases in the policy domain will run up against the principle of open global markets. With respect to the adoption of genetically modified organisms in agriculture, for example, the U.S. has been much less cautious than Europe, with President Bush telling a Biotechnology Industry Organization summit in 2003, "I urge the European governments to end their opposition to biotechnology. We should encourage the spread of safe, effective biotechnology to win the fight against global hunger." European governments, reflecting the hostility of their electorates to genetically modified organisms, reacted angrily to the charge that their cautious approach to an untested technology was starving Africans.

A Complicated Road Ahead

Heated views, heightened tensions, misunderstandings, and megaphone diplomacy are to be expected in these sensitive areas. In the coming decade, certain developments in science and technology will be regarded as amoral in some quarters and shortsighted and arrogant in others, whatever the claims from history that science has been the source of much of our progress. We can expect the backlash to create some unusual and unexpected alliances, and the increasing tension between our capacities and our anxieties will be a core social dynamic. Corporations that are developing and using cutting-edge technology could find themselves caught between the exciting prospects that the technology affords and the deep apprehension that accompanies any new breakthrough.

These issues are putting the structures of democratic governance under strain in many ways. The science on which they rely is often complex and abstruse, mitigating against informed public debate. The judgments are usually ethical rather than technical, financial, or ideological—and our governments are not well set up to deal with such issues. Decisions made in the public interest often have long-term consequences that we cannot calculate with any degree of certainty, and public institutions have traditionally not been long on any degree of foresight beyond the next election. So the mere statement of government policy will no longer be enough to legitimize progress in these sensitive areas. If the public does not trust the science or those in control of the technology, they will not allow it—whatever elected government says. The battle is not, in the long run, for slick lobbying success in the corridors of power but for a genuine consensus of hearts and minds.

Throughout history, one of the most important effects of new technology has been to generate structural economic change. Today, the technologies of communication and connection are fueling the most significant economic transition since the dawn of the industrial evolution: the migration toward an "intangible" economy. Meanwhile, these new technologies are also set to assist with another critical transition in the next decade—from a failing and vulnerable physical infrastructure to one that is safer and no longer crumbling around us.

Chapter 6

Intangible and Physical Economies

In the coming decade, we will witness a continued and accelerating transition from the industrial to the post-industrial era. With it we will experience the further rise of an "intangible" economy, in which the relationship between value and weight continues to break down and an increasing amount of what we consider valuable will be found in things we cannot hold: services, experiences, and relationships. But even as value migrates to the intangible world, the physical world of infrastructure will take on new importance and its maintenance will assume new urgency. Physical infrastructure will experience severe pressures in many parts of the world, becoming even more desperately in need of update and overhaul. We will need to find ways to prevent the potentially catastrophic consequences associated with infrastructural failures in a variety of arenas—most critically, water.

Intangible

> **If you can drop it on your toe, you know it is not a service.**
> *—The Economist*

Throughout the 1990s, observers declared that a "new economy" was unfolding. It was an economy driven by new rules, new metrics, new models, and new players, and it was epitomized by the seemingly gravity-defying dotcom phenomenon. While it is easy today to dismiss the inflated hype of the new economy as a collective hallucination, it was actually more a classic case of category error. Many mistook the dotcom frenzy for the big story when the headline should have been how the Internet was enabling and accelerating an ongoing process of economic transition. For decades now, we have been inexorably evolving from an industrial to a post-industrial economy—an economic and social transition as profound as the shift from the agricultural to the industrial era in the eighteenth and nineteenth centuries.

By far, the most important feature of the post-industrial economy is the declining relationship between physical mass and economic value. As Alan Greenspan has put it, "The per capita physical weight of our gross domestic product is evidently only scarcely higher today than it was 50 or 100 years ago. By far the largest contributor to growth of our price-adjusted GDP, or value added, has been ideas—insights that leveraged physical reality." In the post-industrial economy, value creation is increasingly founded on knowledge, ideas, intellect, and innovation. Developed economies are now dominated by services rather than manufacturing; experiences are purchased and consumed as much as products; the digital bit is matching the physical atom in economic importance; and connections and relationships are becoming as critical as possession and ownership.

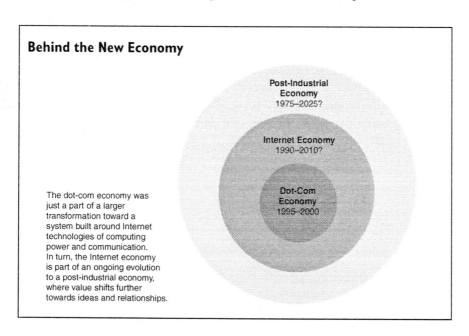

Behind the New Economy

Post-Industrial
Economy
1975–2025?

Internet Economy
1990–2010?

Dot-Com
Economy
1995–2000

The dot-com economy was just a part of a larger transformation toward a system built around Internet technologies of computing power and communication. In turn, the Internet economy is part of an ongoing evolution to a post-industrial economy, where value shifts further towards ideas and relationships.

In other words, value is becoming increasingly "intangible." And while this phenomenon has been widely observed, there is still something not quite intuitive about it. The association between physical goods and economic value is deeply ingrained—hence, the continued widespread assumption that a "real" economy should be built around heavy industry and manufacturing and that "real" employment involves the act of producing tangible goods. (Curiously, there were similar beliefs during the early stages of the transition to the industrial economy. Many members of a widely respected group of French Enlightenment thinkers, the Physiocrats, held that only agriculture—which, after all, was capable of creating enormous harvests from but a handful of seeds—created true economic value.) In essence, however, an economy is really nothing more mysterious than an extremely elaborate system within which people create and satisfy one another's needs and wants. We have long been willing to pay for both the physical and the intangible components of what we desire. But the balance is now tipping steadily toward the intangible.

The Rise of the Intangible Economy

The intangible economy has many overlapping components, and four in particular are worth briefly examining: the rising importance of the service sector; the growing "knowledge intensity" of many products and services; our increasing ability and willingness to pay high premiums for quality experiences; and the importance of aesthetics and beauty as a source of economic value. Together, they are driving and defining significant change in the nature of the economy.

SERVICES

The service sector has experienced remarkable growth for decades—so much so, in fact, that it is now considered the largest and fastest-growing sector of the global economy. Services now account for more than 75 percent of U.S. GDP and more than one-third of global trade. Moreover, because services are increasingly "tradeable"—even though they can't be shipped, they can be bought and sold across borders just like tangible goods—they constitute an increasing portion of global trade. In the last decade, U.S. services exports have more than doubled, now accounting for 30 percent of total exports. Increasingly, intangibles like communications, logistics, and financial services are providing the infrastructural underpinnings for continued growth (and reduced friction and transaction costs) in the global economy.

The shift away from manufacturing and toward the production and consumption of services has been especially marked in the developed world. But services have also taken hold in developing countries. Services already account for roughly 50 percent of developing world GDP; in many countries it is the fastest-growing sector. As electronic connectivity enables more service work to be carried out remotely, this trend will surely accelerate. It will also continue to fuel increasing anxiety in the developed world as more and more high-skill service work is outsourced.

KNOWLEDGE INTENSITY

Knowledge—of how crops grow, how the world works, how to make and use tools, how to fabricate useful products—has always been a critical driver of human economic systems. "Know-how," initially passed on from parents to children and now embedded in increasingly sophisticated technologies, has underpinned agriculture for a thousand generations. The emergence of craft economies was based on the development of better and more specialized knowledge about how to make durable goods that meet our basic needs. The industrial revolution was based on the codification of old and new knowledge to create better and more scaleable technologies and processes.

However, in the last few decades, knowledge has been driving economic value as never before; by the mid-1990s, more than half of GDP in the major OECD (Organization for Economic Cooperation and Development) economics was considered "knowledge-based." In most business sectors in the developed world, the relative significance of physical material to the value of goods (for example, the proportion of the cost of a motor car that is determined by the steel it contains) has declined considerably. We can see this all around us. A modest car coming off the assembly line today has 1,000 times the computing power of Apollo 11 when Neil Armstrong landed it on the moon.

While the remarkable rise in computing power over the last 20 years is responsible for much of the increasing knowledge intensity in our economy and in the goods and services we consume, the trend is far deeper and more ubiquitous. Even a few decades ago, the products that populated our homes seemed relatively simple; it was not difficult to figure out how a kitchen chair was made, or how a simple radio functioned. But today's products are much more complex. It is hard to get a sense of how a video game or a kitchen appliance embedded with sensors and microchips was created and the price at which it can be profitably sold.

In these products, knowledge is just as fundamental an ingredient as plastic and silicon. Deep, embedded knowledge supports the creation—and determines the value—of much that we consume and depend upon.

Knowledge as Value

"Our second growth pathway is knowledge intensity. As a company our technical and market knowledge is unsurpassed in many areas.... We think that the potential in this knowledge should be translated into tangible business value—getting paid for what we know. Knowledge intensity is key to making progress in a sustainability metric we created called 'shareholder value added per pound,' which measures how well a business is creating value for each unit of material output. We are most interested in business that has a high SVA/lb. Unlike the chemicals and materials businesses of the past, where value generation was in direct proportion to raw material and energy throughput and pounds produced, our goal now is to have value creation inversely related to pounds of product manufactured. Knowledge content either reflected in the design and performance of the product, as a brand, or as information that is part of the offering, is one way of getting more value for each unit of production."

Source: Excerpt of a speech by John Hodgson, executive vice president of DuPont, April 27, 2003. Reprinted by permission.

EXPERIENCE

In the developed world in particular, we are witnessing a widespread increase in the willingness of consumers to pay not just for services but for experiences. This trend is more obvious in some sectors than in others. Tourism, for example, is a marketplace of highly designed and packaged experiences, and it is one of the largest and fastest growing industries in the world. Tourism is already the world's largest employer, accounting for one in every 10 workers worldwide. In 2003, 691 million people traveled the world as tourists, spending an estimated $523 billion, according to the World Tourism Organization (WTO). In its long-term forecasts, the WTO projects that international tourist arrivals will nearly triple to 1.56 billion by the year 2020. Another rapidly growing marketplace for experience is spectator sports, with revenues expected to surge to $102.5 billion in 2008, up from $74.6 billion in 2003. It's little wonder that sports stars are joining the stars of another experience industry—entertainment—as among the wealthiest people in the world.

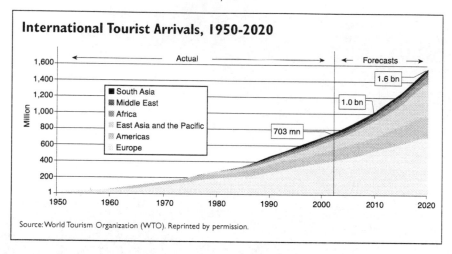

International Tourist Arrivals, 1950-2020

Source: World Tourism Organization (WTO). Reprinted by permission.

Even in less obvious parts of the economy, experience is becoming a big component of value. As Joseph Pine and James Gilmore explain in their book *The Experience Economy,* "The emerging experience economy demands recognizing that *any* work observed directly by a customer is an act of theatre…. Bank tellers, insurance agents, and real-estate brokers engage in theatre when they explain terms and conditions. So do taxi drivers when they converse. Even the trading of commodities in exchange pits is theatre of a particular, attention-grabbing kind."

The authors also posit that the next natural stop in the economic evolution from commodities to goods to services is the emergence of experience as an economic offering in its own right. They illustrate this progression through a simple example: the birthday cake. Prior to the 1970s, most people made birthday cakes from scratch, mixing the ingredients (commodities) themselves. Then came prepackaged cake mixes (goods), which saved time and energy. In the 1980s, ready-made cakes from a bakery or grocery store became the norm; people were now willing to pay for the service of cake-making. Then a leap was made from purchasing the consumption of the cake to purchasing the consumption of the related experience. In the 1990s, an "outsourcing" trend took hold; parents began to hire others to create a "birthday experience" for their children and their guests. Companies like Chuck E. Cheese became favorite places for birthday parties—the primary feature of which was not pizza or cake, but experience. At each step along the way, new and higher economic value was being created and eagerly purchased.

AESTHETICS, BEAUTY, AND ART

As experience becomes an even more important determinant of economic value, so too does aesthetics. The desire to surround ourselves with things of beauty appears to be innate to humans, and our ability to satisfy this urge increases with rising prosperity. This places more emphasis on the design elements of a product or an experience. The aesthetic importance of design is partly related to pure visual appeal (consider the price of a retro-styled toaster relative to a plainer model with equivalent features). But it also extends to simplicity and functionality. The runaway success of Apple's iPod music player, for example, can be largely attributed to its unique combination of appealing aesthetics and visual and functional simplicity. The iPod is not cheaper than competitor products, nor is it so very different in terms of performance. But it is elegant, simple, and intuitive to use, with an interface so well designed that it feels somehow aesthetically "right."

The increased importance of beauty in our lives manifests itself in myriad ways, not the least of which is our increased willingness to pay for it. For example, in the last several years Wal-Mart and other retailers have achieved considerable growth in the sale of flowers—purchased not just for others but increasingly for ourselves. Indeed, the beautification of our homes has risen remarkably in cultural importance in the past decade; witness the proliferation of new paints and painting techniques and the explosion of television shows constructed around decorating and interior design challenges. Products that were once purchased solely for their function are also joining the aesthetic fray. Target now sells teapots designed by famed architect Michael Graves, and clothes fashioned by famed designer Isaac Mizrahi. We can expect to see many more well-designed yet affordable domestic products enter the market in the coming decade.

Perhaps the ultimate expression of the impulse toward aesthetic values and beauty is our relationship to art. Regarded throughout most of history as the preserve of the privileged, art has become more central to developed societies and their economies in recent decades. In the late 1990s, the British government, under the rubric of "Cool Britannia," acknowledged and promoted the critical role of the creative arts, which is now one of the fastest growing economic sectors in the UK—generating annual revenues of $185 billion and employing more than 2 million people nationwide (and providing one out of every seven jobs in London). Seen in this context, the outburst of civic enthusiasm for "The Gates" installation in Manhattan in early 2005 (the first major art happening of the millennium) was a tribute not just to the vision and perseverance of the artists but to the common human aspiration to experience beauty and grace.

Consequences for Business—Rethinking Assets

The shift toward an intangible economy has been changing our understanding of what elements of a business make it most likely to be successful. It used to be that "success" was largely determined by numbers—profitability ratios and projected targets tracked on spreadsheets. But success in the intangible economy is not so easily measured; it is as much qualitative and quantitative. A much wider array of assets, many of them intangible, now underpins economic success. Establishing good relationships—with employees, customers, partners, and supply networks—has grown in importance. Brands have become less about logos and taglines than about generating and communicating trust and credibility; increasingly, they are the vehicles through which business reputations are established and managed. Patents, proprietary information, and other forms of intellectual property, collectively known as "knowledge assets," are becoming as important as the goods and services they help spawn; battles over who owns the rights to what innovation or product are increasingly struggles for rights to the knowledge behind them; and the qualitative skills that humans bring to the table, including their creativity, commitment, flexibility, and capacity for learning and change, are increasingly being treated as key components of a company's success.

We can also see evidence of the rising impact of the intangible economy in the shifting stories of many major corporations over the last half century. General Motors sees greater profits from its financial services arm than from its cars. Nike subcontracts its manufacturing, choosing to concentrate on higher "value add" activities like marketing, design, and logistics. IBM said goodbye to a large and tangible piece of its own legacy when it sold its personal-computer business to Lenovo, a Chinese company, in order to concentrate on its more profitable service and consulting businesses.

Meanwhile, the Internet continues to transform business models and help boost the productivity and profitability of some very traditional sectors. The car insurance company Progressive Corp., for example, pioneered the sale of policies online and the use of digital cameras and wireless Web links to help process claims more quickly—sometimes within 20 minutes. The company's revenues have increased by 20 percent yearly since it went online in 1996, against an auto-insurance industry average of just 5 percent. Not only are old businesses being transformed, but new businesses underpinned by new models are also emerging, especially through the supreme enabler of the intangible, the World Wide Web. Seeds planted a decade ago are starting to flower. The dotcom frenzy may have abated, but even the most retrospectively ridiculed example of '90s hysteria, online pet food retailing, continues to yield nice profits for several competitive companies.

But some of the new models that have emerged over the last decade are more than simple e-tailing. Consider the new categories of business exemplified by these now-household names: Expedia, eBay, Google. Industries that focused on "information gatekeeping," or controlling information that customers want and suppliers want to make available, were among the first to fall to the power of the intangible economy. This was particularly true for the travel industry. Expedia, one of the best known sites for booking travel online, launched in 1996 and was profitable by 2002, a year ahead of schedule. Like the online pet food companies, Expedia's business was primarily about creating a new sales channel for existing goods and services.

Meanwhile, entirely new intangible marketplaces were being created. The primary business of eBay is to enable the trade of largely traditional goods and services, but by doing this online it has created an entirely new virtual marketplace of buyers and sellers—a "global flea market." The company created a dynamic market with an astonishing diversity of products, providing sellers with access to a trusted global "community of consumption" and buyers with access to almost everything imaginable (including some unusual and highly controversial offerings, such as a human kidney for transplant and a "miraculous" 10-year-old grilled cheese sandwich bearing the likeness of the Virgin Mary). It also adds a competitive component to purchasing, as buyers vie to land the best bid at just the right time.

Google represents an even more radical development: a business that deploys extremely sophisticated (and intangible) software to make available to everyone, everywhere, for free, a whole new category of service that did not previously exist—namely, access to a spectacular variety of (intangible) information on almost any topic, prioritized by harnessing the collective (intangible) intelligence of millions of fellow Internet users. Fittingly, Google drives its revenues by "selling" the (intangible) attention of its users to those willing to pay for it. When Google opened its books in order to become listed as a public company in 2004, many analysts were surprised at just how robust the business turned out to be. Founded in 1998, the company has been profitable since 2001 and continues to enjoy solid financial footing even as its offerings continue to expand into new categories; its revenues for the first quarter of 2005 reached $1.3 billion.

Revolutions in Connectivity

Sure to hasten more such developments is the fact that the quality and speed of Internet connections continues to increase. The "broadband revolution" that has been touted for so long is powerfully underway, delivering much faster downloads and always-on connections to an ever-growing online population. In March 2005, the number of broadband subscribers surpassed 150 million—an increase of 51 million since the beginning of 2004. It is expected to exceed 400 million in 2009. More than 51 percent of U.S. households now have broadband Internet connections—up from 38 percent just one year ago. And that growth is not slowing down: by 2009, the number of U.S. households with broadband is expected to top 228 million, up from 81 million in 2003. Also accelerating is the speed of broadband itself. Over the next few years, broadband speeds in the U.S. are expected to soar from today's 1.5 to 3 Mbps to a speed of 25 Mbps—an astronomical leap in speed that will enable all sorts of newer, bigger, and faster interactive offerings, including new forms of rich media and digital video. As broadband speeds up and spreads, it will continue to drive all manners of new growth and to transform and expand our relationship with the intangible.

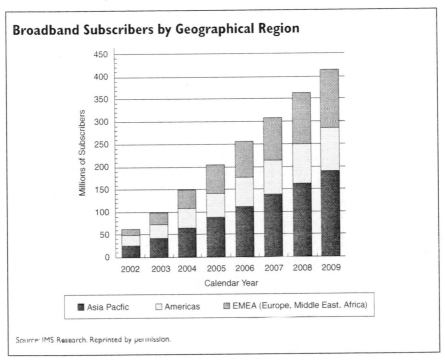

Broadband Subscribers by Geographical Region

Source: IMS Research. Reprinted by permission.

Indeed, some observers suggest that the Internet will soon reach an "inflection point," when high-speed broadband usage will become great enough to trigger profound changes in the ways that we think about and utilize the Internet. The Pew Internet and American Life Project suggests we will soon see the emergence of a "broadband lifestyle," with online entertainment and shopping taking on even more importance, as well as new business models that further expand the Internet's business and cultural potential. As my colleague Andrew Blau has put it, "Broadband's wide use—especially among economically attractive groups such as people with high household incomes or young, well-educated people—will in turn foster business choices that will in the future shape this market around the assumption of widespread access to high-speed connections." If the late 1990s were about the explosion of new technologies and dreams about ways to creatively use them, the 2000s are about making the technology work, putting the ideas into practice, delivering real value, and making real money.

And this is not just a U.S. phenomenon. China alone has 94 million Internet users, almost half of them with broadband connections, and newfound connectivity—email, cellphones, wireless—is spurring new opportunities across the world, even enabling some poorer countries to enjoy an "infrastructural leapfrogging" over wealthier countries. The growth in mobile telephony alone has been staggering. A mere 0.2 percent of the world's inhabitants had a mobile phone in 1991; by the end of 2004, 1.5 billion were mobile phone users, close to one out of every four people on the planet.

Mobile Telephony in Africa

"At the end of 2003, there were 6.1 mobile telephone subscribers for every 100 inhabitants in Africa, compared with 3 fixed-line subscribers per 100. Mobile penetration is much higher in other regions of the world—15 per 100 inhabitants in Asia, for example, 48.8 in the U.S., and 55 in Europe. Even so, there were 51.8 million mobile subscribers in Africa at the end of 2003, reflecting an increase of more than 1,000 percent in five years. Access to mobile telephony in Africa is also almost certainly far more extensive than the subscriber figures suggest, as each handset and subscription has many users."

Source: "Africa: The Impact of Mobile Phones," The Vodafone Policy Paper Series, March 2005. Reprinted by permission of Vodafone Group. Copyright © 2005 Vodafone Group.

New Communities

Intangible technologies also intersect with human values—specifically, they tap into the basic human desire to "belong." As a result, we are witnessing a transformation in social relationships in the form of "intangible communities," often composed of people who have never met and may never do so. Many of these communities are purely social and appear to be creating new and unexpected values, priorities, and behaviors. Instant messaging has become a new and vital form of communication among the young, creating a whole new language (even schoolwork is sometimes written with the terse grammar and abundant abbreviations of "IMese").

"We are now entering a golden era of social software development...and the resulting new products are already building enhanced webs of human connectedness, real social networks."

—Clay Shirky, Internet innovator

Source: *What's Next?: Exploring the New Terrain for Business*, Eamonn Kelly et al.

Blogging, or keeping an online journal that anyone can read, has become an increasingly popular and community-building form of self-expression. In 2004, more than 8 million people in the U.S. alone created their own blogs, and 14 million contributed thoughts or comments to someone else's blog; 32 million U.S. citizens were regular blog readers. The intangible world of chat rooms is also spawning new forms of communication, new kinds of language, and even new kinds of relationships.

The emergence of intangible communities will have other dramatic consequences. For example, the relentless spread of the "open source" approach is creating new "communities of production." Today, open source primarily refers to software and the free publication of source code for others to take and improve upon. Open source harnesses the energy and talents of thousands of contributors, creating products that are often superior to those developed by traditional commercial enterprises. The best known example, Linux, an operating system that competes with Microsoft Windows, has tens of millions of users already. But as my colleague Steve Weber, author of *The Success of Open Source*, has put it, the concept is set to transform other industries as well because it is "a new way of organizing people to create complex products in a knowledge-based economy." This trend toward collective creation is now showing up in realms as diverse as biotechnology research and music production. In the coming decade, we should expect to see open source moving beyond the world of software to start having a transformative impact on many spheres of commerce.

Other social behaviors and dynamics will change as technology creates new ways to communicate and coordinate as well as new forms of activism and "real-time" democracy. Howard Rheingold has written about a new phenomenon he calls "smart mobs," consisting of "people who are able to act in concert even if they don't know each other" through the use of new technologies. He cites as an early indicator a recent incident in the Philippines, in which a million citizens mobilized and forced President Joseph Estrada from office through protests organized and coordinated entirely through text messages. Link this phenomenon to the power of Internet-based advocacy groups such as MoveOn.org and the "flash funding" achieved by presidential hopeful Howard Dean, and the growing potency of intangible communities becomes even more apparent.

Perhaps the most striking example of how virtual creative spaces are driving the growth of new communities and networks is online gaming. Online gaming is already a booming industry in the U.S., and it is even bigger in Asia. By 2009, the worldwide market for online games could reach $9.8 billion—a more than fourfold increase over 2003. Nearly half of this revenue will come from the Asia-Pacific market: Korea, Taiwan, Japan, and China. China alone is projected to become the top online gaming market by 2007.

Online Gaming Around the World

- There are more than 28,000 online gaming parlors in South Korea, one for every 1,700 residents.

- 40 million people in China and South Korea subscribe to the online game "Mu," with an average of 500,000 people playing at any one time.

- America's Army, an online battle game designed and first distributed in 2002 as a recruiting tool for the U.S. Army, now has more than 5 million registered users; it is the third most popular online game in the world.

- In 2003, Thailand imposed a curfew on online gaming from 10 p.m. to 6 a.m., in order to stem what Thai experts call an "addiction" to the Korean role-playing game Ragnarok, which has more than 600,000 registered users in Thailand, many of them children.

Sources: CNet News; America's Army website; GovExec.com; BBC News.

In some games, such as Everquest and Ultima Online, players occupy virtual worlds and create and acquire (virtual) property and rare (virtual) items, often investing considerable time in doing so. A large and growing real-world market for the buying and selling of these entirely intangible "items"—characters, castles, weapons, and more—has emerged. Every week, eBay sees more than 28,000 trades in virtual goods, valued at more than $500,000. "The currency used in the games is also being traded," reports the *Financial Times*. "A block of 100,000 Norrathian Platinum Pieces (the currency used in the EverQuest online game) was sold on eBay for $65, implying an exchange rate of just over 1,538 to the dollar." The *Times* used data on the sales of EverQuest avatars on eBay to calculate the per capita GDP for the imaginary world of Norrath. It was $2,266 per head, making Norrath the 77th richest country in the world.

New Economic Challenges

Clearly, the shift toward an intangible economy has created abundant new opportunities. But it also presents many traditional businesses with serious challenges to their existing economic models. An obvious example is the problems posed to the music and entertainment industries by Napster and other file-sharing services: no matter how much these are regulated, no matter what levels of self-constraint they adopt, the fact is that new technologies profoundly challenge old notions of intellectual property and will inevitably lead to the development of new business models. There were hints of this during the earliest days of the Internet, when frequent references were made to the Internet as the hub of a new "gift economy"— a place of connection where people could help one another without financial gain. The ubiquity of the Internet will continue to undermine traditional economic models of production and transaction.

De-commercialization is not the only economic challenge we will face as we head into the still-evolving frontier of the intangible future. As information spreads and flows, it feeds and speeds competitive pressures, forces up the pace of innovation cycles, forces down the half-life of many goods and services, and leads to rapid commoditization of even the most intelligent products. As the assets underpinning success become increasingly intangible and based on relationship rather than ownership, the smarter and more nimble business strategies must become. The intangible world is with us to stay, and its implications are just now coming into focus.

Physical

The road to success is always under construction.
—Lily Tomlin

The new technologies and connectivities enabling the intangible economy do, however, have tangible underpinnings, and the changes ahead of us will place additional pressure on the already overstressed "physical" infrastructure that makes the intangible possible. Economic progress has never been a straightforward switch from one reality to another; it is always a more evolutionary process in which a new order emerges from the previous one. Agriculture, for example, remains a critical sector even today, 200 years after the industrial revolution—even if it represents a much smaller percentage of our economic activity and wealth. By the same token, the world of tangible things—manufactured goods, natural resources, the physical components of all breeds of business—will not only continue to matter but will grow in importance and priority in the coming decade. This is particularly true of physical infrastructure, the improvement of which could be a tremendous spur for investment, innovation, and quality of life. Without it, the intangible economy and all of its promise would come to a grinding halt.

Developed World Infrastructure: A Perfect Storm Ahead?

People in developed nations have high expectations regarding quality of life. Physical infrastructure—including transportation, health, education, water, and energy—is a core enabler of that. Moreover, today's global economy depends heavily on the developed world's physical infrastructure; its components literally enable the international flow of goods and services. We tend to take this for granted, assuming that this critical infrastructure will always be there and will continue to develop and improve. Yet right now a "perfect storm" of several factors coinciding could dramatically challenge that assumption.

The first factor is simple enough: we have growing expectations of speed and efficiency even while many of our basic physical systems— roads, air traffic, power grids—are reaching the limits of their carrying capacity. Second, new demands for better security are requiring many developed countries to retrofit their existing infrastructure in order to bring it up to new standards, a process that is proving enormously costly. The U.S. government plans to spend $150 million in 2006 just to upgrade the security of the nation's 350 ports, which is a small piece of an expected $4.7 billion homeland security budget for that year that also includes substantial airport upgrades. Third, the maintenance of aging and failing infrastructure is an ongoing challenge. London's subway system still runs through tunnels constructed in the 1860s. Many of the U.S.'s 16,000 wastewater systems are 100 years old, and vast numbers of its treatment facilities are well past their life expectancy; one-third of all U.S. bridges are dilapidated or too weak to bear traffic. As usage of these structures and facilities grows even heavier, even basic maintenance becomes much harder to achieve. Many of our systems run around the clock, making down time for repairs increasingly hard to find.

2005 Report Card for America's Infrastructure

Aviation	D+
Bridges	C
Dams	D
Drinking Water	D-
Energy	D
Hazardous Waste	D
Navigable Waterways	D-
Public Parks & Recreation	C-
Rail	C-
Roads	D
Schools	D
Solid Waste	C+
Transit	D+
Wastewater	D-

U.S. Infrastructure G.P.A. = D

Total investment needs: $1.6 trillion (estimated 5-year need)

Grade definitions: A = exceptional, B = good, C = mediocre, D = poor, F = failing

Source: American Society of Civil Engineers (ASCE). Reprinted by permission of ASCE.

There is also a dilemma between patching up the old infrastructure and upgrading to something new. For example, as both education and healthcare become more distributed and "remote," the nature of required reinvestment in schools and hospitals is becoming less straightforward, often resulting in deferred investments and, thus, deteriorating facilities. Finally, and perhaps most importantly, public policy makers are often prisoners of civic unwillingness to invest in what is not yet overtly broken, unable to address—or sometimes even to recognize—the challenges ahead. In the meantime, highways, schools, airports, railroads, seaports, and hospitals are all feeling the pressure of increased usage, inadequate investment, and natural aging. Attempts at privatization have helped to alleviate some of the worst symptoms but have rarely resolved the deep systemic issues. The health of the infrastructure has suffered as a result.

It Takes Forever to Build New Infrastructure

Large-scale infrastructure projects are getting harder to do and require enormous expenditure:

- The Denver International Airport cost $4.9 billion to build. It opened in February 1995, two years behind schedule and $300 million over budget. It was the first major airport built in the United States in 20 years.

- Rebuilding the eastern span of San Francisco's Bay Bridge is proving the costliest construction project in California history. The price tag is now $5.5 billion—$3 billion more than initial estimates. Construction is expected to be finished in 2011, four years behind schedule.

- New York City's Water Tunnel No. 3 has been under construction for more than 30 years. When completed in 2020, at a cost of $6 billion, the tunnel will have taken a half century to build.

Sources: Autodesk; *The San Diego Union-Tribune*; *Newsday*.

The American Society of Civil Engineers estimates that the U.S. alone will need to invest $1.6 trillion over the next five years in order to raise the condition of its infrastructure to acceptable levels. A lag in the willingness to make such investments is inevitable. But as capacity is exceeded and "tipping points" are reached, congestion, accidents, failures, and underperformance will increase in frequency, magnitude, and visibility. Only then will the mounting shortcomings of infrastructure be taken seriously.

The Intangible to the Rescue of the Physical

The fact that our economic growth is now largely driven by intangible value has blinded us to the looming infrastructural challenges ahead. Yet the very technologies that drive the intangible economy could prove critical in creating new solutions to the problems of physical infrastructure. Perhaps the most obvious example is the overdue upgrade of North America's interconnected electricity grid, which failed spectacularly in 2003, blacking out big swatches of the northeastern U.S. and southern

Canada and plunging 50 million people into darkness. President Bush rightly described the incident as a "wakeup call," dubbing the current electricity grid "antiquated." But new technologies could help run the grid in smarter ways. A combination of distributed sensors that allow the network to stay in constant communication with itself, software that processes the information and keeps the grid in balance, and faster digital switches to shift load from one part of the network to another would make the system more adaptive and resilient. To echo the words of Bruce Germano, vice president of the Long Island Power Authority, it would make the grid effectively "self-healing."

We should also expect to see, and to encourage, more examples of new-economy technologies coming to the rescue of the old. New materials technologies and sensing systems offer "smart" new approaches to legacy problems. For example, construction companies are already able to embed in their cement "smart pebbles" containing tiny sensors that report on the condition of the cement around them, sounding an alert well before failure and making care and maintenance cheaper and more effective. This is part of a trend, which we will see more of in the coming years, of investing in smarter infrastructure that greatly strengthens and improves the longevity of much of our physical world.

New technologies are also enabling existing structures to handle greater volume and capacity—especially in regard to travel and transportation. In Los Angeles, an experimental fleet of buses has been fitted with sensors that communicate with the city's traffic control systems, including the stoplights, in order to smooth passage of the buses and speed up their flow through the streets. The result has been a 25 percent decrease in travel time, as well as increased reliability and capacity of the system. Another important innovation relates to "dynamic pricing" through the use of special lanes on the freeway. In San Diego and Minneapolis, certain stretches of road called "hot lanes" are equipped with traffic sensors that read current levels of congestion and delay. Large roadside screens display a changing price for use of these special, faster lanes, which drivers can choose to enter (paying electronically with their windshield-mounted device) when the price-convenience ratio reaches their own tradeoff level. Again, the net effect is smoother overall traffic flow, with real-time advantages for those willing to pay.

Who Is Responsible—And Who Pays?

Even as the need for infrastructural upgrades becomes greater and more obvious, and the technologies to achieve these upgrades become more effective, questions about responsibility and financing will become increasingly vexed and politically charged, particularly in developed countries. These uncertainties will surely slow the rate of investment needed to smarten these systems. After the electricity blackout of 2003, it became clear that no one knew who bore responsibility for the state of the grid as a whole. The long-running debacle over the privatization of the British railway system offers another example. In the mid-1990s, the British government divided responsibility for the rail system among public and private players. Some were accountable for operating train services, others for maintaining the tracks, and a host of government agencies were in charge of regulating safety, compliance, and efficiency. The policy caused massive confusion, created some perverse incentives, and led indirectly to a number of fatal accidents.

The question of who funds infrastructural investment has proved equally troublesome. Tax-funded government spending is often the most effective way to pay for public goods. But this approach encounters harsh resistance from those who favor smaller government and lower taxation and instead prefer that users bear the brunt of the costs. Sophisticated technologies that allow authorities to measure how much we use roads, bridges, and other infrastructure, and then charge us accordingly, could enable this to happen.

Improving our physical infrastructure will mean continued tension between taxation and private funding and between collective and individual responsibility. We will see a constant search for new arrangements that combine the benefits of private funding with clear accountability. More aggressive privatization will be advocated by some; others will favor shared financing solutions such as bond schemes or the UK's Private Financing Initiative, which transfers much of the risk of construction projects from the public to the private sector. However these debates are resolved, we should expect to see the issue of infrastructural investment emerge as a much more central political uncertainty in the coming decade.

The Developing World: Leapfrogging or Lagging?

The relative absence of legacy infrastructures in developing countries seems to afford them some exciting opportunities—especially in the realm of telecommunications, where mobile telephony has now largely overtaken traditional fixed lines in many countries. In reality, the opportunities for such "leapfrogging" are more limited when considered against the scale of the infrastructural catch-up that is required. In much of the developing world, the challenge is to build an infrastructure almost from scratch and sometimes to rebuild the most rudimentary facilities in the wake of natural disaster or the ravages of conflict. Indeed, the World Bank estimates that developing countries will need to spend, on average, about 5.5 percent of their GDP over the next five years on building and maintaining their infrastructure—a cumulative total investment of $465 billion.

It is certainly true that the sheer scale and cost of these works will drive innovation and experimentation, and there are significant opportunities to build for the present century rather than the last. But the challenges of building, maintaining, and innovating an infrastructure to keep up with galloping demand cannot be understated, and this challenge will be deeply felt in many parts of the developing world in the coming decade.

This issue is already writ large in both China and India, though the lessons emerging from these countries are quite different. China has been engaged in an extraordinary program of infrastructural development for more than 20 years, which has been both a cause and a consequence of its enduring economic growth. Many parts of the country have been physically transformed as a result. In Beijing, so rapid is the building and so extreme the physical changes that the official city website exhorts visitors to use only the most up-to-date maps available to avoid getting lost. The social upheaval involved in such massive and continuous investment in change is readily illustrated by the fact that in Beijing alone, a city of 14 million people, fully 1.3 million migrant construction workers are living and working in the city at any given time. The environmental impact of this galloping industrialization and modernization is also striking. The Chinese government estimates that fewer than half its cities have "acceptably breathable air," and that 90 percent of the water in China's cities is undrinkable.

China's infrastructural investments are having other consequences as well, including a global impact on resource prices, and, paradoxically, new infrastructural shortfalls as new energy needs cannot be met. Since the late 1980s, China has been the world's largest user of cement. It is also by far the largest producer and importer of steel, accounting for one-third of all steel consumption in the world today. China is the fastest growing user of many other commodities as well, putting stress on commodity prices and supply worldwide.

Annual Consumption and Use of Key Resources and Consumer Products in the U.S. and China

Commodity	China	U.S.
Grain (million tons, in 2004)	382	278
Meat (million tons, in 2004)	63	37
Oil (million barrels per day, in 2004)	7	20
Coal (million tons of oil equivalent, in 2003)	800	574
Steel (million tons, in 2003)	258	104
Fertilizer (million tons, 2003)	40	20
Cellphones (million in use, 2003)	269	159
TVs (million in use, 2000)	374	243
Personal computers (million in use, 2002)	36	190
Cars (million in use, 2003)	24	226

Source: Lester R. Brown, "China Replacing the United States as World's Leading Consumer," Earth Policy Institute, February 16, 2005. Reprinted by permission of the Earth Policy Institute (www.earth-policy.org).

Both despite and because of its remarkable investment in infrastructural expansion, China now faces an energy shortfall. Its voracious demand places it second only to the United States as a consumer of energy, though on a per capita basis China still uses only 10 percent of the energy used by Americans. This is proving to be more than the existing energy infrastructure can accommodate, especially as new projects are launched without taking energy availability into consideration. Electricity generation cannot keep up with demand, and rationing is already in place: energy-inefficient factories are being shut down; thermostats are being adjusted in public offices; rain clouds are being seeded in order to lower temperatures—anything to keep the grid running in the face of massive countrywide energy shortfalls. Inefficient but versatile and mobile diesel generators are plugging the holes in many places, creating further environmental damage and rising fuel prices.

What happens when other developing countries embark upon a similar path to that taken by China? This will become a pressing question in the decade ahead—and we will begin to get an early indication of the answer by paying close attention to India. Investment in infrastructural development has been much less aggressive in India than in China over the last 20 years. Yet poor roads, inadequate power supplies, poor transportation, and insufficient commercial and housing space are all growing and challenging impediments to continued growth. Curiously, this is most deeply felt in those parts of India, such as Bangalore, that have been most successful in exploiting the opportunities offered by the growth of the intangible economy. Areas that have become centers for high-end outsourcing have failed to match that success with adequate investment in physical infrastructure. Indeed, some Western companies with interests in these areas have been making their own investments in housing, transport, recreation facilities, and even telecommunications. But such measures are only a small fraction of what is required, and we can expect to see India at the front edge of massive new infrastructural investments throughout the developing world in the next decade.

The Problem of Water

Of all the infrastructure challenges ahead, the greatest will be the availability of water. This problem is not new, but it is growing. Global consumption of water increased six-fold between 1900 and 1995, more than two times the rate of population growth. The world's population is four times greater today than it was in 1900, and yet it consumes nine times as much water. Problems associated with water are caused by a variety of factors, including irrigation (accounting for 70 percent of global freshwater usage), population growth, volatile rainfall patterns associated with climate change, and the cumulative effect of prolonged, unsustainable utilization of underground water reserves.

The UN and Water for Life

Demand for water is rising rapidly. Anticipating a global water crisis, the UN General Assembly proclaimed the period from 2005 to 2015 the "International Decade for Action: Water for Life." The goal of the Decade is "a greater focus on water-related issues, with emphasis on women as managers of water to help to achieve internationally agreed water-related goals." Among those goals is cutting in half the number of people who are unable to reach or afford safe drinking water or who have no access to basic sanitation by 2015. The Decade kicked off on March 22, 2005, with World Water Day.

According to the World Health Organization, more than a billion people today lack access to safe drinking water, while almost 2.5 billion lack adequate sanitation. Five million children die each year from illnesses associated with dirty water. Water tables are falling in much of Africa, parts of Pakistan and India, northern China, the Middle East—and the United States. The World Resources Institute calls water "arguably the world's most pressing resource issue," while UNESCO's director-general talks of a "looming water crisis" and suggests that "the wars of the twenty-first century will be fought over water." Already, water disputes have been the cause of violent conflict and prolonged regional disputes, with the Indus and the Euphrates rivers serving as particularly contested water sources. There is no easy fix to this problem, certainly not in the short term.

Water in 2025

"Global freshwater consumption rose six-fold between 1900 and 1995—more than twice the rate of population growth. About one-third of the world's population already lives in countries considered to be 'water stressed'—that is, where consumption exceeds 10 percent of total supply. If present trends continue, two out of every three people on Earth will live in that condition by 2025."
—Kofi Annan, in *We the Peoples*, 2000

- Number of cubic meters of water available for human use in 1989: 9,000 per person

- Number of cubic meters expected to be available in 2025: 5,100 per person

- By 2025, nearly 230 million Africans will face water scarcity; 460 million will live in water-stressed countries

- Cities are expected to use 150 percent more water by 2025

- Industrial water use in China is expected to grow from 52 billion tons to 269 billion tons by 2025

Sources: "We the Peoples: The Role of the United Nations in the 21st Century," Millennium Report issued by Kofi Annan in April 2000; United Nations Development Programme.

Large infrastructural responses to the problem of water are essential. Yet such efforts often have unintended consequences. Large dams, for example, destroy surrounding areas and can deprive downstream communities of hitherto available water. In Spain, an extremely ambitious plan to reroute the River Ebro through a pipeline from the north to the arid southeast was postponed in 2004, partly due to prohibitive costs but also because of the inevitable destruction of wetlands and the necessity of flooding many valleys and villages in the Pyrenees.

We should anticipate three water-related priorities to increase greatly in importance in the future. The first is better conservation, especially in the U.S. The second is the development and funding of small-scale local solutions to water requirements. Finally, we can expect to see more investment in new technologies for improving water quality cheaply, safely, and at a sustainable scale.

The growth of the intangible economy is an important source of opportunity for many parts of the world. The mobility of employment in a wired economy will equally pose challenges to certain sectors and professions within the developed world. The rising needs associated with physical infrastructure everywhere also generate economic and commercial opportunities. These factors will contribute to the new global patterns of prosperity and decline over the coming decade, which is the subject of the next chapter.

Chapter 7

Prosperity and Decline

In the coming decade, an increasingly global economy will generate different and seemingly contradictory economic conditions around the world. The spread of the market economy—and its substantial reinvention by new entrants—will create new prosperity and opportunity for millions of people, and proponents of free trade will focus on these positive developments. Yet this economic dynamism will also generate friction for many. There will surely be absolute decline in some parts of the world, especially areas already blighted by conflict, corruption, disease, and environmental catastrophe; many people in developing countries will become more aware of their relative poverty as global communication continues to shrink the planet. Relative decline will also be a harsh reality for a growing number of citizens in Europe and North America.

Prosperity

> Upper classes are a nation's past. The middle class is its future.
> —Ayn Rand

The pursuit of prosperity—often measured too simply by the metric of gross domestic product—has long been the peacetime priority for much of the world. In the twentieth century, truly remarkable economic progress was achieved; the global economic output of that single century exceeded the cumulative total output for all previous human history. Most of this phenomenal growth was enjoyed by the developed world, generating extreme gaps in wealth and consumption that have no historical precedents. Five hundred years ago, global wealth was much more evenly distributed. The "new world" had not been settled, average incomes in China and India were roughly equal to those in Western Europe, and the Middle East was arguably the wealthiest region on the planet. Even by the late eighteenth century, the surging Europeans were, per capita, only about twice as wealthy as those living in the poorest regions of the world. Contrast this with the situation just 200 years later. By 1973, the wealth gap between rich and poor countries had increased to 44 to 1; by 1992, it had expanded again to 72 to 1.

Economic Growth Through Deep Time

Year	Population*	GDP per Capita†
-5000	5	$130
-1000	50	$160
1	170	$135
1000	265	$165
1500	425	$175
1800	900	$250
1900	1,625	$850
1950	2,515	$2,030
1975	4,080	$4,640
2000	6,120	$8,175

* Millions
† In year-2000 international dollars.
Source: Bradford DeLong, *Macroeconomics* (New York: McGraw-Hill, 2004). Data from DeLong's estimates and from Joel Cohen, *How Many People Can the Earth Support?* (New York: Norton, 1995). Reprinted by permission of Bradford DeLong.

Spreading Prosperity but Growing Gaps

The reason for this growing gap is quite straightforward. During these recent centuries, Europe and the West evolved and perfected the current capitalist economic system, a system based on markets, strong property rights, relatively open trade, innovative technology, general education, efficient capital allocation mechanisms, and clear legal frameworks. Having created the rules of the global economic game (and introduced them in the nineteenth century by imperial force), it is no surprise that the developed economies enjoyed unparalleled success in the first full century of playing it. But there is nothing inevitable or preordained about the astonishing wealth gaps between today's developed and less developed regions and countries. Such gaps are a relatively new phenomenon, and not one that we should expect or want to endure.

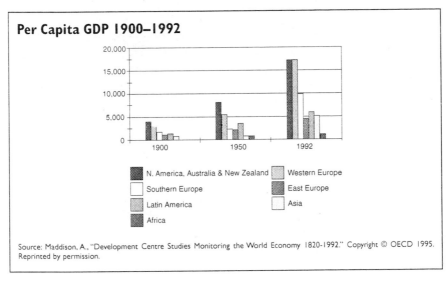

Per Capita GDP 1900–1992

Legend:
- N. America, Australia & New Zealand
- Western Europe
- Southern Europe
- East Europe
- Latin America
- Asia
- Africa

Source: Maddison, A., "Development Centre Studies Monitoring the World Economy 1820-1992." Copyright © OECD 1995. Reprinted by permission.

The increasing gulf between the rich and the poor of the world has led many to challenge the morality and the sustainability of what they regard as exploitative economic globalization and free market trade. Yet the picture is more complicated than it appears. While the rich nations have grown much richer, many of the poorer parts of the world have also been progressing, in many cases quite rapidly. According to the World Bank, countries that integrate more quickly into the global economy fare much better than those integrating more slowly; some of the latter even experience negative growth. Moreover, as economist Bradford DeLong has observed, the twentieth century's other economic system, communism, appears to have significantly suboptimized economic success in regions where it reigned. In 1997, North Korea had a per capita GDP of $700 in contrast with South Korea's $13,590; Cuba had reached $3,100 compared with Mexico's $8,370; and Russia languished at $4,370 compared with Finland at $20,150.

An even more important factor is rate of growth. For most of the twentieth century, wealthy countries grew at a faster rate than poorer ones; GDP per capita tripled in Western Europe between 1950 and 1992, while increasing by only 70 percent over that period in Latin America, for example. But over the last 25 years, by far the most significant growth rates have been witnessed in the developing world, in particular in the two giants that are together home to nearly 40 percent of the world's population: China and India.

Through a mixture of foreign direct investment, trade, the repatriation of capital by emigrants, and local indigenous economic activity, the market system has greatly spread its influence; many more people around the world are now engaged and prospering as players and participants. Despite serious imperfections and inequities, and also some obvious fragility in the global economy today (mounting trade imbalances, growing oil price volatility, etc.), it appears that the spread of global trade and market principles will continue to be a key to prosperity in more and more parts of the world. More countries are joining the World Trade Organization (WTO), including China in 2001. Consumers in poor nations are sidestepping state-run telecom monopolies in favor of private mobile telephony companies. Ten new countries joined the European Union in 2004, including eight that were previously part of the Soviet bloc. From Ljubljana in Slovenia to Tallinn in Estonia, trade, investment, privatization, and deregulation will form the basis for the economic development strategies of that region.

The market economy will continue to expand, reaching areas and lives so far only marginally connected with the global economy. But we should not expect the Western model of capitalism to prevail unchallenged. In the coming decade, market-based approaches will increasingly be flexed to suit the particular circumstances, cultures, and values of specific places. One size will not fit all, and the expansion of market power will involve further experimentation with different forms and models of capitalism, as China, India, and several other large countries continue to carve out their own niches and establish their own terms of engagement in the evolving global economy.

The Changing Shape of Prosperity

The most significant shift in prosperity in recent decades has been the rising economic prominence of several large and influential countries that are now more connected into the global economy than ever before. China and India deservedly take the headlines, but other countries with functioning, growing, and robust economies that include growing indigenous consumer markets, like Brazil, are also "in the game." According to analysis by Goldman Sachs, we can expect these large low-income countries to have as much economic clout as the U.S., Japan, and Europe within the next few decades—and for China to overtake the U.S. as the world's largest economy by 2040.

As recently as 20 years ago, these now-rising nations used foreign direct investment (FDI) as the primary mechanism for establishing connections into the global economic system. Mostly this went into new manufacturing capacity, with powerful American, Japanese, and European corporations using cheap local labor for low-cost and relatively low-value production and assembly. While these nations still actively encourage and attract FDI to fuel growth, they are no longer as dependent on it, and the nature of their relationships with foreign investors is changing.

India, and to a lesser extent China, have started to shift foreign investment up the value-creation ladder from manufacturing to higher-value development and services. India, which is now home to more English speakers (at least 350 million) than the United States and the UK combined, has been particularly successful in this respect, first attracting basic software development, then moving aggressively into customer service and sales through call centers, then expanding into more sophisticated back-office functions like accounting and human resources. Its next move is already on the radar screen. Indian IT companies like Tata, Infosys, and Wipro know that they face cost competition from other sources of cheap skilled labor in China, Russia, and elsewhere. As a result, they are striving to establish themselves as strategic partners to foreign investors, offering high-value services like research, strategic IT consulting, and product development.

Meanwhile, outsourcing in India is also moving up the value chain in some unexpected directions. For the last five years or so, foreign patients who are sick and in need of surgery or other medical care have been traveling to India for medical procedures that are significantly more expensive—even prohibitively priced—in the West. In the U.S., a coronary artery bypass costs about $98,000, but in India it costs just $8,000—less than one-tenth the U.S. price. In the U.S., an echocardiogram costs $800 per scan; in India, the patient is charged 800 rupees, or about $18. As medical care prices soar in the U.S. and the UK's government-funded health service continues to frustrate potential patients with wait lists and delays, seeking critical care in India (and other burgeoning "medical tourism" destinations like Thailand and Malaysia), while still a rare practice, is becoming increasingly popular. India is encouraging the trend by building new hospitals, renovating existing hospitals to Western standards, and offering perks to potential Western patients like free airport pickup and Starbucks coffee. Foreign patient care is expected to bring in $2.3 billion a year to Indian hospitals, according to McKinsey research.

In all likelihood, these various outsourcing strategies will succeed—not least because there is also a push factor at play, as global companies seize the new opportunities that outsourcing offers, such as round-the-clock work. The outsourcing movement has begun to enmesh and integrate company processes across continents and time zones to the extent that future "untangling" becomes more difficult, rendering foreign investors less footloose and more likely to be around for the long haul. The transnational corporation of old is becoming the truly global corporation of today, much to the benefit of low- to middle-income countries. In developed countries, the trend is already causing job anxieties and political headaches. Outsourcing has become headline news in the U.S. and elsewhere. Worried observers bemoan the number of jobs being "lost" to the cheaper, more productive, and often more conveniently time-zoned economies. As strategic and high-value work continues to move elsewhere, this issue will become even more vexing and challenging, doubtless provoking some protectionist sentiments that could complicate the next stages of economic globalization.

Repatriation of Human and Financial Capital

A second kind of "foreign" investment is also helping to transform the economies of China, India, and elsewhere: the repatriation of capital and expertise by people returning to their home countries after study or work overseas, usually in the U.S. Increasing numbers of Western-trained entrepreneurs are choosing to return home to start their next business, and many students educated in the mature economies are keen to put their skills to work in the rapid-growth environment of those still emerging. Between 1978 and 2002, roughly 580,000 students and scholars left China to learn and study abroad. A range of incentives, including special funds to help them start their own companies, has encouraged 160,000 of them to return. More than 15,000 returnees work in the more than 100 "high-tech parks" established by the government and reserved exclusively for companies started by returning overseas scientists and scholars. More than 6,000 firms operate out of these parks, and together they have added an estimated $3.9 billion to the Chinese economy. And 80 percent of Chinese students studying abroad in the U.S. now say they would like to return to China after their studies rather than head for Silicon Valley as so many did in the past. These returnees have been dubbed "sea turtles" after the animals that regularly return to the same beach each year to reproduce. And they are helping China to rapidly increase its technological edge.

Mexican Remittances

"As of the 2000 census, Latinos became the largest minority in the U.S., with Mexican immigrants and Mexican-Americans representing two-thirds of the Latino population. Each month, hardworking Mexicans in the United States send millions of money orders, averaging $200 each, across the border to their communities of origin. These remittances generate more than $9.3 billion a year for Mexico—almost half of the $23 billion total in migrant remittances sent to all of Latin America and the Caribbean. Mexico, a nation of 100 million people, reaps almost as much from remittances as India, with a population of 1 billion. In fact, remittances are Mexico's third-largest source of income, after oil exports and tourism. In the states of Zacatecas and Michoacán, as well as in much of rural Mexico, they exceed local and state budgets."

—Sociologist Xochitl Bada

Source: "Mexican Hometown Associations," from the PBS show *P.O.V.*

Challenging the Rules

The combination of high-quality manufacturing capacity, a rising ability to offer high-value services, the return of capital and expertise, and truly huge domestic markets probably guarantees that China, India, and other emerging economies will be far more influential economic players in the next decade. But another feature of these countries promises even more radical change in the distribution of prosperity around the world: they will not play by the rules established in the boardrooms and political chambers of Europe and North America. Instead, they will challenge these rules forcefully, pioneering new "cultures of capitalism" that suit their unique national interests.

Consider Brazil. As a large country with a proud heritage, Brazil sees itself as something of a renegade or free spirit among nations. It has already shown itself prepared to defy the orthodoxies of the market system. Faced with increasing HIV infection rates, Brazil boldly decided to break the patents on a host of proprietary HIV/AIDS drugs to produce its own much cheaper versions. Brazil's flouting of international intellectual property conventions enraged many rich-country pharmaceutical companies, but Brazil did not back down. In 1997, it began offering free anti-retroviral drugs to all its citizens. By 2000, the AIDS death rate in

Brazil had been cut in half. These dramatic results have powerfully vindi-
cated Brazil's strategy.

In the last decade, China and India have both experienced rapid economic growth without adopting wholesale the dominant Western models
of capitalism. China has dismantled its central planning regime, put in
place a market economy, and become the manufacturing capital of the
world. It has deliberately encouraged international trade and investment
while helping to protect state-owned enterprises that play mainly in the
domestic economy, in order to minimize internal political and social
strife. In the coming decade, China will shift its strategic emphasis from
low-cost manufacturing to faster-growth innovation, shedding its image
as the low-end, cheap-labor link in the value chain. China's launch of a
man into space in 2003 was a vivid symbolic signal of her future leadership intentions.

The Potential of China

"One has to stand in great awe and respect of China's ability to have
unleashed these very dynamic, tectonic market forces and still maintain
the amount of political control they have."
—Orville Schell, China scholar

- China is the world's largest and fastest growing mobile phone market.
  In July 2004, China had 310.2 million mobile phone subscribers—an
  increase of 40.3 million since January 2004. China is expected to have
  730 million mobile phone users by 2020.

- China's middle class comprises nearly 110 million people, or roughly
  19 percent of the population. That number is expected to rise to 40
  percent by 2020.

- More than half of China's 1.3 billion people are under the age of 24.

- The adult illiteracy rate fell from 37 percent in 1978 to 9 percent in
  2002.

- One business park in Shanghai is home to 1,000 software companies,
  10 national medical and biological institutes, and several of the world's
  top 20 pharmaceutical companies.

Sources: Orville Schell; GlobalFluency; *China Daily*; BBC News; United Nations Development Programme
Human Development Index; *People's Daily* (China).

China has also been careful not to get locked into proprietary software standards and solutions, committing itself to Linux rather than adopting a Microsoft platform. Part of the reason for this is pure economics—the costs of scaling, upgrading, and innovating systems are prohibitive under a limited license model, thus the powerful incentive to look for alternatives. But it is also true that China's size and power allow it to ignore international models where and when they threaten its ability to control its own destiny and develop its own alternative structures. Like Brazil, China is starting to set its own standards and make its own rules.

This is of immense significance, yet it is poorly understood in much of the developed world. China is now set to use its scale and power to become increasingly active in challenging the developed world's dominance of the global economy, particularly by setting the global technology standards of the future. It is seeking to establish its own new standards in a great many areas, including RFID tag technology, cellular and mobile technologies, and media products like DVDs. Given its scale, manufacturing dominance, and influence as an exporter, China's national standards could easily become global, affording China extraordinary advantages over the rest of the world—advantages that have hitherto been enjoyed almost exclusively by the developed economies.

India will not lag far behind in using its muscle to promote its own national interests. India's dramatic rise was greatly facilitated in the latter part of the twentieth century by a reduction of the state's size and influence and a lowering of tariffs to encourage free trade. It then focused explicitly on several key knowledge-intensive sectors that played to its educational strengths and its widespread fluency in the English language. India has now become the location of choice for high-technology outsourcing. This has created a thriving knowledge-based economy for the elite while also starting to raise prosperity levels more broadly. A growing middle class—nearly 300 million souls in a country of 1 billion—is fuelling a spectacular consumer demand that has, for example, made India the world's fastest-growing telecom market, with a million new subscribers per month.

But India is unlikely to follow the conventional path of Western-style technology development. Although hundreds of Western corporations have research facilities in India, the country is fast becoming a leader in low-cost innovation. By experimenting with radical new offerings, Indian entrepreneurs are moving into the space where cutting-edge products and services are created for low-income yet technologically sophisticated consumer markets. The Indian Tata Group is working on a compact car that will sell for $2,200—less than half the price of the previously cheapest vehicle in India and able to be assembled by thousands of franchisees across the country. Other developments include low-cost cataract surgery, Linux-based handheld computers, prosthetic limbs, tamper-free electronic voting machines, and online educational programs. These breakthroughs will deliver products and services far more suited to Indian consumers, proving attractive and competitive with much of the high-cost technology typically offered by Western corporations.

Engaging the Base of the Pyramid

Efforts to address the needs of the poorer parts of the world are not confined to India. Asia, Latin America, and Africa could all benefit as global companies start to think differently about these markets. The 4 billion people living day-to-day on paltry wages should be seen as a vital market for goods made to meet their specific needs, not as a population that should be ignored by innovators and capitalists. Indeed, as existing markets mature and grow saturated, it is the disenfranchised masses who hold the greatest promise as customers of the future. C.K. Prahalad's book *The Fortune at the Bottom of the Pyramid* explains this perspective and challenges businesses to meet the needs of this population by redesigning and rethinking core assumptions, not only about their business ideas but about preconceptions of non-Western markets as well.

The outsourcing of manufacturing has helped spur some of this innovation. For example, the U.S. company Whirlpool found that when it shifted manufacturing capacity to Brazil and China, local designers became interested in adapting U.S. models to local needs. One result is what the company advertises as the world's cheapest automatic washing machine, launched in 2003. Sales have been good in Brazil, where in 2003 only a third of its households owned a washing machine (yet washing machines are the second most-coveted item by low-income consumers, behind cellphones). Whirlpool is confident that the washing machine will find footing elsewhere as well, among the vast numbers of people in China, India, and elsewhere where washing machines are still considered and priced as luxury items.

Another example of a business that is directly targeting "base of pyramid" needs is Adaptive Eyecare, a British company with a simple and inspirational mission to provide glasses to the 1 billion people in the world who need corrective lenses but cannot afford them. The diagnostic process involved in eyesight testing and the custom grinding of lenses to address the revealed deficiencies are time-consuming and expensive. Adaptive Eyecare, through smart but very low-tech innovation, has transformed these processes with a simple, inexpensive product that anyone can use. The company has created eyeglasses with double lenses. There is a variable gap between those lenses into which the wearer can inject a small quantity of clear silicon oil. Gradually adjusting the distance between the lenses has the effect of adjusting the focal length of the lens; the wearer simply injects or withdraws the oil until the glasses give them the best possible vision, thus combining diagnosis and manufacture in one simple operation. The process takes only a minute, and the result is completely adjustable. Best of all, each pair of glasses costs approximately $1.

We can expect to see more of this kind of innovation in the coming decade, rethinking challenges from first principles in order to bring products and services within reach of the 4 billion people living on the edge of the market. Business processes that are more sensitive to diverse cultures and values will develop, as capitalism is modified and adapted in a constantly evolving global economic system.

Reinventing Capitalism

Part of the adaptation process will certainly involve a greater urgency to adjust market models to benefit those who are struggling to reach even the first rung of the growth and development ladder. Sometimes this will mean looking anew at the fundamental building blocks of capitalism.

Peruvian economist Hernando de Soto argues in *The Mystery of Capital* that the West has evolved an unplanned and invisible yet essential web of laws, expectations, entitlements, and relationships that support the ownership of property, thereby making capitalism as we have come to know it possible. Yet in many developing nations, vital elements of that system do not exist—not a surprising fact, given that most of us in the West barely understand how our own system works. As a result, de Soto claims that well-intentioned efforts by the International Monetary Fund, the World Bank, and other agents that disseminate the Western capitalist model are doomed to failure, or at best suboptimal success.

De Soto points to a regime of enforceable property rights as one of the founding conditions for the capitalist system. He estimates that in the developing world today, $8 trillion languishes unexploited in informal property—potential capital from which to generate new wealth and opportunity. He has suggested concrete rationales, policies, and actions to release this massive latent potential. His argument is attracting a great deal of attention, and former U.S. president Bill Clinton has called his work the most significant systematic development in economics for years. These ideas will certainly inform the debate and influence the policies of the next decade of globalization.

Reforming Trade Policies

There is genuine possibility that many of these new twists on capitalism can deliver a more prosperous future for billions around the world. However, some of these benefits might be threatened if there is little progress regarding one of the most powerful drivers of capitalism: the spread of free trade. Free trade underpins the promise of the market model, and it is endlessly espoused by developed nations. But they are keener to advocate the medicine for others than to consume it themselves. Round after round of WTO trade talks have failed to live up to their promise, foundering principally on the politics of agriculture.

Developing nations want tariff-free access for their agricultural goods to markets around the world. Meanwhile, the U.S. and EU are striving to maintain large farm subsidies in order to sustain their internal productive capacity and placate their farmers, creating small but highly influential pressure groups on both sides of the Atlantic. According to the WTO, rich countries now spend $1 billion a day subsidizing their agricultural sectors. The European Union's Common Agricultural Policy gives $2 a day to every cow in Europe—an amount greater than what more than a billion humans on the planet live on per day.

Agricultural trade is not the only source of perceived injustice—poorer countries seem disadvantaged across other industries, too. Bangladesh, primarily a textile exporter, pays significantly more in tariffs to the U.S. than France does, even though its exports are less than one-tenth the size. U.S. imports of underwear from Cambodia are subject to greater tariffs than Japanese steel. The World Bank has calculated that trade protection in rich nations costs developing countries more than $100 billion a year, twice what they currently receive in aid. This issue is far from being resolved, but there has been progress. Following setbacks in WTO talks in Cancun in

2003, where rich and poor nations clashed on the question of agriculture support, trade negotiators have now agreed on a framework that could eventually lead to the elimination or reduction of most farm subsidies.

The developed world has benefited greatly from global trade for more than a century. But it will continue to do so only by acknowledging the legitimate aspirations of the rest of the world to become true partners and participants in a growing global economy. This will absolutely require the developed world to give ground on agricultural support. It will also require the acceptance of many other inevitable economic shifts that favor the developing world across all sectors of the economy—including the transfer of high-value work and the emergence of powerful new competitive regions capable of innovating and driving the global economy in the future, not just providing cheap labor and large consumer markets. The next decade should produce positive gains in prosperity for the rich and poor alike. But there will be serious challenges for all along the way, and the developed world will have to start the painful process of letting go of its longstanding sense of entitlement. It is time for others to start catching up.

Decline

> There are people in the world so hungry that God cannot
> appear to them except in the form of bread.
> —Mahatma Gandhi

While millions of people are set to benefit from the spread of prosperity, millions of others will experience the opposite: a decline in living standards. For many this will be absolute—a devastating drop from what they have previously known. For others it will be relative; it will come in the form of a painful sense of standing still or inching forward while others race ahead.

Poor—and Getting Poorer

According to the United Nations, the number of people living in poverty (defined as living on less than a dollar a day) is falling. But it is still 1.3 billion people—roughly a quarter of the global population. The UN's Millennium Development Goals promise to halve that number by 2015, and progress is being made in that respect. But other data suggest that the plight of the poor has actually worsened. Despite the efforts of international institutions such as the World Bank, the IMF, and the UN, and the stepped-up efforts of some global corporations, 21 countries worldwide exited the 1990s with decreased levels of development. During the 1980s, only four countries tracked by the UN Development Programme showed similar decade-long declines.

Overall Growth Has Masked Declines for Many

With economic growth increasing in the developing world, are poor countries set to achieve rising prosperity? It may appear so, but a different story emerges when heavyweights India and China are removed from the developing world tally and population growth is taken into account. Per capita GNP has actually fallen in many countries, further increasing wealth disparities.

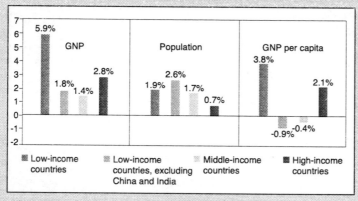

Source: Tatyana P. Soubbotina with Katherine Sheram, "Beyond Economic Growth: Meeting the Challenges of Global Development," The International Bank for Reconstruction and Development/The World Bank, October 2000. Reprinted by permission.

Looking forward, it seems inevitable that some countries in sub-Saharan Africa, Central Asia, and the Middle East will continue to struggle. The latest UN Human Development Index, which measures a combination of life expectancy, education, and income per capita, shows that almost all the countries at the bottom of the index are in sub-Saharan Africa. Income in half of the countries in Latin America and the Caribbean declined or stagnated during the 1990s. Eastern Europe and Central Asia both showed an overall decline in the Human Development Index over the same period. In the coming decade, some nations and regions, mired in prolonged crisis, will again see no benefit from global expansion and more flexible models of capitalism.

In some instances, it might be fair to attribute this decline to the overly strict application of Western-style economic policies. The "Washington Consensus," a highly influential doctrine emphasizing fiscal discipline, privatization, and competitive exchange rates, has certainly led to economic instability and a rising sense of injustice in some countries. The IMF and the World Bank have been accused of setting the rules of the game mainly to serve the interests of rich countries rather than poor. Joe Stiglitz, Nobel Prize-winning economist and former chief economist at the World Bank, put it starkly: "Globalization has left many of the poorest in the developing world even poorer. Even when they are better off, they feel more vulnerable."

But international economic policies are by no means a full explanation for decline. For the poorest, most troubled places, it is more often the devastating convergence of poverty, disease, drought, famine, ethnic rivalry, ongoing conflict, and poor governance that consigns millions of people to a lifetime of distress and deterioration.

Battling Disease, Corruption, and Conflict

Of particular concern is the scale of the AIDS crisis, which is now exceeding even the worst-case scenarios of a decade ago. UNAid projects that between 2002 and 2020, 68 million people will die from AIDS in the developing world—more than three times as many as have already perished—and life expectancies will drop precipitously. Meanwhile, influenza is on the rise, new outbreaks of Ebola are occurring, and malaria continues to run rampant. Polio, a disease that the World Health Organization had hoped to eradicate from the planet by 2000, is experiencing a resurgence. There were 1,185 new cases of polio in 2004, and since early 2004, the disease has spread to 16 previously polio-free countries.

Top 15 HIV/AIDS Prevalence Countries (end 2003)

Africa

Rank	Country	Percent of Population
1	Swaziland	38.8
2	Botswana	37.3
3	Lesotho	28.9
4	Zimbabwe	24.6

continues

Top 15 HIV/AIDS Prevalence Countries

Africa

Rank	Country	Percent of Population
5	South Africa	21.5
6	Namibia	21.3
7	Zambia	16.5
8	Malawi	14.2
9	Central African Rep.	13.5
10	Mozambique	12.2
11	Tanzania	8.8
12	Gabon	8.1
13	Côte d'Ivoire	7.0
14	Cameroon	6.9
15	Kenya	6.7

Outside Africa

Rank	Country	Percent of Population
1	Haiti	5.6
2	Trinidad and Tobago	3.2
3	Bahamas	3.0
4	Cambodia	2.6
5	Guyana	2.5
6	Belize	2.4
7	Honduras	1.8
8	Dominican Republic	1.7
8	Suriname	1.7
10	Thailand	1.5
10	Barbados	1.5
12	Ukraine	1.4
13	Myanmar	1.2
14	Jamaica	1.2
15	Estonia	1.1

Source: 2004 World Population Data Sheet, Population Reference Bureau. Reprinted by permission.

Diseases produce longer-term economic catastrophe as well as immediate human tragedy. The sub-Saharan African labor force is diminishing, with enormous consequences for production, savings, and investments.

Not surprisingly, countries hard-hit by AIDS and other diseases are finding it difficult to sustain their already-low levels of economic activity. Years of development, training, and education are being lost forever. Healthcare, military, and police systems already crumbling will be hard-pressed to cope. Even if mortality rates are slowed, the systemic effects will last for generations.

Poor countries' hopes have also been dashed by widespread corruption and ongoing conflict. Research by the World Bank Institute points to something called the "400 percent governance dividend," which holds that countries that tackle corruption and improve the rule of law can increase national income by up to four times and reduce child mortality by as much as 75 percent. Corruption is not by any means only a developing world problem. But countries like Nigeria, Bangladesh, and Haiti regularly top the league tables, and fully half of all developing countries score less than three out of a possible "clean" score of 10 on the corruption scale. The WBI calculates that more than $1 trillion is paid in bribes globally each year.

Conflict is also a serious source of economic disruption and decline. Eleven percent of the countries ranked in the top half of the 2003 Human Development Index experienced armed conflicts during the 10-year period 1994–2003, but 43 percent of those in the bottom half were at war at some point during that period. The legacies of these struggles—landmines, cluster bombs, uncontrolled access to weapons—will ensure that suffering is locked in for many years to come. There are typically around 30 significant conflicts (those with over 1,000 casualties, military and civilian) raging in the world, and the vast majority of them are being fought within nations rather than between them. Many conflicts are long-enduring, such as the on-off struggle between India and Pakistan in Kashmir or the Israel-Palestine conflict. Others are the legacy of past state-building, like the areas of central Africa where the Democratic Republic of the Congo, Burundi, Rwanda, and Uganda meet, with fighting now spilling over into Sudan; there have been more than 20 major civil wars in Africa since 1960. Whatever the causes of internal conflicts, their consequences are clear: human misery in the short term, and chronic economic underperformance over the long term.

Current Conflicts Around the World

Algeria	Insurgency	1992 →
India	Assam	1985 →
India	Kashmir	1970s →
India	Naxalite Uprising	1967 →
Indonesia	Aceh	1986 →
Indonesia	Kalimantan	1983 →
Indonesia	Maluku	1999-2002
Indonesia	Papua / West Irian	1963 →
Israel	Al-Aqsa Intifada	2000 →
Ivory Coast	Civil War	2002 →
Korea	Korean War	1953 →
Liberia	Civil War	1999 →
Moldova	Transdniester	1991→
Namibia	Caprivi Strip	1966 →
Nepal	Maoist Insurgency	1996 →
Nigeria	Civil Disturbances	1997 →
Peru	Shining Path	1970s →
Philippines	Moro Uprising	1970s →
Russia	Chechen Uprising	1992 →
Somalia	Civil War	1991→
Spain	Basque Uprising	1970s →
Sudan	Second Civil War	1983 →
Thailand	Islamic Insurgency	2001 →
Turkey	Kurdistan	1984 →
Uganda	Civil Conflict	1980 →
United States	Afghanistan	1980 →
United States	Djibouti	2001 →
United States	Iraq	1990 →
United States	Philippines	1988 →

Source: GlobalSecurity.org, March 2005. Reprinted by permission.

Relative Decline: Grinding Poverty Amid Growing Plenty

Even for places and people that have enjoyed some measure of economic progress, any sense of growing prosperity may feel limited next to the runaway and increasingly visible success of others. For example, income per person in the world's 20 poorest countries has risen over the last 40 years—but only by one-fourth, from $212 in 1960–62 to an only marginally less appalling $267 in 2000–02. In contrast, the richest 20 nations have seen their income per head triple from $11,417 to $32,339 in that same time period. As President Bush prepared to tour Nigeria, Senegal, Botswana, and Uganda in 2003, the combined income of those four countries was less than the combined income of the 400 richest Americans.

There are growing inequalities within countries as well. The impressive growth figures for many rapidly developing economies often mask huge inequalities and social tensions, in particular between the urban rich and the rural poor. In China, urban incomes are more than three times greater than the incomes earned by rural workers. In Russia, the richest 10 percent now earn 23 times more than the poorest 10 percent, up from just 3.2 times more back in 1980. Russia currently ranks 82nd on the CIA's list of the nations with the highest per capita GDP, yet it has the fourth-highest number of billionaires in the world. Only the U.S., Germany, and Japan have more.

Decline in Rich Countries

Many people in the developed world have experienced and will experience a sense of relative decline as they witness much faster rises in the income of others. For example, in 1979, the after-tax income of the top 1 percent of the U.S. population was 23 times greater than that of the bottom 20 percent. In 2000, it was 63 times greater. It seems likely that this trend will continue in much of the developed world. But many citizens of the richer countries will not be immune from experiencing absolute decline in prosperity, as economic pressures and restructuring combine with demographic forces to lower living standards.

Parts of the U.S. and Europe have already suffered through difficult economic transitions. The twin drivers of change in the global economy—trade and technology—have taken a particularly heavy toll on traditional industries like agriculture and manufacturing. Inevitably, some localities suffer disproportionately, even if they are in otherwise thriving countries. As business realities have changed, many places have lost their economic function—like Flint, Michigan, after the U.S. automobile industry declined, and the coalmining areas of the UK after Margaret

Thatcher shifted the nation's energy policies away from coal and toward natural gas. Indeed, recognizing the friction burns associated with economic restructuring—as well as the need to maintain a rough parity between different areas in order to operate as a "single economy"—the European Union has long provided special "structural fund" assistance to those places with less than 75 percent of the average EU GDP.

We should expect, with the entry of the typically poorer accession countries into the EU, that structural funding will be significantly squeezed for the poorest parts of the established EU, most notably Greece, Spain, Germany, and Italy. Meanwhile, U.S. corporations will continue to relocate significant aspects of their work while facing increasing competition from developing countries, putting pressure on particular employment categories and geographical areas.

Moreover, there are concerns about the long-term financial weaknesses of traditionally powerful European economies like Germany, Italy, and France. Like most of their neighbors, these countries designed very generous welfare systems at a time when the worker-to-pensioner ratio was about four to one. But demographic shifts and restrictive immigration policies are radically altering that ratio. In Germany, if current trends continue, there will be one German worker for every pensioner by 2020. By 2030, nearly half of Germany's adult population will be over 65, and the number of people of working age will fall from 40 million to 30 million. As a result, current benefit levels could become unsustainable over the longer term; health and wealth benefits have been overpromised and will be increasingly costly and difficult to deliver, especially as baby boomers approach retirement. We should expect to see some gradual clawing back of benefits, especially retirement benefits, over the coming decade—accompanied, understandably, by political furor and an increasingly heated European debate about immigration policies.

Clearly there will be regions, demographic groups, and a great many individuals in the developed world experiencing real decline in prosperity in the decade ahead, and this will become an increasingly high-profile and politicized issue in many countries. But we should also be prepared for the possibility of radical relative decline. While we are unlikely to see absolute decline in GDP in any part of the developed world, we are likely to see several wealthy countries experience very low rates of growth relative to the rest of the world. For example, many European nations, partly because of their longstanding economic strengths in manufacturing and traditional industries, have probably underinvested in renewing the industrial practices and economic base necessary for the years ahead. Meanwhile, the exodus of their young and talented people to more dynamic countries is likely to accelerate, reinforcing the possibility of economic stagnation. In an increasingly competitive global economy, with hungry and ambitious emergent players starting to succeed over more complacent incumbents, this combination of challenges could place significant pressure on the economies—as well as the political systems and civic cohesion—of these and other developed countries.

These structural weaknesses are not confined to Europe. Japan has suffered low levels of economic growth for over a decade, and there are mounting reasons not to take for granted the longer-term economic health of the United States. Important financial weaknesses could result in severe economic setbacks in the decade ahead. In 2004, the U.S. account deficit climbed to almost 6 percent of its GDP, or $650 billion—and there are strong indications that this will grow still larger in the coming years. The inevitable result will be a continued decline in the value of the U.S. dollar. If this fall happens abruptly—brought on, perhaps, by Chinese banks withdrawing their investments—the U.S. economy could suffer inflation and higher interest rates, plunging businesses and debt-ridden consumers into a crisis of confidence. The mounting U.S. fiscal imbalance makes the picture worse. In early 2005, the Congressional Budget Office forecast that federal budget deficits would reach $2.4 trillion over the next decade. The possibility of painful declines in U.S. economic standards in the coming years is very real indeed.

The Poverty Imperative

In a world in which new global players enjoy rapid economic growth and challenge the rules of the game while the developed world faces new economic challenges, it is inevitable that there will be calls from some quarters for a radical review of aid programs and developed-world funding for poorer regions. However, such arguments seem unlikely to prevail. There are no simple solutions to the complex problems of disease, conflict, disaster, and corruption, and conditions in some parts of the world will likely get worse before they get better. By the end of this decade, the continuing plight of some regions in steady decline will be more visible on the agenda of pressing global issues—not least because these will become increasingly "disorderly" places from which the rest of the world cannot isolate itself. We cannot safely ignore areas of extreme poverty and related disorder in a connected world in which, as one foreign policy analyst crisply put it, "a country without much law and order can still have an international airport." Tackling global poverty will be as much an act of self-interest as altruism in the coming decade—and it will rise in priority.

This pattern of spreading prosperity yet rising decline is closely linked to the continued growth of the human population, which has been increasing at an accelerating rate for several centuries. This is leading to perhaps the most dramatic and pressing of all the dynamic tensions—the interplay between people and our planet.

Chapter 8

People and Planet

In the coming decade, we will develop a deeper understanding of how to meet our growing needs and wants while protecting our planet and its ability to provide a home for future generations. We will begin to see the interrelatedness of the human economy and Earth's ecosystems more clearly and realize that there may be planetary limits to our growth. As a result, we will take the concept, if not the practice, of sustainability more seriously. However, we will also begin to understand the profound autonomy of the planet—its long cycles of change and transformation that occur independently of our presence and our actions. We will then reach a collective realization that is more ancient wisdom than modern worldview—that the planet does not belong to us but we belong to it, and it will survive and change no matter what we do, while the opposite may not be true.

People

Two fundamentally different stories have been enacted here during the lifetime of man. One began being enacted here some two to three million years ago by the people we've agreed to call Leavers and is still being enacted by them today, as successfully as ever. The other began to be enacted here some ten or twelve thousand years ago by the people we've agreed to call Takers, and is apparently about to end in catastrophe.

—Daniel Quinn, *Ishmael*

Since the advent of agriculture, the human species has been busily expanding its influence and imprint on the planet. Humans have grown steadily in number for centuries. They have also evolved a system of existence and consumption that many have worried may soon become

153

unsupportable. Our unbridled pursuit of rapid economic growth over the last 100 years, combined with our sheer force of numbers, has put the planet under considerable stress, setting the stage for dramatic challenges to unfold.

In the last 300 years, the growth in human population has been explosive. In 1700, Earth was home to around 600 million people. By 1800 it was 900 million, and by 1900 it had doubled to 1.7 billion. During the last century alone, the population has nearly quadrupled to the current 6.5 billion. Every year, another 78 million people are born onto the planet. The world population is expected to increase by 50 percent to 9 billion by 2050.

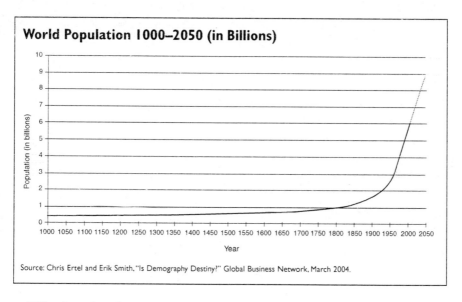

World Population 1000–2050 (in Billions)

Source: Chris Ertel and Erik Smith, "Is Demography Destiny?" Global Business Network, March 2004.

Whether the planet can continue to support this burgeoning population has been a topic of concern not for decades, but for centuries. In 1798, the Englishman Thomas Malthus, in his "Essay on the Principle of Population," expressed his worry that "the power of population is indefinitely greater than the power in the Earth to produce subsistence for man." In 1968, Stanford biologist Paul Ehrlich voiced a similar concern in his bestselling book *The Population Bomb*, in which he suggested that the 1970s and 1980s would test the limits of the planet's capacity to support its human inhabitants. Four years later, the Club of Rome published "Limits to Growth," an alarming report on the rate at which global resources are being depleted as more and more people consume nearly everything in greater and greater quantities. In the decades since, the challenges associated with a growing global population have been widely acknowledged to the point that they have now entered mainstream civic consciousness.

Yet there has also been something of "the boy who cried 'Wolf!'" to these cautions and warnings. Malthus is often dismissed as a dreary pessimist whose dire predictions have still failed to materialize 200 years (and a sevenfold increase in population) later; Ehrlich's warnings were made less credible when he famously lost a bet with economist Julian Simon over predicted shortages in natural resources; and the Club of Rome's report has been criticized as overly pessimistic for failing to take into account ever-improving technologies and efficiencies that have allowed the human population to continue to grow without serious constraint. But most important is the fact that the population has begun constraining *itself.* The long-predicted overpopulation of the planet is no longer expected to happen. Demographers now agree that the rate of population growth will not, in fact, continue to accelerate. Rather, it will slow down—and it may even start to reverse.

Many nations in the developed world have been experiencing declining birth rates for several decades. Some have even fallen below replacement levels, meaning that they are producing fewer than the 2.1 children per woman required for the population to hold steady. Throughout the developed world, the very real prospect of depopulation is raising some puzzling new questions. For example, Italy, with only 1.2 births per woman, expects to experience significant population decline soon. It is only beginning to grapple with the economic and social implications of that decline, and it is not the only nation being forced to do so. As Phillip Longman writes in *The Empty Cradle*, "The global fall in fertility, even if it does not continue to deepen and spread, is creating a world for which few individuals, and no nations, are prepared.... Population growth and the human capital it creates are part of the foundation upon which modern economies, as well as modern welfare states, are built."

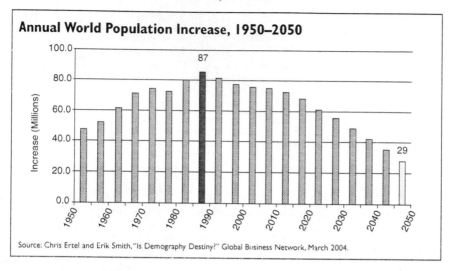

Annual World Population Increase, 1950–2050

Source: Chris Ertel and Erik Smith, "Is Demography Destiny?" Global Business Network, March 2004.

Birth rates are now falling throughout much of the developing world as well, largely as a consequence of higher survival rates, spreading prosperity, expanded educational opportunities for women, and a widespread shift from rural to urban dwelling (children are less useful in cities than on farms). Therefore, the birth rate is falling not just regionally, but globally. The global average birth rate in 1970 was 4.5 children per woman; today it is 2.7 children per woman. In response to this trend, the UN revised its global population projections downward, from 12 billion by 2050 to the 9 billion mentioned previously. It may not end there.

However, the fact that the planet will be less overcrowded than previously anticipated should not lessen our concern about our impact on the planet. Far from it. Population pressure is only one of myriad issues that give rise to troubled interactions between people and planet. Real challenges still lie ahead of us, and their solutions will demand levels of creativity, flexibility, and intentionality that humans have yet to display.

Four trends in particular will converge to drive change in the decade ahead: (1) the growing imbalance between the number (and age) of people living in the developed versus the developing world; (2) a global shift in the direction of human migration; (3) the widespread, worldwide human migration from the countryside to the city; and (4) growing evidence that our relationship with the planet may be reaching a tipping point. Indeed, we may be approaching a time when the planet will turn to the billions of voracious humans riding on its back and say, "Enough." Each of these trends will be an important shaper of our future.

Rich Old Millions, Poor Young Billions

In 1960, one-third of the world's population lived in the developed world; today it is one-fifth. In the next decade, the balance of population will shift even further toward the planet's less prosperous regions. Age distribution is also growing more uneven globally. In the developed world, increased life expectancy and falling birth rates are creating more elderly populations. Today, one out of every five people in the developed world is over 60; in 2050, it will be one out of every three. By that time, nearly 10 percent of the developed-world population will be over 80.

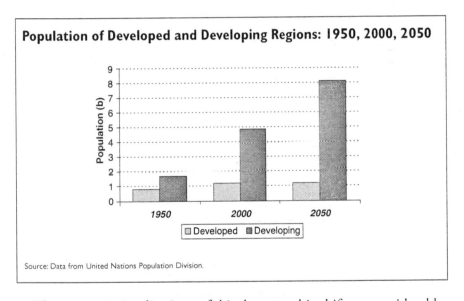

Population of Developed and Developing Regions: 1950, 2000, 2050

Source: Data from United Nations Population Division.

The economic implications of this demographic shift are considerable. Despite the trend toward deferred retirement, this older age bracket will at some point cease to be economically productive—perhaps just as they begin to require expensive healthcare. What this will mean for medical insurance, long-term care, and pension provision is particularly troubling for Europe. Right now, Europe has 35 pensioners for every 100 people of productive working age; that ratio is projected to shift to 75 pensioners for every 100 workers by 2050. The U.S. is expected to experience similar stress as its over-65 population nearly doubles from 12 percent to 21 percent over the same time period.

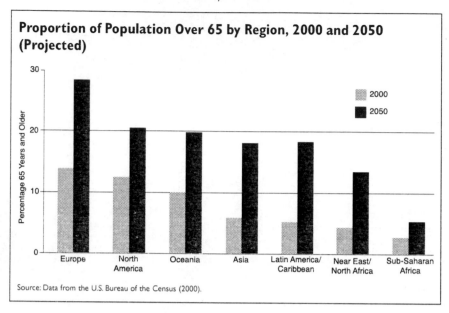

Proportion of Population Over 65 by Region, 2000 and 2050 (Projected)

Source: Data from the U.S. Bureau of the Census (2000).

As the age pyramid of the developed world grows increasingly top-heavy, the age profile of much of the developing world (notably East Asia and sub-Saharan Africa) will remain more youthful. According to UN projections, *99 percent* of all global population growth between now and 2050 will occur in the developing world, predominantly in its poorest nations.

Many people living in areas of the world that are primed for considerable economic growth and development will bring with them an increased demand for energy, which could have profoundly negative consequences for the planet if not properly managed. They will impose additional stress on already-strained economic, physical, and social infrastructures, and the increased economic activity and consumption will generate massively-increased environmental and resource pressures. Unfortunately, the developed world has set a model for natural resource consumption (and consumption in general) that the developing world simply cannot follow. Today, the planet's 1 billion wealthiest people consume more than 50 percent of the world's energy supply, while the 1 billion poorest use only 4 percent. The wealthiest 20 percent of people also consume more than 85 percent of all goods and services, while the poorest 20 percent consume just over 1 percent. As sustainability expert Mathis Wachernagel put it, "If everybody on the planet lived like the average American, we actually would need about six planets. But we only have one."

This is most obvious (and most problematic) when you consider current patterns of energy consumption. The acceleration in energy consumption in the West during the last century was extremely rapid, and we may be witnessing the same surge now in the developing world. From 1950 to 1970, per capita consumption of oil in Japan increased from one barrel to 17 barrels; from 1900 to 1970, U.S. consumption increased from one barrel to 28 barrels per person. Today, China uses 1.7 barrels per person, but it is already the second largest oil importer in the world and its energy needs are rapidly spiking.

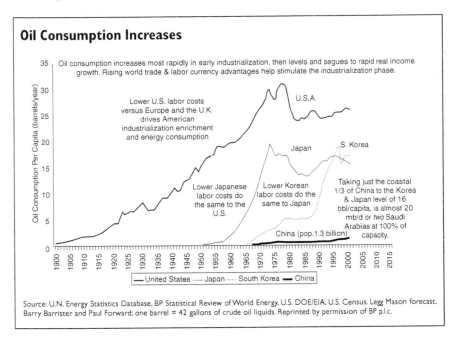

Oil Consumption Increases

Oil consumption increases most rapidly in early industrialization, then levels and segues to rapid real income growth. Rising world trade & labor currency advantages help stimulate the industrialization phase.

Lower U.S. labor costs versus Europe and the U.K. drives American industrialization enrichment and energy consumption

U.S.A.

Japan

S. Korea

Lower Japanese labor costs do the same to the U.S.

Lower Korean labor costs do the same to Japan

Taking just the coastal 1/3 of China to the Korea & Japan level of 16 bbl/capita, is almost 20 mb/d or *two* Saudi Arabias at 100% of capacity.

China (pop.1.3 billion)

— United States — Japan ⋯⋯ South Korea — China

Source: U.N. Energy Statistics Database, BP Statistical Review of World Energy, U.S. DOE/EIA, U.S. Census. Legg Mason forecast, Barry Barrister and Paul Forward; one barrel = 42 gallons of crude oil liquids. Reprinted by permission of BP p.l.c.

Resource constraints are only part of the story: massive environmental damage is an equally alarming prospect. Many developing countries, most notably China, are already experiencing significant environmental problems (and profound health consequences, such as increased lung disease from polluted air) that will increasingly accom-pany rapid economic growth in areas with very large populations.

We must be prepared, then, for the demographic inevitability of a continuing bifurcation of the world between "rich old millions" and "poor young billions"—with consequential economic challenges at one end of the spectrum and environmental challenges at the other. This bifurcation will also further reinforce another shift well underway toward new patterns of human migration.

Migration: A Rising Flow from South to North

Today, more than 175 million people on the planet reside in a country other than the one in which they were born. In more than 50 countries, legal and illegal migrants account for more than 15 percent of the population. Nearly 10 percent of people living in the developed world were born in another country, while just over 1 percent of people living in the developing world are international migrants—suggesting, not surprisingly, that many of the world's migrants are leaving their home countries in search of economic opportunity.

Immigration is not a new phenomenon, yet its patterns are clearly changing. For much of the twentieth century, migrants generally moved from East to West, particularly from Europe to North America. Today, the global migration pattern is much more South to North. In 1930, for example, there were more foreign-born people in the U.S. from Italy than from any other country—1.8 million Italians in a U.S. population of 122.8 million. In 2000, it was Mexico, with 7.8 million Mexicans living in a U.S. population of 281.4 million. This South to North movement is steady, strong, and global, with thousands of migrants flowing from Latin America to the U.S. and from North Africa, the Middle East, and Eastern and Southern Europe to Northern and Western Europe. As Asian countries continue their rapid development, there will be higher levels of migration from the less-developed parts of South Asia to the more quickly-advancing northern regions.

Migrants (Millions) by Region of Destination: 1960–2000					
Region	1960	1970	1980	1990	2000
World	75.9	81.5	99.8	154.0	174.9
Africa	9.0	9.9	14.1	16.2	16.3
Asia	29.3	28.1	32.3	41.8	43.8
Europe	14.0	18.7	22.2	26.3	32.8
USSR (former)	2.9	3.1	3.3	30.3	29.5
Latin America & Caribbean	6.0	5.8	6.1	7.0	5.9
Northern America	12.5	13.0	18.1	27.6	40.8
Oceania	2.1	3.0	3.8	4.8	5.8

Source: Joseph Chamie, "International Migration: The Redistribution of Humanity," Global Business Network, May 26, 2005. Original data from the United Nations Population Division.

The sheer number of international migrants is also growing—it has more than doubled since 1970—and the momentum is unlikely to decline in the decade ahead. More affordable travel continues to bring emigration within reach for more and more people, and immigrants tend to encourage others to follow them. Globalization is weakening boundaries, increasing connectivity across traditional borders and reducing cultural barriers. The emergence of more regional blocs, if they follow the example of the European Union, will generate more opportunities for legal migration. Meanwhile, growing populations in the less-developed South will become increasingly aware of opportunities in the more developed North, while aging northern populations will require more workers willing to take on lower-compensated work in their local service economies. From a pure supply and demand perspective, the likely outcome is increased migration, both legal and illegal.

But migration is an emotional topic that generates considerable political heat. Consider, for example, the rising unpopularity of immigrants in Europe, where "in every country except Bulgaria, immigrants are seen as having a bad influence on the country," according to a recent Pew Global Attitudes Project survey. Or consider the strong U.S. reaction to the Mexican government's decision to publish and distribute its "Guide for the Mexican Migrant," a 31-page handbook offering safety tips and advice for those considering an illegal crossing of the U.S.-Mexico border. Mexican officials defended the publication as a public service, likening it to distributing AIDS information to drug users. Opponents in the U.S. dubbed it a "how-to manual for illegal aliens."

As these rising tensions suggest, "migration management" will become an even more serious social, political, and economic issue around the globe, and a source of heightened tension between northern and southern neighbors, in the coming decade.

From Countryside to City

Complicating the migration map is another shifting pattern of human movement, this one from rural to urban environments. Initially triggered by the Industrial Revolution, the shift from country to city has been progressing steadily and globally for almost 200 years. In 1860, just 20 percent of Americans lived in cities. Today, it is more than 80 percent. As industrialization spreads globally and cities become central gathering points where economic opportunities beckon, the movement to cities will grow even stronger. As my colleague Erik Smith, a demographer, points out: "For the first time in the entire history of humanity more than half the people on the planet will live in urban spaces. More importantly, many will live in 'mega-cities,' the likes of which have never been seen." In 1985, there were only nine cities in the world with more than 10 million inhabitants. By 2015, there will be more than 20 cities of this scale, more than three-quarters of which will be in the developing world. A third of those cities will be home to more than 20 million people.

In fact, these mega-cities are already emerging. Sao Paulo and Mumbai both have roughly 18 million inhabitants; Shanghai has about 14 million, and Lagos roughly 13 million. Such concentrations of urban settlement are unprecedented. Moreover, projections for their 2015 populations are extraordinary: Mumbai to 22 million, Sao Paulo to 21 million, Lagos to 16 million.

The process of rapid and extreme urbanization has been especially notable in India and China. India now boasts 32 cities with more than a million residents; by 2015 it will increase to 50 cities. China already has more than 160 cities with populations of more than 1 million, and it is home to five of the world's 20 fastest-growing cities that today number half a million inhabitants, many of which have experienced staggering growth over the past few decades. A new social group in China known as the "floating population," consisting predominantly of young migrants who live in the countryside but travel to cities for work, is taking on considerable scale. In 1993, the group numbered 70 million. By 2003, it had swelled to 140 million—accounting for more than 10 percent of China's population and 30 percent of its rural labor force.

Over the coming decade, we will witness the continuing concentration of a growing human population in increasingly massive urban spaces, mainly in developing countries that are experiencing rapid increases in economic activity and consumption. Cities will be acute testing grounds for sustainable resource use and the capacity of our governance systems to manage the many environmental and social pressures that arise from such intensive cohabitation.

A Lesson from Ur

Hopefully we've developed a better instinct for self-preservation than our ancestors of 5,000 years ago. It is striking today to read Brian Fagan's tale of the history of the ancient city of Ur in Sumeria, in what is now Iraq. Five thousand years ago, shifts in the climate caused the agricultural village populations in southern Mesopotamia to congregate in cities as a means of cushioning the effects of periodic droughts. By 2800 B.C., 80 percent of Sumerians lived in cities. But by 2000 B.C., that pattern of living had collapsed. A prolonged drought cycle overwhelmed the area, war over the scarce resource of water ensued, and the population scattered back into smaller settlements, moved to more defensible ground, or perished. It was "the first time an entire city disintegrated in the face of environmental catastrophe," Fagan explained in his book *The Long Summer*. "The intricate equation between urban population, readily accessible food supplies, and the economic, political, and social flexibility sufficient to roll with the climatic punches had been irrevocably altered."

The Unfolding Impact of People on the Planet

There are inevitable demographic factors in play that will further complicate and challenge the relationship between humans and the planet. However, there is also growing evidence that we may already be having a greater, more adverse impact than we realize, and that even without these further demographic changes, our exponentially growing consumption patterns may be encountering their limit. Such fast and drastic growth can be psychologically deceptive, as demonstrated by the "lily pond effect." Suppose a lily in a pond reproduces enough new lilies to double its overall size each day, so that in 30 days it covers the entire pond. On the twentieth day, how much of the pond is covered by lilies? Most people guess around one-tenth of the pond, but the answer is less than one-thousandth. Not until day 29 is the pond half full. As this demonstrates, we can get fairly far into a process of exponential growth—and awfully close to an overwhelming, even catastrophic, situation—before it is visible to us.

The fact that the size of the human economy is increasing while the size of the Earth's ecological systems remains fixed will be another continuing source of tension between people and planet in the decade ahead. For example, the mounting imbalance between oil demand and oil resources has sparked debates about the "end of the oil age" that are distinctly reminiscent of the old "limits to growth" arguments. Experts like Amory Lovins of the Rocky Mountain Institute note that since the planet's "easy" oil has been extracted already, the costs of reaching and refining sufficient new reserves may become untenable, forcing a shift to alternative fuels and innovations in transportation and manufacturing.

But energy is only part of the picture. Many of our human practices have been shown to be in profound tension with the planet, and ultimately threatening to ourselves. Excessive consumption is demonstrably depleting the world's natural resources and significantly degrading the environment. The evidence is compelling. Every 20 minutes, a species of animal or plant life disappears from the planet, with more than 26,000 species lost every year.... More than 80 percent of the Caribbean coral reef cover has vanished since the 1970s.... Fifty percent of the world's wetlands have been destroyed since 1900.... Fifty percent of the world's fish species are either fully exploited or depleted.... Twenty-four billion tons of fertile soil disappears each year.... Around one-third of the planet's land surface is threatened by desertification.... Eighty percent of the world's original forests have been cleared or degraded, and more than 40 million acres of tropical forest are lost each year.... Water tables are already alarmingly low in many parts of the world, yet will decline by an additional one-third over the next 20 years.... Demand for water has more than tripled over the last 50 years.... A billion people are regularly exposed to levels of indoor air pollution 100 times higher than World Health Organization recommendations, causing 2 million deaths annually.... Each year, three times more rubbish is discarded in our oceans than the total weight of all fish caught.... Americans throw away 2.5 million plastic bottles every hour, a signal of a looming waste management crisis in the developed world that more landfills alone cannot address....

And perhaps most serious of all, we can see increasingly clear and uncontested evidence that we are directly contributing to global climate change (discussed further in the "Planet" section). As the Intergovernmental Panel on Climate Change, a network of internationally recognized climatologists established under the auspices of the UN, concluded in its 2001 assessment report, "There is new and stronger evidence that most of the warming observed in the last 50 years is attributable to human activities."

A Growing Awareness of Human Impact

Today, we have far more information to help us understand how human activities are changing the planet.

1890—1990s	Increase Factor
World Population	4x
Total World Urban Population	13x
World Economy	14x
Industrial Output	40x
Energy Use	13x
Carbon Dioxide Emissions	17x
Water Use	9x
Marine Fish Catch	15x
Bird and Mammal Species	0.99x
Blue Whale Population	0.0025x

Source: J.R. McNeill, *Something New Under the Sun*. Copyright © 2000 by J.R. McNeill. Reprinted by permission of W.W. Norton & Company Inc.

What is less clear is how we are going to change those activities in order to forestall or even thwart some of the looming problems that we have set in motion. Perhaps, on that front, we might take a lesson from other species that have evolved less damaging relationships with the planet. As *Cradle to Cradle* authors William McDonough and Michael Braungart put it: "All the ants on the planet, taken together, have a biomass greater than that of humans. Ants have been incredibly industrious for millions of years. Yet their productiveness nourishes plants, animals, and soil. Human industry has been in full swing for little over a century, yet it has brought about a decline in almost every ecosystem on the planet."

Rising Awareness, Rising Action

It seems clear that many people around the world, alarmed by our circumstances and our growing list of environmental offenses, are seeking and creating paths forward to a more sustainable future. This is particularly true among younger generations. Surveys and studies suggest that in the U.S., members of the "millennial" generation—those born after 1982, and the largest population of teenagers since the baby boomers—

are taking environmental issues very seriously. William Strauss, one of the world's leading authorities on U.S. generations, says that millennials are much more focused than earlier generations on issues of equity and responsibility, with environmental awareness being a key issue. Surveys reveal that a 10 to one majority believe that their generation, not older generations, will do the most to protect the environment over the next 25 years. A similar willingness to take responsibility for environmental change is being expressed by another influential and expanding segment of the U.S. adult population dubbed the "cultural creatives." This group of 50 million and growing, identified by sociologists Paul Ray and Sherry Anderson, cares deeply about nature and is prepared to make personal tradeoffs for the sake of ecological balance.

This rising desire to find more sustainable paths is not confined to the West. A nascent "third sector" is emerging in developing countries as well, empowered by increased connectivity and communications. At the 2004 World Social Forum—the global activist's alternative to the World Economic Forum that attracts more than 80,000 delegates from around the world—protecting the "immune system" of the planet was a leading priority, positioned in the broader context of self-determination and anti-corporatization. Also in 2004, the Nobel Peace Prize was awarded to Wangari Maathai, a Kenyan environmental activist who founded the Green Belt Movement, a pan-African network that not only planted millions of trees but explicitly linked the values of sustainable development with democracy and peace. "Today we are faced with a challenge that calls for a shift in our thinking, so that humanity stops threatening its life-support system," said Maathai in her eloquent acceptance speech. "We are called to assist the Earth to heal her wounds and in the process heal our own—indeed, to embrace the whole creation in all its diversity, beauty, and wonder. This will happen if we see the need to revive our sense of belonging to a larger family of life, with which we have shared our evolutionary process."

We are, in fact, seeing growing evidence of more sustainable approaches not just among citizens and advocates, but among manufacturers and businesses. Arguably, the most critical of these are efforts to create product manufacturing processes that minimize resource use and reduce waste. These efforts are largely based on the notion of "industrial ecology," introduced in the early 1990s by Hardin Tibbs and others and now a discipline in its own right, taught in environmental design and engineering programs worldwide. As landfills overflow, we are coming to realize that throwing things "away" in fact means stockpiling them around us. In the coming decade, we will be forced to take the mantra of "reduce, reuse, recycle" seriously, with increasing responsibility in this arena borne by manufacturers rather than consumers.

In many areas, consumers will become more like "service users," using a product for a set period before returning it to the manufacturer for recycling and reuse. When we start to design with this longer lifecycle in mind, we can move from "down-cycling," in which each new use of the materials leads to lower quality, to "up-cycling." We will also start to think less in terms of a "cradle to grave" lifecycle for a product and more in terms of a "cradle to cradle" approach, with the end of a product's life simply signaling the start of another incarnation of the same materials.

The Energy Imperative

In the coming decade, a shift in our energy habits will be accelerated by a number of undeniable factors, the most important of which is the growing body of scientific evidence that global carbon emissions continue to play a serious and alarming role in the destabilization of the Earth's environment. The International Energy Agency estimates that global energy demand will continue to grow throughout the next 25 years, increasing almost 60 percent by 2030, with two-thirds of new demand coming from developing countries. Right now, the world relies on carbon-emitting fossil fuels for 80 percent of its energy, and carbon emissions are on track to double by 2050 if significant measures are not taken. This conflict between meeting the needs of an energy-hungry world and limiting carbon emissions to mitigate global climate change will continue to create significant pressure for governments, corporations, and citizens to change their energy consumption patterns in the decades to come.

Some shifts in models and mindsets are already taking shape, albeit slowly. New solutions to our energy problems are emerging, many of them focused on lowering consumption by boosting the efficiency of everyday products and technologies. In the past few decades, energy efficiency has been boosted in virtually every household appliance. Fluorescent light bulbs now use 75 percent less energy than Edison's incadescents. In the last 25 years, the efficiency of refrigerators has increased threefold. Currently, much attention is being paid to the development of ultra-light vehicles that not only require less energy but also use alternative or hybrid fuel sources, thereby reducing our use of and dependence on oil. As Amory Lovins writes in his book *Winning the Oil Endgame*, "Fully applying today's best energy efficiency technologies in a doubled-GDP 2025 economy would save half of the projected U.S. oil use."

The Oil Endgame

"The cornerstone of the next industrial revolution is…winning the oil endgame. And surprisingly, it will cost less to displace all of the oil that the United States now uses than it will cost to buy that oil. Oil's current market price leaves out its true costs to the economy, national security, and the environment. But even without including these now 'external-ized' costs, it would still be profitable to displace oil completely over the next few decades. In fact, by 2025, the annual economic benefit of that displacement would be $130 billion gross (or $70 billion net of the dis-placement's costs). To achieve this does not require a revolution, but merely consolidating and accelerating trends already in place: the amount of oil the economy uses for each dollar of GDP produced, and the fuel efficiency of light vehicles, would need only to improve about three-fifths as quickly as they did in response to previous oil shocks."

Source: Armory Lovins, *Winning the Oil Endgame: Innovation for Profits, Jobs, and Security.* Reprinted by permission.

Another important development is the growing attention being paid to laying the groundwork for an eventual shift to a "hydrogen economy," in which hydrogen would replace oil and gas as our primary fuel source. Extracted from gasoline, natural gas, water, nuclear, or any renewable resource, hydrogen stores energy more efficiently than current batteries, burns twice as efficiently in a fuel cell as gasoline does in an internal com-bustion engine (more than making up for the energy required to produce it), and leaves only water behind. While hydrogen vehicles and fuel-cell power already exist, the science is still evolving, and convincing con-sumers, manufacturers, product designers, politicians, and those in the energy business to collectively evolve toward a new energy platform will be far from easy.

Yet as my colleague Peter Schwartz argues, hydrogen might be the most viable energy solution available to us. "Oil is an indulgence we can no longer afford, not just because it will run out or turn the planet into a sauna, but because it inexorably leads to global conflict," he wrote in a 2003 *Wired* cover story on hydrogen. "What we need is a massive,

Apollo-scale effort to unlock the power of hydrogen, a virtually unlimited source of power." Schwartz estimates that achieving a hydrogen economy in 10 years would cost roughly $100 billion. So far, that level of commitment has not been forthcoming. But more and more, the question is shifting from *whether* hydrogen will happen to *when*.

Evidence for Global Warming

- Atmospheric concentrations of greenhouse gases have increased from around 280 ppm 200 years ago to 370 ppm today. It is expected to rise to somewhere between 500 and 900 ppm by 2100.

- Carbon dioxide emissions are 17 times higher today than at the start of the twentieth century, with sulfur dioxide emissions 13 times higher.

- The earth's global mean surface temperature has increased by more than one degree Farenheit during the twentieth century.

- Sea levels rose by 10-20 cm during the same period.

- Arctic ice thickness has decreased by 10-15 percent since the 1950s.

- According to NASA, the 10 warmest years on record have all occurred since 1980.

Sources: Conference on Human Health and Global Climate Change (1996), National Academy of Sciences; U.S. Global Change Research Information Office; Science and Development Network; NASA.

Meanwhile, we are finding creative (albeit stopgap) ways to reduce the damage caused by carbon emissions—for example, by capturing and storing emitted carbon before it can affect the atmosphere by essentially incarcerating it underground or in the ocean. The current technologies to do this are messy and expensive, but some promising experiments are underway. Recently, eight of the world's leading energy companies decided to coordinate their carbon sequestration efforts, setting up the CO_2 Capture Project in hopes of reducing the cost of carbon capture. Meanwhile, large-scale projects to store carbon in geological formations are also underway, most notably in Statoil's Sleipner natural gas field in the North Sea and EnCana's Weyburn oil field in Saskatchewan, Canada.

Another development is the continuing search for viable alternative energy sources, particularly renewables like wind and solar power. Vast improvements have been made in solar cell efficiency in the last few years;

the cells can now be made from much cheaper materials, which would make solar power prices competitive with grid electricity. In December 2004, Germany opened the largest solar energy plant in the world, spanning 30 acres. Since 1998, German chancellor Gerhard Schroeder's Social Democrat-Green coalition has worked to turn Germany into the world's leader in renewable energy. Schroeder's politically risky move to increase taxes on petroleum products freed up billions to spend on wind and solar projects while reducing consumption of conventional fuels. Meanwhile, Scotland is fast becoming a pioneer in harnessing wave energy and has recently opened a massive marine energy center to develop and test commercial-scale devices for capturing tidal energy and converting it into useable power.

Nuclear power is also reemerging on a big scale as a cleaner—and safer—alternative to coal, gas, and oil. For example, China is deep in development of next-generation nuclear reactors. France already derives more than 75 percent of its electricity from nuclear energy; Belgium derives 58 percent, and South Korea, 40 percent. The U.S. lags at 20 percent, but even that number is impressive considering the red flags and visions of Three Mile Island still triggered whenever the word "nuclear" is mentioned. As Peter Schwartz puts it, "Nuclear is here, now, in industrial quantities." And its importance among alternative energy options will only increase in the coming decade.

Ultimately, as science writer Janine Benyus has argued, the simple rule for any organism is to "keep yourself alive and keep your offspring alive— meaning your offspring a thousand generations from now." For humans, the sheer scale of that challenge will become more evident, more vexing, and of greater concern in the coming decade than at any time in our history. Yet developments already in play suggest that a shift in our collective mindset toward optimism and the belief that we can achieve greater sustainability than many currently presume might be possible. Such a shift could change the tone of our global dialogue about sustainability from one of fear and recrimination to one of greater hope and common purpose.

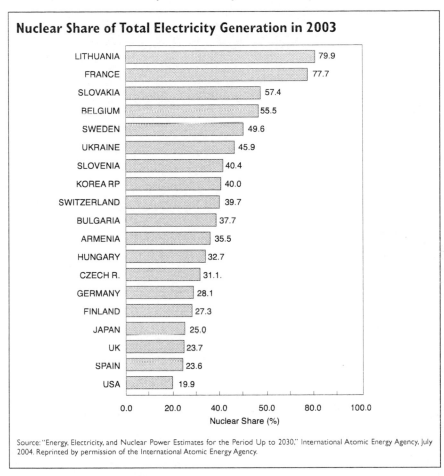

Nuclear Share of Total Electricity Generation in 2003

Country	Nuclear Share (%)
LITHUANIA	79.9
FRANCE	77.7
SLOVAKIA	57.4
BELGIUM	55.5
SWEDEN	49.6
UKRAINE	45.9
SLOVENIA	40.4
KOREA RP	40.0
SWITZERLAND	39.7
BULGARIA	37.7
ARMENIA	35.5
HUNGARY	32.7
CZECH R.	31.1.
GERMANY	28.1
FINLAND	27.3
JAPAN	25.0
UK	23.7
SPAIN	23.6
USA	19.9

Source: "Energy, Electricity, and Nuclear Power Estimates for the Period Up to 2030," International Atomic Energy Agency, July 2004. Reprinted by permission of the International Atomic Energy Agency.

Planet

> Nature always bats last.
> —Unknown

In the years ahead, we will begin a new chapter in our relationship with the planet, one in which we come to better understand that we do not inhabit an inert piece of rock—and that we alone do not trigger every change on our planet. We will come to challenge the modern view of mankind as somehow separate from and dominant over nature, master of our environment, pilot of "Spaceship Earth." We will realize that there is actually a hidden egotism in the call on mankind to "save the planet," as the planet continues to act on its own behalf. The idea of sustainability, which essentially calls on us to pay attention to the planet to save our own civilization, is closer to the mark, but it still assumes that we hold all the cards and must learn to play them better. While that is an important step forward, it is also the start of a longer cognitive shift. We are in the early stages of rediscovering the ancient wisdom that nature holds its own hand of cards and gets to play them at will. We belong to the planet, not the other way around.

Our Changing Relationship with the Planet

Three important factors will drive this imminent shift in our relationship with the planet. The first is that we will continue to experience natural disasters in many parts of the world in the years ahead. With more people concentrated in tight spaces and spreading into new spaces, the impact of these disasters on human life will be increasingly severe. As we build homes on 100-year flood plains or grow populations of millions in cities built on geological fault lines, this deepening impact is inevitable.

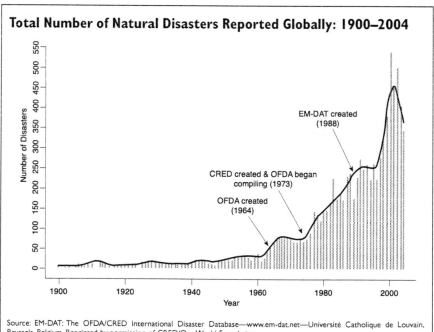

Total Number of Natural Disasters Reported Globally: 1900–2004

EM-DAT created (1988)

CRED created & OFDA began compiling (1973)

OFDA created (1964)

Number of Disasters

Year

Source: EM-DAT: The OFDA/CRED International Disaster Database—www.em-dat.net—Université Catholique de Louvain, Brussels, Belgium. Reprinted by permission of CRED/Our World Foundation.

Moreover, in our increasingly interconnected world, awareness and psychological reactions to these events will be greatly amplified. The December 2004 tsunami that devastated so many coastal areas around the Indian Ocean and killed hundreds of thousands of people provoked an enormous global outpouring of grief, concern, and help, with $4 billion pouring into the region within a few weeks of the catastrophe. We have no reason not to expect further large-scale natural disasters, as well as the heightened awareness they bring of the extraordinary and seemingly random power of the planet to exert itself at will, with little if any warning.

Second, in recent years, we have massively boosted our surveillance of the planet and our ability to track and understand its flickers, fluctuations, lurches, and leaps. Satellites are capturing images of ice caps and global vegetation patterns; unmanned submarines are traveling around the Gulf Stream measuring temperature, pressure, and salinity; land-based sensors are growing in number all across the world—and all that they are learning is being connected and analyzed by powerful computers. Such wide-ranging surveillance is rapidly deepening our knowledge and understanding of the various planetary shifts occurring around the globe.

Third, as we learn more about our impact on the planet and particularly its climate systems, we are also learning interesting things about the ways in which the planet also determines its own climate. There is no question that humans are major contributors to climate change. Indeed, there is now nearly global scientific consensus that we are living through a period of manmade and gradual global warming. In the last 150 years, carbon dioxide concentrations in the atmosphere have jumped from 280 parts per million (ppm) to 370 ppm, almost entirely due to human industrial activity. This increase has continued to push global average temperatures ever upward, creating new and different weather patterns in many parts of the world: floods, droughts, changes in vegetation, glacial melting, and heat waves. Furthermore, the warming trend is not slowing. If atmospheric carbon dioxide reaches 560 ppm, which it will if our emissions continue along their projections, the global temperature could rise 20 degrees—a warmth level not experienced on Earth since the time of the dinosaurs. As David King, chief scientific adviser to the British government, stated in early 2004, "Climate change is the most severe problem that we are facing today, more serious even than the threat of terrorism."

But while climate change is largely the result of human handiwork, it is not entirely so. The planet it also an actor in this play, reading its own script. Big temperature swings are not new to the planet. In fact, scientists are now learning that they happen more frequently (and suddenly) than previously suspected. In 1999, a team of Russia scientists drilled a 3,623-meter ice core into the Antarctic ice pack; the recovered core effectively tells the story of 420,000 years of climate change. In 2004, another ice core was taken from a different Antarctic plateau that could be "read" for weather changes dating back 740,000 years. These efforts led to the creation of the oldest continuous climate records to date. And what those records tell is that over this considerable time span, the Earth experienced eight ice ages and eight "interglacials"—warming periods with temperatures similar to ours today. In addition to major transitions from glacial to warm periods about every 100,000 years were many smaller, more frequent transitions. The evidence is growing that most of these changes were relatively sudden, occurring over years or decades rather than centuries or millennia.

Other scientific studies are revealing more pieces of the planet's volatile climate story. It appears that the Gulf Stream—which keeps the Northern Atlantic much warmer than it would be otherwise and accounts for the relative warmth of Northern Europe compared with Canada at the same latitude—has failed, quite suddenly and quite regularly, about every 5,000 years, with serious consequences for global weather patterns. Historically, when the Gulf Stream fails, the climate shifts over the course of a single decade to cooler, dryer, and windier conditions across the entire Northern Hemisphere, creating hard winters, violent storms, and droughts. We have not had a Gulf Stream failure for more than 8,000 years, but there is strong evidence that the conditions that could create another failure in the near future are coming into place. In May 2005, scientists discovered that one of the primary "engines" driving the Gulf Stream—the sinking of giant, frigid columns of water in the Greenland Sea—has weakened to less than a quarter of its usual strength. If it continues, this weakening could trigger an abrupt climate change scenario that would turn Northern Europe into Siberia within several decades and create volatile patterns of heating and cooling worldwide, causing food and water shortages, floods, and economic and political instability.

So, should Northern Europeans be considering a move across the Atlantic, and seek residency rights in the U.S.? Maybe not. Other research suggests that there have been five major droughts on the U.S. landmass over the last 2,000 years, each covering larger areas and enduring much longer than the drought that gave rise to the Oklahoma Dust Bowl of the twentieth century. Noted scientist Bill Calvin, author of *A Brain for All Seasons: Human Evolution and Abrupt Climate Change*, has described them as "droughts that won't quit" and predicts we will experience more of them in the future. Historic climatic events of this sort, he explains, are often highly localized and carry the threat of long-term devastation; they create a "flip-flop" in the climate of a particular region, possibly rendering it inhospitable.

Looking forward, it is very likely that parts of the Earth will undergo periods of very abrupt climate change. The U.S. National Research Council cites evidence that about half the North Atlantic warming since the last ice age was achieved in a single decade, and posits that because abrupt changes usually happen when climates are under stress, the global warming trend we are already experiencing will "increase the possibility of large, abrupt, and unwelcome regional or global climatic events"—and not just more warming, but "weirding" as well. As environmentalist Paul Hawken has put it, "One of the problems with global warming is that it's a misnomer…. It's not that everything is going to be hot and humid—it's going to be more volatile."

In the 1950s, there were 13 "extreme weather events"; in the 1990s, there were 72. Insurance against these devastating episodes is becoming more expensive and harder to find. In the first 10 months of 2004 (before the South Asia tsunami), natural disasters cost the insurance industry more than $35 billion, up from $16 billion in 2003. Overall economic losses for this 10-month period, many of which were not insured, totaled roughly $90 billion—up from $63 billion in 2003 and among the highest on record.

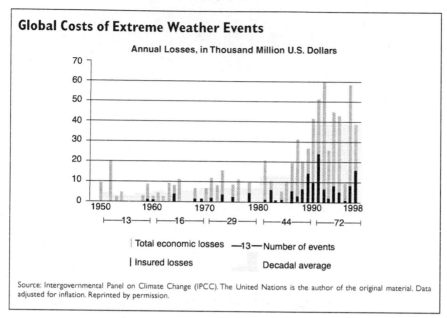

Global Costs of Extreme Weather Events

Annual Losses, in Thousand Million U.S. Dollars

Total economic losses   —13— Number of events

Insured losses   Decadal average

Source: Intergovernmental Panel on Climate Change (IPCC). The United Nations is the author of the original material. Data adjusted for inflation. Reprinted by permission.

Acknowledging Complexity, Avoiding Paralysis

It is essential that we come to understand and acknowledge this more complex picture of climate change, in which the planet itself is a meaningful participant, outcomes are varied and differ from place to place, and bizarre weather events become more commonplace. Simplistic perspectives on this issue could prove extremely damaging—witness, for example, Russian president Vladimir Putin's remark at the end of 2003 that "an increase of two or three degrees wouldn't be so bad for a northern country like Russia. We could spend less on fur coats, and the grain harvest would go up." Even if meant to be humorous, such comments reveal a clear misunderstanding of the scale and nature of the challenges we could *all* be facing.

Equally, many of those who advocate radical changes in lifestyle and economies to drastically reduce carbon emissions may also be jumping to overly simple conclusions. For example, the relationship between carbon and temperature seems in danger of reaching an unprecedented tipping point, bringing the climate to a state where it reverts to pre-ice-age insta-bility. But what if climate follows a nonlinear path? Theoretically, it is con-ceivable (though not likely) that an injection of CO_2 at the present high point may stop it from falling as it has done repeatedly before. The point is that *no one knows for certain*, which makes our continued efforts to understand the complexities of climate change all the more paramount.

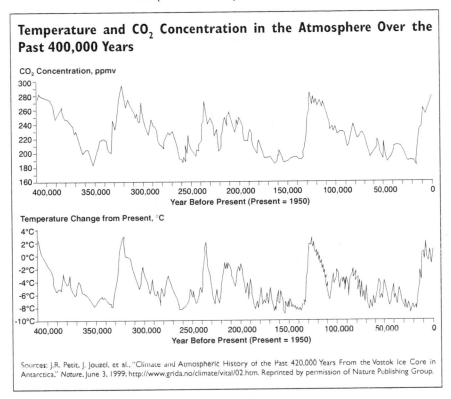

Temperature and CO_2 Concentration in the Atmosphere Over the Past 400,000 Years

CO_2 Concentration, ppmv

Year Before Present (Present = 1950)

Temperature Change from Present, °C

Year Before Present (Present = 1950)

Sources: J.R. Petit, J. Jouzel, et al., "Climate and Atmospheric History of the Past 420,000 Years From the Vostok Ice Core in Antarctica," *Nature*, June 3, 1999; http://www.grida.no/climate/vital/02.htm. Reprinted by permission of Nature Publishing Group.

In the next 10 years, we will increasingly come to regard our planet as a complex living system, one in which humans play an important role and which they influence but do not control. In the 1970s, James Lovelock offered the metaphor (rejected and much vilified, but perhaps worth revisiting in the years ahead) of "Gaia." He suggested that "the Earth may be alive: not as the ancients saw her—a sentient Goddess with a purpose and foresight—but alive like a tree. A tree that quietly exists, never moving except to sway in the wind, yet endlessly conversing with the sunlight and the soil. Using sunlight and water and nutrient minerals to grow and change. But all done so imperceptibly, that to me the old oak tree on the green is the same as it was when I was a child." A shift toward regarding our planet as a complex living whole will help us to better understand its needs, its patterns, and its future.

However, it is equally essential that we do not slip into "paralysis by analysis," frozen into inactivity because we do not fully understand the Earth's changing climate. There is some danger of this today, with many in the developed world resistant to making changes that cannot be absolutely proven to be required (except, perhaps, in hindsight) while many in the developing world are, quite reasonably, unwilling to compromise or constrain their own growth paths in ways that the West did not.

Five Tracks to the Future

In the decade ahead, I believe that our knowledge and actions regarding the challenging state of the planet will develop along five tracks. The first track is *learning,* and here we are already making strong progress. Our understanding of climate patterns is evolving. We are tracking and sensing the Earth's climate systems in ever-expanding ways. We are paying attention to weather events and discovering their connections in an attempt to understand them at a more systemic level. We are observing, measuring, and assessing planetary changes as they occur. And we are modeling and simulating our planet's climate system in increasingly sophisticated ways. But learning requires, quite literally, the ability to change our minds, necessitating an openness and spirit of inquiry that has not always characterized civic, political, and even scientific dialogue on this critical issue.

The second track is *mitigation*—in particular, a serious global effort to constrain carbon emissions. As Brian Fagan has said, "The times require us to learn the vagaries of the global climate, to study its moods, and to keep our skies relatively clear of excessive greenhouse gases with the same diligence, and for the same reasons, that the Mesopotamian farmers five millennia ago had to learn the moods of the Euphrates and keep their irrigation canals reasonably free of silt. If they didn't, the gods grew angry." Today, we are stumbling along this mitigation track, unclear of our destination and bickering about who should go first and how quickly to proceed. But at least we are proceeding.

The Kyoto Protocol is a prime example. The treaty, which took effect in February 2005, sets country-by-country targets for cuts in carbon emissions. Although the U.S., which alone produces 36 percent of the industrial world's emissions, refused to sign the treaty, much of the rest of the world has made the bold and collective choice to address global warming while it still can. Columnist and friend Gwynne Dyer nicely summed up Kyoto's importance: "Kyoto is the first legally binding international treaty on the environment.... Getting countries to surrender their national sovereignty over domestic industrial policy in this way was so unprecedented—but so vital to dealing with a global problem like climate change."

The third track will be *retrofitting*—figuring out how we might continue to occupy parts of the planet even as they come under increasing pressure, which they surely will. To some extent, we have been retrofitting against nature for thousands of years, especially in the construction of coastal defenses as the sea has encroached upon inhabited areas. But the future scale of our work in this regard is without precedent, although there is hope that large-scale retrofitting can be achieved. Maldives, a country of more than 1,000 coral islands nestled in the Indian Ocean southwest of India, is the lowest-lying nation on the planet; its capital, Male, is only 3 feet above sea level. Faced with destruction by rising sea levels, the country's president, Maumoon Abdul Gayoom, decided to create an entirely new island, Hulhumale, at a height of 6 feet above sea level. The project cost more than $60 million so far and is already home to more than 1,000 people (in 2040, when the island is complete, it will be 150,000). The island was unexpectedly tested by the December 2004 tsunami; it survived with only very minimal damage while the rest of Maldives was devastated.

The fourth track, sadly, will be *retreating*, for there will be land that cannot be saved for human habitation. In some areas, the rising cost of coastal defense is prompting a policy of returning land to the sea. But in the years ahead we will be forced to leave land that has been inhabited for millennia. The 155,000 Inuit in Canada, Alaska, Greenland, and Russia face the very real prospect of the devastation of their culture, which is so intimately linked with their geography. For years, Inuit hunters and elders have observed melting permafrost, glaciers, and sea ice; unpredictable and unusual weather patterns; changes in vegetation; and the appearance of new species never seen before, including barn owls and mosquitoes. They fear that their way of life may disappear, and, tragically, they might be right.

Finally, the fifth track will be *transcending*—imagining and preparing for radically different approaches to configuring human life on this planet, or even possibly elsewhere. We will not have to embark upon anything dramatic in the decade ahead. But we *will* begin to explore more creative ideas as our understanding of the deep tension between people and planet increases. In addition to implementing aggressive new energy strategies, these might include designing huge engineering feats like giant mirrors to deflect the sun's rays. It is possible that we will even start exploring, in more practical terms than we have to date, how we might manipulate the atmosphere and environment of another planet to support the continuance of our species—"terraforming" other worlds, as science fiction writers describe it.

The evidence suggests that in the coming decade and beyond we will see our planet and our civilization challenged in unprecedented ways. If we think we live in powerful times today, the planet may be on the brink of telling us: "You ain't seen nothing yet." How we respond will define the coming century, as well as the evolution of our sense of "we" in an increasingly interdependent world. The promise is that in coming together globally to address shared challenges that we cannot blame on one another, our argumentative species may achieve a level of unity and coherence that has thus far eluded us.

Section 2

What If?: Changing for the Challenges Ahead

The road to wisdom? Well, it's plain and simple to express. Err
and err and err again but less and less and less
—Piet Hein

The dynamic tensions set out in the previous chapters provide a framework for recognizing and tracking the big, contextual forces that are
reshaping the world today. The better we understand the nature, power,
and curious duality of each of these forces, the better we can filter the signal from the noise and make greater sense of what is happening around
us, as we head into a world where:

- We enjoy unprecedented **clarity**, driven by abundant information, powerful analysis, ubiquitous connectivity, and
  remarkable transparency—while these same forces also
  empower **craziness**, as every storyline and conspiracy theory, no matter how bizarre, can be supported by some distortion of real data and spread like a virus.

- **Secular** ideals continue to drive much of modern civilization, especially with regards to governance and commerce—
  yet have to coexist and coevolve with powerful, and powerfully different, **sacred** worldviews.

- The U.S. seems set to call upon its unmatchable military **power**, yet may face challenges that hard power alone cannot meet even as its soft power weakens—contributing to a growing sense of **vulnerability** in the Western world as a variety of looming threats come into sharper focus.

- Technology **acceleration** proceeds apace, providing us with ever greater power to manipulate our world and increasingly to manipulate nature and the very essence of life itself, triggering increased (but globally uneven) moral, ethical, and pragmatic concern and **pushback** against the untrammeled pursuit of science.

- The economy becomes increasingly **intangible** as the relationship between mass and value continues to decline in a world of services, experiences, and virtualization—yet the **physical** economy also matters more as we have to renew and create critical infrastructure everywhere.

- **Prosperity** spreads further around the globe as new players exert increasing influence on the world economy—while **decline** in some countries and regions and among certain groups leads to increased polarization between those doing well and those faring poorly.

- The needs and expectations of **people** lead to an increased mandate to pay serious attention to the principles of sustainability—yet the **planet** exerts its own clear authority and autonomy, leading to deeper and more urgent concern about the robustness of our civilization's footprint.

There are great opportunities and promises here. We can expect unprecedented (though by no means perfect) transparency in world affairs, greatly improved prospects for more and more of us to share in the prosperity of our times, and scientific breakthroughs that can help feed and cure us in new and better ways. These are real and important reasons for optimism. Yet we can also expect to find ourselves concerned with a set of mounting challenges that we must address in the years ahead.

These challenges come into sharper focus when we consider some of the interactions *between* the tensions. For example, the spread and democratization of the tools of biotechnology will likely create new vulnerability to bioterrorism. The rise of competing sacred worldviews will serve to promote a sense of separation and vulnerability. The polarization between the haves and the have-nots will be extremely visible in a world of heightened transparency—which will lead to new forms of discontent and provoke faster innovation to address the unmet needs of billions. As the U.S. deploys its power in troubled regions, its actions—and its inevitable transgressions—will be scrutinized, captured, disseminated, and amplified around the world, possibly provoking deeper resistance (for example, some of the troubling images from Abu Ghraib have become almost totemic, featured even in art and graffiti in many parts of the world). Spreading prosperity and consumption, especially of fossil fuels, will deepen climatic problems, which will in turn accelerate the search for new innovation in energy technologies and solutions. The emergence of powerful new global players with less rigid and well-established systems of property rights, combined with the increasing value of knowledge in the intangible economy, will raise serious questions about the viability of existing global approaches to protecting intellectual property. Finally, all the dynamic tensions will combine in myriad ways to generate increasing geopolitical tensions, security challenges, and new risks.

Rising to New Challenges

History is truly in motion—and our powerful times seem to bring challenges of such magnitude and diversity that even trying to think seriously about the future can feel overwhelming. But we are an inventive and determined species, and I have no doubt that we will make important changes that will enable us to walk new paths into an uncertain future. In particular, we will see significant new developments in two critical arenas: how we *relate*—the realm of governance—and how we *create*—the realm of innovation. The following two chapters address each of these in depth.

Questions of governance revolve around how we order our rules and norms, regulate ourselves, and relate to one another such that we not only spread the achievement of the traditional purposes of good governance— security, economic progress, protection of rights—but also achieve greater global coherence in tackling the growing challenges of our world. Innovation is about how and where we create new approaches, solutions, goods, and services—particularly those that address the needs of people in less-developed parts of the world, create more sustainable ways of prospering on our planet, and spawn the long overdue transformation of our approaches to education and learning. Contending with the complex challenges posed by governance and innovation is within our grasp, but it will require new approaches and new mindsets, as well as a departure from some of our entrenched ways of thinking. This does not always come naturally, as illustrated by the following story.

In the early days of World War II, the British army was perplexed. Using heavy artillery unchanged since the Boer War (except now drawn into place by mechanical trucks instead of horses), British gunners found themselves unable to match the volley rate achieved by their German counterparts, who were using similar artillery. Puzzled and unable to identify any deterioration in their load-aim-fire routine, the army turned to the new discipline of time-motion studies to discover the source of its relative underperformance.

A hired expert in this field quietly observed their routine. He took primitive moving-film images and studied them repeatedly. He soon spotted an element of their ritual that he could not logically explain: just before the gun fired, two soldiers stepped out of the procedure, backed up, and stood at salute until the firing was over, then stepped back in to assist again with the routine. It was an obvious inefficiency, the expert thought. Being unfamiliar with military matters, he assumed there must be some compelling rationale to explain it. So he showed the film to an elderly artillery colonel, who watched once, pondered what he had seen, asked for it to be played again, and then began to laugh. "Yes, I know what they are doing," he said, "and no, they don't need to do it—not anymore. They are holding the horses, lest they startle!" In the coming decade, if we are to meet the challenges of our times, it is important that we are able to "let go of the horses" and accept the need for change.

Organizing for Change

However, before exploring the realms of governance and innovation, it is important to consider another "both/and" dynamic tension that underpins the evolution of both: *the ongoing developments in how we structure, lead, and work in our organizations.* It is easy to forget how recently autonomous organizations arrived as powerful actors in the world. Only in the last few centuries did a significant role emerge for independent entities that did not fall under the dictate of ruler or church, able to make (within certain social and legal constraints) their own decisions and pursue interests and opportunities of their choice. It is primarily in the last

100 years that we have formed a mental model of how an organization ought to function and be structured—a model that is now only partially accurate, because our organizations have been evolving rapidly in different directions as the knowledge economy has firmly taken hold.

Most organizations have experienced significant change over the last two decades. However, our default mindset is to think of organizations as hierarchical, centralized, and top down, even though many organizations also manifest new and even opposite characteristics: networked, decentralized, bottom-up. Both models—what I call "citadels" and "webs"— typically coexist in the same organization.

Citadels are orderly, rational, and robust. You can almost visualize organizations with high walls around them and gates at each end for bringing in required resources and shipping out finished products. Citadels have been developed and refined over the past century, which is why they feel natural and intuitive. Authority is clear and rarely challenged; decisions are made based on clear data provided by experts; plans are constructed to allocate resources and drive all activity; structures and systems are clear cut; success can be readily and definitively measured, and comes from repeating tried and true methods and procedures; work is routinized into crisply-defined jobs; assets are owned and have clear book value. The prevailing—and enduring—metaphor of the citadel mindset is of the organization as a machine—something to be constantly calibrated, endlessly measured, rigidly structured for optimal efficiency, situated within value "chains," and occasionally re-engineered. (Just think of most organizational charts, which look like wiring diagrams or assembly instructions.)

The citadel model was developed during and for the industrial era, when the Taylorist notions of organization were helping us usher in a new world of mass production and automation. This model is incredibly good at securing efficiency, productivity, quality, and focus, but has evident limitations in our knowledge-intensive and dynamic world. Yet the citadel is so embedded in our consciousness that we often find it hard to understand and accept the importance of the much more fluid, self-organizing, and decentralized organizational models that have been emerging in recent decades—and that will be required to meet our complex future challenges. The shift toward incorporating elements of both the efficient citadel model and the more fluid web model will accelerate further as organizations increasingly harness, integrate, and align human talents rather than simply control and standardize routine and physical human activity.

Webs, on the other hand, are messy, dynamic, ambiguous, tangled, far less obvious and familiar, and much harder to grasp. It is often difficult to figure out where they end and where the organizations with which they interact begin. They require more but less formal connection and communication (often virtual and technology-enabled), self-organization around agreed principles and intentions, and continuous strategic conversation to discover new knowledge and understanding through the integration of multiple perspectives. Relationships and responsibilities are fluid; structures are flexible and evolving; work can be multifaceted and constantly changing. Success is often predicated upon innovation, with as much emphasis on discovery of the new as exploitation of the known. Speed and creativity are highly valued. Leaders encourage inquiry—What must we learn more about?—which in turn requires their willingness to confess ignorance. The balance sheet generally contains a lot of intangibles. In this changing context, the organizational metaphors are biological ones. We cannot really "build" effective organizations: they grow. We cannot always reengineer them: they adapt and evolve. They are more like organisms than machines. They are generally not stable links in solid value chains, but rather exist as part of the ecology of evolving value systems that are iterative, not linear, and characterized by complex relationships and interactions.

As with the other dynamic tensions explored earlier in this book, we must recognize the "both/and" quality of these two models; both have strengths and weaknesses, and both will exist in most organizations in a hybrid form. But we should also be prepared for growth in the relative importance and spread of the "web" model. Citadels were supremely effective in the industrial economy, when the key purpose of organizational design was to control production processes, optimize the traditional factors of production, and manage the *hands* of those who worked there. But as we are witnessing all around us, the characteristics of the web model are more suited to the newer imperatives to create, combine, and apply knowledge and ideas to innovate new forms of value, respond rapidly to environmental changes and consumer demands, integrate complex processes, and attract and lead the *minds* of the key value creators. These are essential if we are to rise effectively to the challenges of our times.

Moreover, the web model encourages and enables collaboration across organizational boundaries. This is a key future characteristic of both governance (where we will likely see much greater dependence on multi-actor initiatives) and innovation (where networked, bottom-up, and open source production processes will become increasingly important). In thinking about each, it is best to keep in mind this need for both citadel and web structures and behaviors in our organizations—and to recognize that the power and impact of the latter may be far greater than our default expectations might lead us to anticipate.

Chapter 9

Governance

Amid the destruction following WWII, a new world order was formed. We faced a dangerous rivalry between two global superpowers, the deployment of the atomic bomb, Western Europe in ruins for the second time in less than 30 years, and new nation-states formed by peace treaties. Nonetheless, the world (with strong American leadership) evolved a new system of institutions, relationships, treaties, regulatory frameworks, and checks and balances that sustained a new global order for 40 years.

Some elements from this era remain. However, when the Cold War ended, the world entered a new and calmer period of change. There was little violence and destruction, and in sharp contrast to the urgency felt in the late 1940s, a sense of complacency settled in. The West lacked the impulse to proactively design and create the conditions for a new global political arrangement. Instead, during the late 1980s and throughout the 1990s, it appeared that a new global order was emerging organically and inexorably through the convergence of inevitable and historic forces related to the power of the market, the supremacy of democracy, and the innate human urge for freedom and autonomy.

In fact, a new story of the future emerged as we prepared for a new millennium, and it flowed quite naturally from the fall of the Berlin Wall: Western capitalism had won an "either/or" battle for the future of the planet, and its attendant concepts of democracy, open trade, free markets, and free choice would shape the world from here on out. Economic factors would set the future on its course; the spread of wealth and opportunity would be the vanguard, and political and social changes were bound to follow. Adam Smith's "invisible hand" was quietly recasting the globe in a Western image. His disciple, Margaret Thatcher, had been right when she had made her famous "TINA" proclamation: "There Is No Alternative." Throughout the 1990s, this orthodoxy evolved as the shared story of our times.

Shrewd commentators captured the mainstream spirit well in pithy phrases. John Williamson's notion of a "Washington Consensus" set out the preferred policy model for achieving growth in Latin America and, by extension, the wider developing world. The core characteristics of this consensus revealed an overwhelming confidence in open markets: fiscal discipline, tax reform, trade and interest-rate liberalization, opening up to foreign direct investment, privatization and deregulation, transparent and secure property rights. At the end of the Cold War, when President George H.W. Bush proclaimed the creation of a "new world order," he was not signalling the overhaul of our transnational political, legal, and institutional frameworks. Rather, he was conveying the underlying assumption of the times: that the emergence of global commerce and the empowerment of the institutions that make it possible would provide the core platform for a new, largely self-organizing order based on economic globalization and market forces.

While this belief had its critics and doubters, they were mostly shouting from the fringes. Even traditionally left-leaning political parties throughout the world embraced the new capitalist order. Yet valid concerns were raised. Some doubted the degree to which governance instruments and approaches evolved 40 years earlier for a quite different era could sustain and support the new order that was unfolding. Some observed that the liberation of markets, driven by powerful corporations and international organizations, also served to create complex, interconnected global economic and social systems that could not readily be controlled and were responsive to many different, even opposing, forces. Others were concerned that it took centuries for the West to evolve the elaborate infrastructure, laws, cultures, norms, and social systems to support its capitalist model, yet the forces of globalization, rapid technological advances, increased connectivity, and mounting transparency were unfolding and spreading so fast that new entrants were attempting to accelerate their own evolution into a mere decade or two.

Today, such concerns have proven prescient. Indeed, even the very market-oriented mechanisms for world order that we patiently fashioned over the latter years of the twentieth century are showing signs of strain. The rules and regulations, international standards, trade laws, and financial institutions designed to deliver friction-free commerce are in danger of being undermined by corporate accounting scandals and by powerful interests like China or Brazil taking their own stand against the international system.

An Emerging Global Governance

The current world order cannot take us through these powerful times and will undoubtedly evolve considerably in the decade ahead. As this reality has grown clearer, the concept of "global governance" has gained increased attention. The phrase is not the same as "global government"— a term that conjures images of sinister black helicopters and conspiracy theories for world domination on the one hand and utopian visions of a benign and wise authority providing coherence, order, equity, and justice on the other. In today's discourse, global governance does not assume a centralized authority wielding traditional hierarchical power. But in truth, it is easier to define what global governance is not than what it is; no widely accepted definition has yet emerged. Perhaps the best high-level definition can still be found in "Our Global Neighborhood," the 1995 publication prepared by the Commission on Global Governance for the fiftieth anniversary of the United Nations: "The development of global governance is part of the evolution of human efforts to organize life on the planet."

That we have not yet arrived at a more precise definition is symptomatic of the *emergent* quality of global governance today. A new order is already starting to unfold around us, yet it is not being explicitly or consciously designed. This *de facto* global governance is coming about because of experimentation across a diverse range of processes, approaches, policies, actions, and actors that are overlapping and interlocking in a complex and evolving system. There are strengths in the emergent quality of the global governance system. Indeed, there is arguably a strong role for Adam Smith's "invisible hand" here as well— especially given that Smith coined the term to refer to the positive force of human nature, not the power of the market itself.

However, it is becoming clear that we cannot expect this piecemeal system to fully self-optimize to confront the challenges of our times. Rather, increasingly coherent and mutually compatible elements of our global system that support shared security, prosperity, and inclusion must move closer together and establish common ground for tackling and avoiding systemic crises.

There are two related issues today that are driving the need for new approaches to global governance, and both of them require us to "let go of the horses." The first is that our current expectations and norms regarding governance are far too dependent upon the concept of the nation-state that emerged from the Treaty of Westphalia three and a half centuries ago. The second is that the global issues we must address are interconnected and multifaceted, and therefore do not conform even remotely to national boundaries.

Nation-states, especially the wealthier ones, tend to set their own rules and guard their autonomy, choosing on a case-by-case basis whether to join treaties and conventions and abide by international standards. They continue to have extremely important sway over multilateral institutions; the voting rights at the United Nations, the World Bank, and the International Monetary Fund, for example, all privilege the most powerful nations. Yet while the concept of the nation remains dominant, there has been relatively little true innovation in the exercise of national governance. Granted, great strides have been made in the spread of some form of democracy (around 140 of the 193 countries in the world hold regularly scheduled multi-party elections) and the increasing focus on exporting "good governance" to underperforming countries. But while transfer of best practices has increased, the development of new practices in national governance has not. Rather, considerable experimentation and changes in governance approaches are occurring at the global, regional, and local levels. Moreover, much of the new energy, action, and direction-setting in the world are coming not from nations or even governmental institutions but from other actors—especially global corporations and nongovernmental organizations, whose legitimacy is still informal at best.

Meanwhile, many pressing issues are clearly transnational or global in character. Even those domains traditionally associated with governance—security, prosperity, and inclusion—do not lend themselves to straightforward nation-state resolution in an increasingly open global economy. Clearly the state has already lost its monopoly on the use of force; you no longer need an army or a military-industrial complex in order to deploy and project force in the world. Terrorist movements are not state-based and operate outside our normal conventions; modern weapons technology has made it possible for small groups of well-organized people to challenge the state's monopoly on waging war; and security is made much more complicated by the fact that some parts of the world have not been even remotely integrated into the global commons, and consequentially present threats everywhere. In effect, there are persistent zones of chaos within our global order—and we know that we can no longer afford to ignore faraway parts of the world of which we know little. Chaos elsewhere will have an impact on security everywhere. As Thomas Barnett observed in *The Pentagon's New Map*: "Show me where globalization is thinning or just plain absent, and I will show you regions plagued by politically repressive regimes, widespread poverty and disease, routine mass murder, and—most important—the chronic conflicts that incubate the next generation of global terrorists."

In fact, very few problems that threaten to become chronic systemic crises lend themselves to purely national responses. Environmental issues—pollution, climate change, the loss of biodiversity—observe few borders. Arms proliferation, human smuggling, the drug trade and other forms of increasingly globalized crime, the occurrence and spread of infectious disease—each of these problems is rising in urgency, yet few would argue that they are being dealt with effectively or conclusively.

The important issues of our times are transnational or global in nature and are not easily or best solved by national governments. Yet our governance systems are heavily biased toward protecting the power of the nation-state. Today, much of the formal power in the world lies with national governments that lack the capacity to address the planet's central challenges. This is a fundamental weakness of our current situation.

So what should we expect to see unfold in the coming decade and beyond to address global governance? History would suggest three dominant approaches to the achievement of coherence and order, and we should look first to them. The first, *hegemony*, is based on the overwhelming power of a single authority that has tended toward imperial status, the British Empire being the most recent and global example. The second, *balance of power*, arises when competing powers arrive at a mutually contained form of stalemate (based on matching national strengths and/or the development of competing alliances) that, for a while at least, creates stability; the Cold War was the most obvious and recent manifestation of this. The third approach, *multilateralism*, is based on achieving alignment and accord through mutual interest and compromise; it involves developing an international system based on balancing interests, accommodating and managing differences, and protecting and sustaining peace according to agreed upon protocols, regulations, and principles. The League of Nations was the first global attempt at this approach; its successor, the United Nations, is the current manifestation.

Today, as we evolve toward that promised "new world order," all three of these approaches are in play—and in rather new and interesting ways. Currently, the U.S. can be rightfully regarded as the world's sole super-power—a hegemon. Yet the U.S. is not motivated by a conventional desire for imperial power but by a twin desire (simultaneously noble and self-interested) to enable the spread of democracy and to avoid the terrible costs of disorder. In his essay "History and Hyperpower," Eliot A. Cohen wrote, "In the old days the great powers—for reasons of pride, greed, and sheer competitiveness—desired colonies. In the twenty-first century, in contrast, the projection of power into another country results not from the lure of profit or ambition but from the fear of chaos." Cohen went on to identify U.S. hegemony as the only possible form of global order in the years ahead, and proposed that the only uncertainty is how well this is exercised: "The real alternatives, then, are U.S. hegemony exercised prudently or foolishly, consistently or fecklessly, safely or dangerously." Perhaps he will be proved right, but it may not be safe to assume that the rest of the world will gladly accept this global order for long.

Other nations are actively anticipating and planning for a future in which they can provide countervailing weight and authority in the world, enabling a return to a global order based upon balance of power or through the strengthening of multilateral institutions of governance. China in particular is systematically working to establish a leadership role in Asia and elsewhere in the world that will accelerate its emergence as a balancing power for the future. Meanwhile, innovations and experiments in multilateralism are also underway. Naturally, the United Nations and its champions continue to argue for more power being vested in global institutions and treaties—and we should expect to see continued efforts in that direction.

Perhaps even more interesting are the experiments in multilateralism currently lighting up around the globe, many of which are organized around either issues or regions. For example, there appears to be increasing alignment and support behind achieving the United Nations' Millennium Development Goals, which encourage all countries to work together to solve target issues, such as poverty eradication. And there are promising signs that multiple actors and agents are learning to collaborate to address overwhelming and devastating problems, as they did in response to the tsunami at the close of 2004.

But the most mature, interesting, and innovative approach to new governance is the ambitious—and frequently fraught—experiment of the European Union. The EU involves a remarkable new level of multilateralism, with national authority subsumed within a powerful regional governance system. But it is also a new form of balance of power—at the level of voluntary, self-creating, regional blocks rather than nations or empires.

Despite continuing and profound challenges, the European Union is emerging as a more sophisticated example of regional governance than many thought possible even a decade ago. Currently comprising 25 nations with others queuing to come in, it is a highly organized and codified network that allows the mutual interference of one state into another's sovereign affairs. By recognizing a context greater than the nation-state, this cross-boundary system of governance has eroded the notion of national boundaries even while retaining them. It has developed complicated but effective governance principles, elaborate voting mechanisms, and a commitment to helping grow prosperity across the continent. This is an entirely new blend of orderliness and diversity (sometimes called a "flexible geometry"). Its importance is often underestimated by observers in the U.S and even within Europe—not least because its ongoing progress is regularly punctuated by periods of crisis and confusion, the most recent example being a series of popular national votes against a proposed new constitution. Such setbacks should not blind us to the importance of this bold and continuing innovation in governance, and the degree to which its key features might underpin broader global governance in the future. As Jean Monnet, one of the founders of the original European Community after World War II, concluded his memoirs, "The Community itself is only a stage on the way to the organized world of tomorrow."

There are a range of models for organization and action today that will play a role in shaping the future of global governance. Yet none seems poised for total success. The U.S. has found in Iraq stark evidence of the limitations of military might when it encounters deep-rooted resistance. Moreover, the deployment of hard military power appears to be in some danger of undermining its softer political influence. On the other hand, "Old Europe," China, and Russia are very far from being capable, even collectively, of balancing the enormous military and political power of the

U.S. The United Nations and its multilateral offspring appear less confident and less surefooted than ever in today's complicated and turbulent environment. The European Union experiment still proceeds by trial and error, two steps forward and one step back, and has a long way to go before it will provide a new global template. But even as it matures, it will likely set the standard for regional coherence more than global approaches. Latin America, for example, is watching and learning from the EU as it considers and designs its own regional structures.

Local Innovations in Governance

Where else might we look for breakthroughs? To find the answer, we must first slide down the spatial level from global, regional, and national to look at what is happening with local governance. Because it is at the local level that we are seeing a blossoming of new approaches, an outbreak of innovative civic participation that may offer insight into the future of global governance.

- In July 2002, in a large hangar at New York City's Javits Center, 5,000 citizens from all walks of life attended an event organized by the Civic Alliance to Rebuild Downtown New York. Seated at tables of 10, they were asked to consider and comment upon ideas for redeveloping the World Trade Center site. At each table, debates were "sober, thoughtful, and civil," reported Pete Hammill in the *New York Daily News,* "We have a word for what they were doing. The word is democracy…. The energy in the room could not be photographed but it was as real as the tables and chairs and computers. Later in the day, the collective verdicts were announced, expressions of the visions and ideas of the assembly. All reflected a critical intelligence."

- In 2003, the government of British Columbia established the Citizens' Assembly on Electoral Reform, comprising 160 citizens chosen at random to make recommendations for a new voting system for the province. Ten months later, after serious deliberation and review, they agreed by an overwhelming majority to propose a novel, customized system that combines instant runoff voting with proportional representation. The premier of Ontario has since announced his intention to set up a similar assembly for his province—adding to Ontario's "citizens' juries," which are already at work reviewing the optimum means of funding political campaigns.

- In the Chinese town of Zeguo, the young Communist Party secretary recognized that, "No matter how smart we are, we officials have limited information. The easiest way to avoid mistakes is by having more democratic decisions." He decided to poll 257 randomly selected citizens who were well briefed on the positive and negative aspects of various proposed municipal projects; they then voted on which should proceed. Other experiments in local direct democracy are occurring all over China.

- Across Latin America—most notably in Brazil, Guatemala, and Mexico—local governments are adopting innovative approaches to engaging their citizenry in participative forms of democratic governance. In his 2003 paper "Deliberative Approaches to Governance in Latin America," Andrew Selee of the Woodrow Wilson Center observed that these experiments are being conducted by "political parties of widely different ideological stripes," and are often motivated by "the need to shore up the legitimacy of governments before an increasingly mobilized and skeptical citizenry." According to Selee, there are some clear patterns to be discerned across these efforts: they involve continued and ongoing participation in civic and political processes rather than one-off voting at elections; they enable citizens to engage in collective dialogue and even decision-making on policy and resource allocation issues; and they change the old "top-down" communication and power dynamics between elected bodies and society.

Examples like these are almost endless, and together they point to something interesting—we are clearly witnessing an explosion of innovations in democratic participation at the local level around the world. This form of participation is sometimes referred to as "deliberative democracy" because it typically involves deeper and more sustained deliberation among representative citizens than traditional voting enables. This phenomenon will no doubt continue to grow, spread, and change the way we think about democratic government. But can this type of innovation and participation scale to more actively engage civic society in global governance?

Evidence suggests that this is already happening—and with potentially profound implications for the emergent systems of global governance. In their 2000 book, *Critical Choices: The United Nations, Networks, and the Future of Global Governance*, Wolfgang H. Reinicke and Francis Deng argue that "creative new arrangements are needed urgently to allow governments, other organizations both public and private, and individuals around the world to work together to address pressing global problems—from weapons control, to the lack of adequate global labour standards, to climate change—as they arise." They go on to suggest that a valuable new arrangement can be found in global public policy (GPP) networks. The best known and most referenced example of a GPP network is the International Campaign to Ban Landmines, which continues to make strides in its attempts to garner universal international support for its 1997 Mine Ban Treaty. So far 152 states have joined the treaty; China, Russia, and the U.S. are notably absent as signatories.

Most GPP networks share certain characteristics. They often cross national boundaries and are typically "trisectoral"—they connect people and organizations from government, business, and civic society. They make extensive and creative use of information technology. And they are effective because they bring together and mobilize the resources of diverse and often oppositional groups and stakeholders to address problems no single actor can resolve alone.

Taking the view that traditional arrangements cannot address the growing list of world problems, the World Bank's Jean-François Rischard advocates a much more deliberate, formalized, and systematic use of networks. In his book, *High Noon: 20 Global Problems, 20 Years to Solve Them*, he proposes creating a series of dedicated "global issues networks," or GINs, made up of government experts, members of international civil agencies, and delegates from the business community and facilitated by a global multilateral institution, such as the UN or the World Bank. Over a period of several years, these GINs would work to develop a "rough consensus" regarding their particular issue (peacekeeping, conflict prevention, combating terrorism) and then consult with thousands of interested parties globally, through electronic meetings, to arrive at the norms, procedures, and rules relevant to governance of that issue. The results would apply to all actors globally. The GINs would then assume the role of monitors, assuring transparency around any violations of the agreed-upon rules and ensuring compliance.

Whether such formal arrangements are ever put in place, Rischard highlights certain core ideas that are very likely to manifest in the future: empowered networks that include nongovernmental actors; the use of electronic forums to reach out to many thousands of people globally; the gradual evolution, by stakeholders, of new, shared standards; and the use of connective and transparent technologies to encourage changes in the behavior of important contributors to complex problems.

A Rising "Second Superpower"

But while organized multi-actor networks are undoubtedly significant, they should not distract us from the emergence of an apparently rather *disorganized* phenomenon—a connected, active, global citizenry that is able to discover, articulate, and perhaps even increasingly enforce its will. In the dynamism of mid-eighteenth century Europe, Adam Smith iden-tified a new pattern of chaotic but productive commercial activity in which everyone seemed to be connected through complex, humming webs of transaction. Individuals interacted with one another and with institutions to combine labor, coordinate financial exchanges, and barter—all in the pursuit of creating value and producing wealth. His insight was the foundation for the new social science of economics, and it changed our understanding of the production of wealth as the achieve-ment of a nation's entire population.

Smith captured well the shift in his era toward the collective, self-organizing creation of value. Today, a similar and equally profound shift may be underway with respect to the global collective creation of *values*—a shift that will transform our sociopolitical spheres just as the rise of self-organizing commerce and trade transformed the economic.

Martin Albrow provided us with a clear line of sight on what was to come when he observed the following in 1996 in his book *The Global Age*: "The decline of the nation-state leaves intact its greatest achieve-ment, the civic education of its populations, which have become not just the human resources of consumer capitalism but also the citizens of the world state. The decline of interest in national politics is paralleled by the rise of involvement in movements that seek to mobilize opinion on a worldwide basis on issues that nation-states have regarded as marginal to their own agendas."

The worldwide civic movement has become more vibrant and coher-ent. It is empowered by a potent mixture of global transparency, turmoil, turbulence, and the essential human impulses to connect, transcend boundaries, and make a difference. Enabled by email, texting, blogs, and instant messaging, many millions of people are connecting and commu-nicating across time and space, yet with a mass intimacy that is swiftly evolving shared consciousness, insight, conviction, and passion. In the words of Harvard Law School's James Moore, we may be witnessing the birth of a "second superpower...a new form of international player, constituted by the 'will of the people' in a global social movement...made up of millions of people concerned with a broad agenda...a surprisingly agile and muscular body of citizen activists who identify their interests with world society as a whole—and who recognize that at a fundamental level we are all one."

This "second superpower" is already finding its voice (as witnessed by the coordinated global demonstrations against the launching of the war in Iraq). But will an increasingly connected global citizenry also find the *power* to influence the world in the future—and will the forces that enable it drive a healthy diversity of political perspectives and beliefs? The answers may already be unfolding. This global citizenry is already providing a strong and lively check on the power of the media and formal governing institutions, ensuring that information flow is less centralized and "one way." In some cases this leads to stories that the mainstream media only runs when outside pressure (often in the form of an alert blogging community) forces it to do so. For example, when U.S. Senator Trent Lott made some rather controversial comments during his colleague Strom Thurmond's one-hundredth birthday party, the incident was ignored by the national media until bloggers elevated the story—which, of course, led to Lott's resignation as Senate majority leader. In March 2005, the White House even admitted a blogger to its press briefings for the first time.

In other cases, this new force makes itself felt as a corrective to major media stories. The most important feature of the furor surrounding Dan Rather's CBS report on George Bush's National Guard service, which turned out to be based on forged documents that had not been properly scrutinized, had little to do with the story itself but rather the real-time, blog-provoked challenge to the documents that instantly undermined the established media giant's story. Unlike the Trent Lott case, this incident was a powerful example of a correction by a mainly conservative community.

A new, collective, co-creative, sense-making medium is clearly emerging, one that is diverse in its perspectives, ubiquitous in its scope, and energetic in its scrutiny and its communication. From consciousness and dialogue springs action and change. As we are already seeing, the global citizenry will play a profound, if as yet uncertain, role in the emergent systems of global governance. In addition to nations, regions, global institutions, corporations, and NGOs (all, in their way, top-down, hierarchical, and more or less centralized), a new bottom-up, distributed, multiheaded, multidimensional, and hard-to-fathom player is entering the game. Watch this space.

Chapter 10

Innovation

We are accustomed to looking to the West and the rest of the developed world for innovations and breakthroughs—after all, developed nations have been responsible for nearly all major innovations in the last century, achieving huge supremacy even over the Soviet Union from the 1960s onward. We also expect these innovations to be substantiated—if not initiated—by significant corporations or institutions. Certainly, most will continue to follow this pattern in the coming decade. But we should also be prepared to witness, as well as celebrate and promote, important innovations from two rather different sources: people working their passion, or entrepreneurial spirits with the energy, creativity, and effectiveness to generate new and potentially transformative products, services, and approaches; and places finding their power, or those parts of the world that are ready to "come of age" as creators, to be exporters as well as importers of breakthroughs. We should look particularly for innovations from these unexpected sources in three critical areas: addressing the unmet needs of the 4 billion people still ill-served by the global economy, creating more sustainable solutions, and improving approaches and technologies for education and learning.

Innovating for "The Base of the Pyramid"

The renowned Indian business professor C. K. Prahalad has long urged Western corporations to take seriously what he calls, in the title of his latest book, *The Fortune at the Bottom of the Pyramid*. His thesis (explored briefly in Chapter 7, "Prosperity and Decline") is a compelling one. Part of his case derives from Abraham Maslow's analysis of the human hierarchy of needs: as we satisfy our basic needs for food, shelter, and security, we also look to satisfy the higher-order needs for fulfillment and self-actualization. In the developed global economies, corporate competition is fierce and focused on the innovation needed to find ever more ingenious ways to meet and extend those higher-order needs. This is the world of cheaper, better, faster—the world of increased functionality, regular upgrades, and the design of products we never even knew we needed until they came into existence. It is a cutthroat marketplace, but a highly profitable one; after all, there is a fortune at the top of the pyramid.

But there is also a market for the satisfaction of unmet needs at a more basic level. The profit margin may be slimmer, but the numbers are potentially huge: 4 billion people around the world waiting to have their needs at the lower end of Maslow's hierarchy met by a market that so far has largely ignored them. In Chapter 7, I offered an example of a major corporation seizing this opportunity: Whirlpool now offers a basic, cheap washing machine that was first manufactured for Brazil and is now destined for other developing markets. In his book, Prahalad shares a number of similarly compelling innovations—driven by local businesses and entrepreneurs as well as global corporations. Yet it remains to be seen to what extent the latter will open up to such opportunity. Many may find it difficult to focus on the kinds of innovation needed to survive and prosper at the top of the pyramid while at the same time developing the models and practices needed to make an impact at the base. Instead, we might see more evidence of passionate entrepreneurs and local businesses more fully engaging with Prahalad's vision of "eradicating poverty through profits."

This is one reason why we should start to look beyond the developed markets for the capacity to create value in new and more appropriate ways for local conditions. Another is the strong motivation for countries growing their economies for the first time to learn from the mistakes that others have made in their development. This ability to learn and to leapfrog offers a distinct advantage for those not already locked into specific markets, production processes, and business models. The sheer weight of numbers in the rapidly growing economies of China, India, and elsewhere, and the extraordinary density of urban population in mega-cities, also provide hothouse pressure for innovation.

People Working Their Passion: Meet Ralf Hotchkiss

The Whirlwind Wheelchair program is the brainchild of Ralf Hotchkiss, an engineer at San Francisco State University and a recipient of numerous accolades, including the Kilby International Award for innovation. Ralf was injured in a high-school motorcycle accident and has been in a wheelchair ever since, but that did not reduce his passion for high-performance engineering: he quickly became a connoisseur of high-end, high-tech wheelchair design. When his wheelchair was damaged during a trip to Nicaragua, a group of disabled local teenagers patched it up for him in the way they were used to repairing their own wheelchair, damaged time and again on the uneven local terrain. They had to be resourceful, because four of them shared one chair.

There are up to 20 million people in developing countries who need wheelchairs, but only about 1 percent own or have access to one. The chairs created in the developed world and "passed down" to developing countries are often unsuited to rougher terrains. Hotchkiss tells of the common sight he encounters on his travels of piles of wheelchairs rusting outside local hospitals—old models donated by Western countries but next to useless on the potholed sidewalks of the average African village or Central American township. But Ralf had seen in these Nicaraguan teenagers the engineering skills and capacities to maintain an appropriate machine—if they could only get their hands on one.

So he proceeded to work with his new friends to design a wheelchair that they could build and maintain themselves, using local materials and local tools (for example, bending the rim round a suitable tree trunk provided a pretty good wheel round). The result was a high-performance chair that costs a fraction of the price of its industrialized equivalent, can be built with little training and no special materials, and can be repaired by the local blacksmith. Hotchkiss rides one himself, and he is a demanding consumer. Whirlwind wheelchairs have been introduced in more than 45 countries, and chair repair workshops run by locals trained by Hotchkiss are now operating in some two dozen countries, including Zimbabwe, Sri Lanka, Uganda, Vietnam, Cambodia, Honduras, and Guatemala.

PLACES FINDING THEIR POWER

Developed nations, especially in the West and Japan, have enjoyed a stranglehold on scientific and technological innovation for so long that they are almost wholly unprepared for meaningful new developments to emerge from elsewhere. But "elsewhere" sees it differently. Many developing nations and regions are investing significantly in front-edge scientific endeavors, developing new capabilities and platforms that could enable them to play a much greater innovative role over the coming decade. Some are in the early stages of developing their capacity, while others appear ripe to find their power in the near future. The former is epitomized by Africa, the latter by India. Both are worth some reflection.

Since the mid-1990s in Africa, a powerful idea has been slowly taking root and spreading: the vision of an "African Renaissance." In the spirit of this goal of rebirth and renewal, the Organization of Africa Unity (OAU) mandated the heads of state of Algeria, Egypt, Nigeria, Senegal, and South Africa to create an integrated development framework for the continent. This resulted in the New Partnership for Africa's Development (NEPAD) in 2001, which has recently developed a coherent plan for boosting science and technology across Africa. An important component of NEPAD is the establishment of four new "centres of excellence" in Africa, the first of which has already opened: a new biosciences facility for eastern and central Africa, located in Nairobi and aimed at generating new solutions to African food-related problems, developing nutrient-rich plants resistant to stress and disease, and creating vaccines for livestock diseases.

Of course, Africa's potential emergence as a player in leading-edge science is not purely driven by public agencies; an increasingly vibrant commercial sector at the forefront of science and technology is also finding its feet. For example, South Africa's Electric Genetics Corporation is a pioneer in the field of computational genomics; since 1997, it has been providing the pharmaceutical, biotechnology, and genetics markets with genomic data-analysis systems and validated drug targets. South Africa has also been active in developing close collaborative scientific links with other developing countries, especially India and Brazil, many of them predicated on open access databases and open source software. Such collaboration heralds the prospect of increasingly open (and hence self-reinforcing) alliances in scientific efforts in the developing world.

India, with a longer history of investment and commitment to scientific leadership, has also made significant strides in recent years. This is partly a result of progressive government policies that, since the late 1990s, have placed strategic emphasis on several key technology areas, including biotechnology, vaccines, advanced batteries, and space and defense. The government's primary focus has been on tackling real human needs and improving lives. Nowhere is this more obvious than in ISRO—the Indian Space Research Organization, which describes itself as a "space program for the people" and has for the most part eschewed large prestige projects for practical undertakings. For example, India deploys its satellite network to link patients in remote rural areas to doctors in hospitals and research centers. Recently, as part of the peace-making process, this program has started to connect medical centers in Pakistan to those in India.

The private sector is also playing a role in ensuring India's place as a future technology leader. For example, from 1990 to 2002, R&D-to-sales ratios in many leading pharmaceutical and agrochemical companies tripled from less than 2 percent to almost 6 percent. In the field of solar energy, more than 20 Indian manufacturers have a combined production capacity of around 20 MW a year—already the fourth largest national capacity in the world—and almost a million commercial photovoltaic systems have been designed and installed throughout the country.

Most importantly, though, India is already proving itself able to create genuinely innovative products and services appropriate for and accessible to people living on relatively low income. C.K. Prahalad provides us with a number of examples in his book, one of the most striking of which is Jaipur Foot, "the world's largest prosthesis provider, with more than 16,000 prosthetic fittings each year." For those requiring a lower limb prosthetic in India, the functional requirements are much greater than in the West. For example, the user has to be able to walk on uneven ground, often barefoot, squat on the floor, and sit cross-legged, and typically requires the fitting to be completed in one day rather than multiple days because of the expenses associated with travel and work absence. Jaipur Foot has invented a new lower limb that addresses these needs, and it performs equal to or better than those available in the United States. It is now on the market in 16 countries. Almost unbelievably, it costs just $30—orders of magnitude less than the average cost of the lower-performing versions available in the U.S.

The capacity of Indian entrepreneurs and companies to innovate new products is migrating into areas of high technology previously dominated by the developed world, including automobiles and computers. The Indica, a compact hatchback developed by India's largest automobile manufacturer, Tata Motors Limited, and retailing for about $7,500, is a hit in India, increasingly popular in Europe, and poised to enter the Chinese and South Korean markets. No doubt Tata's new $2,200 car, mentioned earlier in this book, will meet with similar global success. Among its many cost-saving innovations, the car will be distributed to franchisees across India in kit form, saving shipping costs while generating local employment opportunities in assembling the cars.

An even more intriguing example of the imminent wave of Indian innovation can be found in the Amida Simputer, an astounding product developed by four scientists from the Indian Institute of Science in Bangalore who formed a new company called PicoPeta Computers. Their original idea was to develop an appropriate and extremely inexpensive handheld computer for mass use in India, called the Simputer. By 2001, the idea had attracted considerable positive attention, but it soon became bogged down in funding problems, false starts, and delays. Perhaps that was what enabled its developers to arrive at such radical and innovative upgrades. The Amida, launched in 2004, is not just a simple and inexpensive computer, but a technological *tour de force*. PicoPeta Computers describes it as "the most versatile, most mobile personal computer in the world." The handheld device runs on Linux and features a fully functional web browser and built-in applications designed for people with limited education. It recognizes multiple languages and dialects and even allows you to scribble on the screen and email your handwritten messages. It is "the world's first and only computer that responds to your gestures"; flick your wrist, and the page turns. The Amida is a truly unique and visionary product. Even before it has achieved its economies of volume, it is retailing at about $300. The device demonstrates that innovations from within the developing world might soon enough not simply undercut Western technology but transcend it, creating new benchmarks for the entire world.

Sustainable Solutions

As emphasized in Chapter 8, "People and Planet," the concept of sustainability will be central to all parts of the world in the years ahead. Currently, it is primarily perceived as a defensive and reactive notion—limiting damage, preventing loss, and slowing deterioration. However, as the imperative takes hold, it is likely to assume a more proactive and energetic character, concentrated on the opportunities for growing and spreading prosperity globally while working in true harmony and partnership with nature.

And yet it is clear that as the rest of the world makes its inexorable progress toward Western standards of living, we will require powerful innovations that minimize the environmental consequences of this historic march. Sustainability will become even more politically charged and sensitive as the developing world consumes and requires more and more energy—much of it in the form of coal, often the cheapest and most available source of energy and yet one that comes with a high environmental cost. Nowhere is this clearer than in China, where environmental problems are growing worse the more (and the faster) it develops.

Yet there are reasons to be optimistic that the emergent economies might manage to develop themselves along a more sustainable path and gain real advantages by doing so. With less installed base and fewer legacy systems, they can design more efficient and sustainable processes and products. They will also have clearer evidence of the potential consequences of environmental carelessness and can piggyback on existing "green" technologies, materials, and processes. They may be able to adopt patterns of recycling and reuse that have eluded the West. Many of the economies now taking off have a long history and culture of mending, tending, and making do; they are not "throw away" cultures. They have a chance to design and build more environmentally benign buildings—an area of considerable attention today, especially in China. However, the most essential area for innovation that will enable a sustainable future for the planet is in the field of energy. Here again, people working their passion and places finding their power will have an increasingly important role to play.

People Working Their Passion: Meet Brian Sager

Brian Sager is a renaissance man: scientist, entrepreneur, and composer of new classical music. His energy and enthusiasm are remarkable and infectious. Spend an hour with him and you will find your head swirling with ideas, concepts, and possibilities. But he is focused and clear in his intention. As cofounder and president of the startup company Nanosolar, he is determined to help lead the way in deploying nanotechnology in one of its most promising areas of potential application—the transformation of solar energy.

Nanosolar is the perfect example of innovation driven by a combination of science, business, and passion. Sager was convinced that if solar cells could be manufactured at a much lower cost, they could become commercially competitive with other sources, not just in the U.S., but in the developing world as well. Cheap, clean energy not only represents a huge market opportunity, but it also has the potential to transform lives without damaging the environment.

After visiting scientists around the world, Sager and his team developed and patented a new technology that produces ultra-thin, light-weight, low-cost solar cells by depositing a semiconductor "paint" onto a thin metallic foil using a high-speed, roll-to-roll manufacturing process, much like how a newspaper is produced. At a time when the world requires nothing less than a genuine revolution in the critical field of clean and ubiquitous energy, Sager believes Nanosolar has the technology to seriously contribute to making it happen—very soon, and at a price the whole world can afford. For him, this business satisfies his three personal objectives: to have a positive, sustained impact on the world; to stretch himself and his colleagues as far as possible as scientists, innovators, and entrepreneurs; and to leave a meaningful legacy for his family.

PLACES FINDING THEIR POWER

All over the developed world, people are experimenting with, creating, and improving ways of producing energy without producing more carbon dioxide and other pollutants. Strides are being made in many fields. Solar power, especially with nanotechnology innovations, is clearly one of the most promising areas; it will not be too long before we see some form of nanosolar cells being embedded in building and roofing materials. Wave and tide power also appear to hold very substantial promise in many coastal areas. As mentioned in Chapter 8, Scotland is emerging as a leader in this technology. South Korea has also launched an ambitious tidal power project expected to generate in excess of 250 megawatts. Meanwhile, the largest tidal power project in the world, expected to generate 300 megawatts, is underway at the mouth of the Yalu River in China. Wind power also continues to see innovation and improvements in efficiency. Microturbines using bio-gas (converted from manure by new anaerobic digesters) hold real potential, especially for rural areas, and are being piloted in India. And, at the very modest levels required to recharge batteries for a host of portable devices, even children's playsets—see-saws and swings—are being designed to capture energy from playing youngsters.

While the leading edges of these technologies are coming from the developed economies, taken together they provide a real opportunity for developing countries to leapfrog over the West's dependence on expensive, centralized electric grids. Just as wireless telecommunications and cellphones have allowed many parts of the world to achieve widespread telephone connectivity without expensive wired copper networks, so a variety of new energy technologies can be creatively combined in developing countries to achieve distributed, sustainable micropower solutions to meet growing energy demands. Again, solar seems to have the most potential in this respect. Therefore, it is especially interesting to note not just the emergence of increased investment and research in solar technologies within India and China (whose technologies today are less efficient than those of Europe and the U.S., but significantly cheaper), but the establishment of solar technology links and collaborations within the developing world. China, for example, has trained hundreds of technicians from Africa and Latin America in programs for solar power heating and irrigation and has committed to training 10,000 more African technicians by 2010.

Whether improvements in these alternative energy technologies (and corresponding improvements in efficiency of energy consumption) will be fast enough and radical enough remains to be seen. In the meantime, China is placing a huge bet on nuclear power. While the prevailing mood in the West has swung away from the promise of nuclear energy over the last few decades, there is currently a contentious and sometimes fierce debate about its potential revival. Even James Lovelock, the widely revered creator of the Gaia hypothesis, has come out strongly in favor of nuclear power, declaring in May 2004 that "civilization is in imminent danger and has to use nuclear—the one safe, available energy source—now or suffer the pain soon to be inflicted by our outraged planet." Many environmentalists, as well as some celebrated visionaries on energy solutions, such as Amory Lovins, strongly dispute the validity of the nuclear solution—the debate is likely to heat up further as the nuclear option continues to receive fresh scrutiny.

Meanwhile, China is taking the plunge. Not only has it announced plans for 30 new reactors over the next 15 years, but it is considering recommendations to build more than 200 plants by 2050, which would together generate 350 gigawatts of electricity. And as Spencer Reiss pointed out in a 2004 *Wired* article, China is taking an extremely innovative approach to nuclear power: "China's leaders are pursuing two strategies. They're turning to established nuke plant makers...but they're also pursuing a second, more audacious course. Physicists and engineers at Beijing's Tsinghua University have made the first great leap forward in a quarter century, building a new nuclear power facility that promises to be a better way to harness the atom: a pebble-bed reactor. A reactor small enough to be assembled from mass-produced parts and cheap enough for customers without billion-dollar bank accounts. A reactor whose safety is a matter of physics, not operator skill or reinforced concrete. And, for a bona fide fairytale ending, the pot of gold at the end of the rainbow is labeled 'hydrogen.'"

The most potentially transformative aspect of this innovation is the prospect that these new high-temperature reactors can not only create abundant electricity but, by enabling thermochemical water splitting, also serve to produce huge quantities of hydrogen. That, in turn, could provide the fuel for the fuel cells that could ultimately power China's inevitable hundreds of millions of cars—without destroying its own, and the entire planet's, environment. There is a very significant gap between here and there, and there are serious questions to be answered about the wisdom and efficacy of the nuclear path. However, China might be on the brink of an innovative leap that could shape the story of energy in the twenty-first century.

Education and Learning

It is not new to argue that education and learning are the critical success factors in today's changing world. It is often argued that competitive nations operating in a global economy are essentially engaged in learning races—the society that can most rapidly adapt its skills, knowledge, and capacities to a changing world wins. It is perhaps no surprise, then, that Britain's prime minister, Tony Blair, described his top three priorities in government as "education, education, and education."

As the importance of education and learning increases, so does the need for significant innovation in the substance and pedagogy of our educational systems. We are not short of research evidence on the ways in which our existing systems need to adapt. A recent OECD study, for example, noted that our understanding of what learning is, how the brain functions, and the multidimensional nature of "intelligence" is unsurpassed in human history. This new knowledge suggests the need for rapid advances in our educational practice—"discontinuous change...revolution, not reform," the OECD concluded.

We also know that simply learning facts is no longer a sufficient educational objective. Information is readily accessible in searchable databases, making the rote learning of facts increasingly obsolete. Also, the specialist knowledge that we acquire has a time-limited applicability outside of the academy. For example, recent estimates by engineers found that the technical knowledge of engineering graduates is very close to obsolete immediately upon graduation from college. Hence, the professional engineering licenses that used to grant lifetime approval to practice are now becoming time-limited in many states, renewable only on proof that applicants have spent time in "continuous professional development" to update their skills. In other words, we need to move toward a model of "lifelong learning" for everyone. An important part of the shift is to move from an educator-centric model to a learner-centric model.

Moreover, living and working in a knowledge-intensive society and economy requires a broad base of abilities, including solid interpersonal and communication skills, the ability to work well in teams, the capacity to function in ambiguous situations, problem-solving skills, creativity, flexibility, and self-motivation. From Howard Gardner, we have learned about the range of critical human intelligences beyond the linguistic and logical/mathematical intelligences that schools teach and test. From

Daniel Goleman we have learned the important of "EQ"—emotional quotient—as a different but equally important measure of intelligence as IQ (which, incidentally, was originally developed in France as a test to help educators prepare farm workers for factory work).

Yet for all of our knowledge and awareness of the need for innovation, the education systems of the developed world appear stubbornly resistant to change. It would be inaccurate and unfair to suggest that there has been no innovation in education in recent years. There are hundreds of thousands of dedicated, creative teachers across the globe that are experimenting with and improving their approaches every day. Many new initiatives have been launched to discover and disseminate better ways of educating children and creating the enabling conditions for all of us to become "lifelong learners." Promising inroads have been made in the application of new technologies to accelerate learning. Still, progress has been slower than one might expect in such a high-priority area. Our educational institutions are often prisoners of their own legacies, trapped in long-established procedures and norms; civic expectations of accreditation and grading constrain experimentation; and legitimate performance and accountability concerns have led to an extreme focus on metrics, measurement, and testing that unintentionally freezes innovation and reduces teaching time.

However, one developed country has proved itself willing to embark in a new direction in education: not surprisingly, it is Singapore, which has a long record of looking eagerly forward rather than nervously backward. In 1997, Prime Minister Goh Chok Tong launched the "Thinking Schools, Learning Nation" program—a brave and concerted attempt to move beyond what the Education Ministry describes as the "efficiency-driven phase" of development in the education system to an "ability-driven" one. Efficiency in education has produced great gains in Singapore, as it has in the U.S., Europe, and elsewhere. But it has also rewarded the pursuit of the average.

With characteristic determination, the Singapore government has introduced a number of changes to stimulate a reorientation of the system. It has reduced curriculum content by 30 percent to free up time for thinking, reflection, and cross-disciplinary and self-directed learning and to signal to teachers that something different is expected of them. Central inspection has been replaced by a system of self-assessment based on the European Business Excellence Model, with a 50 percent focus on results and the rest on processes—teaching methods, pupil empowerment, and leadership. There is no big stick and plenty of mutual support: every school has its assessment validated by the Ministry within five years, but only when the school thinks it is ready.

People Working Their Passion: Meet Nelly Ribot

As a teacher of English as a second language in Argentina, Nelly Ribot resonated with the idea of "multiple intelligences" developed by Howard Gardner, Daniel Goleman, and others. She applied this concept in a highly integrated and experiential unit on "Helpers" (community workers like police, firefighters, and doctors) that she created for her 6-year-old students, many of whom were also struggling with their own native language. The lesson began with field trips, where the eager children met and saw these men and women in action. They captured their experiences in "My Little Journal," creating flash cards with words and pictures, and "My City in a Box," building the structures they visited out of little boxes and brightly colored paper. Through "The Helpers Band" they not only learned about and tried different instruments, but also made up and sang songs about the helpers. In "How Many Helpers?" they used math to count and sort the different types of workers they'd encountered. For the "I Am a Helper" activity, they wrote dialogues in English and acted out being helpers and even role-played motor activities (like firefighters racing down a street) in P.E. For "The Helpers Mural," the children drew human bodies and painted on detailed uniforms, excitedly discussing their art work in English. The last activity "Look at Yourself in the Mirror," was held in Spanish and helped the students identify the values of the helpers—like courage and helpfulness—as well as the values that they held and hoped to achieve.

Professor Ribot's simple innovation around multiple intelligences sparked tremendous learning and enthusiasm on the part of her students and reflects the passionate creativity of countless teachers around the world, forging new ways to tackle the learning imperatives of the future. "Winds of change are also blowing here in Argentina," she observed. "Awareness of the fact that education needs to be transformed is increasing. It is my opinion that MI is a perfectly acceptable addition to our school curriculum and an invaluable tool for educational transformation. I hope that many other teachers will want to face the challenge. It's absolutely worth the effort."

Source: Nelly Ribot, "My Experience Using Multiple Intelligences," New Horizons for Learning website (http://www.newhorizons.org/trans/international/ribot.htm).

All of this is rather counterintuitive in a culture that has pursued the goals of efficiency-driven education for 20 years. But teachers and officials together looked at future trends, gave themselves the chance to "dream" (their word), and are no longer satisfied with what has gone before. And the changes are beginning to deliver. After a recent inspection visit, the International Academic Advisory Panel praised Singapore for the transition it has made, for the absence of the strong and stifling bureaucracy they had expected to find, and for the confident, outward-looking, and world-ready students who so impressed the visitors. Robert Brown, provost of MIT, said: "The changes in the Singapore higher education system in the last five or six years have been aimed at increasing the breadth of the students. Those are really good changes and necessary, in a world where you need to create very highly educated but very flexible human beings."

While Singapore has managed to find an educational path to the future by walking it, few other developed nations appear poised to follow. Again, the truly important innovations in education and learning may come from people working their passion and places finding their power.

PLACES FINDING THEIR POWER

Today, the developing world seems primed for a "Cambrian explosion" of innovation and experimentation in the field of education and learning. The main factor driving this is an enthusiastic demand for education among people who can see the promise of a different, more prosperous future for those with the knowledge and skills to participate in it. Motivated learners, as any teacher can affirm, eventually create fertile conditions for learning—even in otherwise challenging circumstances. Consider Africa, where demand for basic education has exploded in recent years. In Uganda, a new government came to power in 1996 and promptly announced that education would be provided free to four children from each family. The following year, school enrollment almost doubled. Across Africa, several countries have abolished fees for education over the last decade, with similar results: huge increases in the numbers of children, most of them desperately poor, arriving at overcrowded, even overwhelmed, schools. Teachers often stand in front of classes of 100 or 200 students. Not surprisingly, grades have fallen, and many students fail each year and have to repeat. But the point is that so many of them do. Even in these circumstances, many millions of children who last year or the year before were working to help support their families are today walking miles to participate and to learn, while parents willingly accept the sacrifice of their children's labor in return for their better futures. If necessity is indeed the mother of invention, it is inevitable that these circumstances will provoke meaningful innovations in approaches to education and learning in Africa.

Perhaps there is a lesson to be learned from India, where a new satellite exclusively dedicated to education and teaching has been launched. Dubbed the "Edustat," the satellite aims to tackle the problems of illiteracy and a shortage of trained teachers by using powerful spot-beam technology that can be captured by small satellite dishes to transmit educational programs to 1,000 rural schools (soon to be extended to 10,000 schools). The technology even enables interaction between these distant schools, with, for example, a teacher at one location able to answer a question for a student at another; each is connected to a hub that is, in turn, connected directly to the satellite. Eventually, the Indian Space Research Organization believes that a fleet of similar satellites could be launched to deliver an equivalent service across the entire country, assuming other actors, including industry, can supply the ground-based equipment.

A very different innovation in India demonstrates the power of education that is explicitly directed at fostering stronger communities and improving quality of life for learners and their neighbors. Barefoot College, launched in 1972 in the village of Tilonia, Rajasthan, was founded on the premise that solutions to rural problems lie within the community, not with external "experts." Created by a voluntary agency called the Social Work Research Centre, the college describes itself as "a place of learning and unlearning. It's a place where the teacher is the learner and the learner is the teacher. It's a place where no degrees and certificates are given because in development there are no experts—only resource persons. It's a place where people are encouraged to make mistakes so that they can learn humility, curiosity, the courage to take risks, to innovate, to improvise, and to constantly experiment. It's a place where all are treated as equals and there is no hierarchy."

Consistent with this "learning by doing" ethos, the 80,000-square-foot campus was built entirely by local people, who also installed and maintain its solar energy system. The school also manufactures solar lanterns that are now in use at 200 night schools throughout the country. It has trained many rural youths as "barefoot solar mechanics" without help from urban professionals, created practical solutions to local problems related to drinking water and healthcare, and catalyzed and enabled other, similar Barefoot Colleges in locations across India, all of which share its powerful philosophy, innovative learning approaches, and commitment to having a deep and positive impact on local communities. There is something profound about the resonance between this radical, self-organizing, bottom-up initiative and the findings of the UNESCO Task Force on Education in the Twenty-first Century, which summed up the future curriculum as follows: "learning to know, learning to do, learning to be, and learning to live together."

India is also home to innovations in learning and education that run along more traditional lines, and has paid particular attention to spreading the benefits of the digital age. In 2002, the state government of Kerala launched one of the most ambitious "e-literacy" initiatives in the developing world. The goal of the Akshaya Project is to teach basic computer and Internet literacy to at least one member of each of the state's 6.5 million families in an effort to "propel Kerala as India's foremost knowledge society." Just two years later, on November 12, 2004, one of Kerala's 14 districts, Malappuram, announced that it had become the first district in India to become fully e-literate, with over 600,000 people trained in the basics. Sixty percent of those trained were women, and the 15-hour courses cost about $3 per student.

But perhaps the greatest technology-enabled learning revolution could unfold in China, driven by the needs of its globalizing industries. My colleague Jonathon Levy, a learning strategist at Monitor Group, has observed that in the critically important arena of business education and training we are in the middle of a transition from faculty-centered teaching to "more robust, just-in-time personalized support," much of which is available online. But in the developed countries, trapped by our legacies and our faculty-oriented mindsets, we are still muddling toward a new model for corporate learning. On the other hand, as Levy observes: "China knows it must rapidly retool for the knowledge economy of the twenty-first century. Its people are aware that they face a dangerous lack of skills and knowledge at a critical time of increased expansion and global competition." It is already making investments and conducting experiments. Having demonstrated its ability to build full-fledged cities from farmland in just a few decades, and having become the manufacturing capital of the world almost from scratch in the same timeframe, could China be home to the next generation of corporate learning systems? It certainly cannot be ruled out, and it could be an important accelerator of the country's rise in the century ahead. How might those of us in the West respond to such developments? Perhaps first by acknowledging the irony of the fact that the constraints in our own learning systems might best be addressed by developing the capacity to learn from others.

If our future is filled with challenge, it is also characterized by remarkable possibility. The innovations that will help us both harness our opportunities and respond to challenges will, happily, come from far more sources (many of them quite surprising) than we might expect. While more distributed and diverse sources of discovery and change will no doubt trigger anxiety, even consternation, especially in the West, these may well prove to be not only beneficial, but also our collective salvation.

What's Next?: Scenarios for the Next Decade

The dominant intellectual strategy that people bring to the
future is denial.
—Peter Schwartz

As we head into this period of powerful turbulence and significant change, there is a high degree of uncertainty as to precisely how the world will evolve. We are already seeing experimental forms of organizations, increasingly fluid and virtual, coexisting with more traditional and top-down models. Important innovations are emerging faster and from a wider variety of sources than ever before. And our current global governance arrangements (piecemeal at best, incoherent at worst) are proving increasingly inadequate to address the complex challenges of our times—let alone turn them into opportunities. We have to figure out how to live together on this planet with all our differences, even as we learn how to cope with the fact that the biosphere itself is changing all around us. We must address inequalities in a world where they are ever more visible and apparent. We must find ways of making energy and water available wherever they are required. We have to resolve the inevitable tensions that will come as new powers continue to grow in strength and together face failing nations, security risks, and the threats from new diseases. Rising to these challenges holds extraordinary promise for a century of achievement and progress that would make the developments of the twentieth century pale in comparison. Failure to do so could lead to dire circumstances for us all.

It is increasingly evident that the status quo cannot deal adequately with these powerful times: we must not only prepare for, but hope for, an imminent era of transformation in global affairs. What shape this will take is unclear. However, we can identify three different models that are credible foundations for a new order rooted in the questions raised here. Each of these models will be in play over the coming decade, and elements of all three will inform our future. However, one will most likely dominate in the coming decade, providing primary shape and substance to the rest of this century—which one prevails is anyone's guess. These three models for what the future might hold are *scenarios*—not predictions. They are alternative, equally plausible, and quite different hypotheses about what might happen. They are designed to stretch our thinking, challenge our assumptions, and help us prepare for multiple possibilities instead of assuming a single future or simply waiting, like Pandolfo Petrucci, to react to whatever the fates might throw our way.

The Critical Uncertainties

Today there are two critical questions (derived from the tipping point challenges of governance and innovation and the underlying changes in organizational models) that can help us frame these alternative scenarios.

The first concerns the types of organizations, patterns of relationships, structures, and interactions that will provide coherence and drive the future: *Will the most effective sources of leadership, innovation, and change be primarily centralized and "top down" or decentralized and "bottom up?"* Will the centralized social, organizational, and governance models, characterized by central plans and blueprints, large hierarchical institutions, and top-down coordination and regulations, endure? Or will the future be driven by more fluid and decentralized alliances, emergent networks, and the bottom-up integration of energy around compelling and widely spread insights and ideas?

As an historical example of the latter, think of the first century of Christianity—a word-of-mouth, bottom-up movement, underpinned by powerful and challenging new ideas and ideals, driven by committed individuals and groups, that slowly but steadily spread and grew, changing the societies it reached. Contrast those early years with the eventual establishment of the Church of Rome, a vast hierarchical, structured, ordered, and extremely centralized institution that also had enormous impact across Europe and much of the world. Today, the differences between the bottom-up and top-down models are exemplified by Falun Gong and the Communist Party in China. The former is a nimble, informal, networked movement based on powerful ideas and shared practices that touch tens of millions; the latter is a powerful and controlling institution whose structures reach into and influence every part of Chinese society.

Which will prove more powerful and have the greater impact in the coming decade? We can be sure that we will witness a great deal of centralized, top-down activity *and* a tremendous amount of experimentation and action across decentralized networks; both forms will be embraced within businesses, governments, and civic society. Moreover, information and communication technologies are significantly enabling both models to succeed and spread.

Yet the sheer scale of the global issues we face may encourage us to adopt more centralized, hierarchical, and top-down solutions as we seek order, coherence, and consistency. There is plenty of evidence to suggest that we are reaching for control in a seemingly chaotic world. In the domain of commerce, for example, we see many industries continue to consolidate as corporations achieve scale and capture new and converging technologies through mergers and acquisitions. We can also see an impulse toward the more rigorous protection of intellectual property rights and the pursuit of closed and proprietary standards in many areas of technology. Even some of the most innovative companies, like Apple, are thriving largely through a top-down strategy of controlling everything from the hardware to the user interface to the web service; the runaway success of the iPod and the iTunes store is a case in point.

In the domain of governance, the strong pull toward centralization and top-down approaches is equally widespread and can be an effective platform for collaboration and progress. In China, rural electrification took off at an astonishing speed after the government inaugurated a massive investment in hydropower. In the U.S., the creation of a structurally integrated, centralized Department of Homeland Security and the appointment of an intelligence "czar" were attempts to streamline and improve the war against terror. The oft-maligned WTO is poised for further expansion, and the prospect of membership—highly attractive to less developed countries—is being used as a political bargaining chip with recalcitrant nations like Iran. Europe is likewise initiating highly centralized political initiatives, ranging from labor to standards and tariffs to the environment—which are all aimed at securing a powerful and integrated economic union. European nations also remain champions of rigid global policy frameworks and protocols, like the Kyoto accords. In civic society, we can observe a trend among nonprofits to adopt more conventional organizational forms, install rigorous planning and evaluation functions, and seek regulatory solutions in their areas of concern.

Simultaneously, there is considerable evidence of a strong impulse toward decentralized, self-organizing networks and bottom-up approaches. Globalization and technological connectivity have created a more effectively networked world that will be enhanced further as wireless networks, mobile telephony, and related developments spread. These are creating the conditions for the global emergence of decentralized, real-time, and aligned movements and ideas. Examples abound. For years, the Search for Extraterrestrial Intelligence (SETI) has been supported by millions of individuals who donate their home computers' downtime. The Internet has enabled remarkable coordination of global protest movements. Cellphones and instant messaging permit the instantaneous spread of ideas and opinions. In 2003, marketers and promoters of the movie *The Hulk* blamed its dismal box office sales on bad word-of-mouth spread by kids instant messaging their friends on opening weekend that the movie was dreadful.

On the other hand, businesses like TiVo take advantage of this open, connected reality by encouraging hackers to modify its product, thereby accelerating development while also conferring a leading-edge credibility that would be hard to acquire through marketing alone. Online gaming is exploding around the world, creating new forms of community and social interaction as well as sizeable virtual economies. Highly effective nongovernmental initiatives like the International Campaign to Ban Landmines have been launched by exploiting the potential of technologies and networks. During the 2004 U.S. presidential election, Internet-based fundraising catalyzed large numbers of new politically active citizens. Proliferating peer-to-peer technologies have forced the music industry to establish draconian control measures that appear doomed to fail. Many commentators anticipate a vital social and economic role for social networks and "smart mobs" that emerge—and disperse—almost instantaneously. The open source movement has demonstrated the remarkable creative and productive power of distributed networks of talent, often motivated not by profit but by the ability to contribute and excel. Never before in human history has there been such powerful potential for a "bottom-up" world to emerge, and it will surely bring many surprises.

Even so, it remains extremely uncertain whether the potential of the bottom-up, decentralized, networked model will prove to be a true source of profound, global transformation, or whether it will produce only incremental change. If the former unfolds, then we are heading into a fascinating and uncharted scenario I refer to as *emergence*—a bottom-up, networked world in which power shifts away from the center to become more broadly distributed than ever before.

On the other hand, if the center holds and our more familiar top-down models prevail, we must pose our second fundamental question: *Will the United States exert more or less influence globally?*

Evidence can be found and arguments made in support of either outcome. There are many reasons to believe that the role of the U.S. in the world will further expand. The U.S. is so influential today that very significant reversals would be required to undermine it. In particular, the U.S. economy has been the world's powerhouse for at least two generations. With 5 percent of the world's population, the U.S. accounts for more than 30 percent of its GDP, and New York City remains the undisputed center of the global financial system. The U.S. is also the center for innovation, accounting for fully 40 percent of the world's expenditure on research and development. It remains a remarkably entrepreneurial nation, with hotspots of new business startups, powered by the strongest venture capital system in the world, clustered around key cities like Boston, Seattle, Austin, and San Francisco. Its market system has a demonstrated tolerance for failure; it even appears willing to allow large corporations to succumb to competition instead of bailing them out, ensuring a churn and dynamism that is the envy of many other countries. U.S. brands are known across the world and enjoy a special prestige in many regions. The U.S. occupies a privileged place in setting the world's standards—technological, regulatory, and infrastructural—that bestows advantage in both the present and the future. It is currently shaping the standards that will underpin the evolution of cyberspace as an economic medium. The U.S. is already a leader in the emerging technologies that seem poised to drive the next bursts of economic growth, including sensors, wireless networks, distributed supercomputing, and biotechnology.

The U.S. has also demonstrated a continuous creativity that has driven both its economy and its ability to adapt. Through technological innovation and commercial imagination, the U.S. has been at the forefront of economic change, spawning the new "creative industries" that are so central to the intangible economy. This has enabled the U.S. to sustain and renew its economic vitality and leadership—but it has also ensured the growth and spread of its cultural impact globally. American film, television, and music have been expanding into new markets for decades, and have quietly but effectively promoted American values, worldviews, and even brands. Moreover, the entertainment industry has been a major and growing part of the "experience economy," and looking forward, the new media opportunities in a world of growing bandwidth seem quite likely to be harnessed by U.S. companies and talent.

The U.S.'s economic and cultural influence is compounded by both its military strength (unassailable for at least a decade) and the political muscle that these other assets inevitably secure. But there is a greater, and quite explicit, aspiration that today animates the second administration of George W. Bush—one that, if fulfilled, could ensure the enduring influence of American models of capitalism and democracy for the remainder of this century and beyond. If the U.S. succeeds in its attempts to deploy (in the words of Secretary of State Condoleezza Rice) "transformational diplomacy" to engender radical change in all those parts of the world that are still struggling to find their way into the future, the American "rules of the game" could prevail globally long after the U.S. has ceased to enjoy its current levels of influence. That is the ambition of American leadership today—and it is the cornerstone of a very plausible future. The U.S.'s economic, cultural, military, and political influence are certainly strong enough, and its models of capitalism and democracy are perhaps attractive enough in some critical parts of the world (for example, Eastern Europe and parts of the Middle East), that a *New American Century* is an entirely credible scenario. Importantly, this is *not* a scenario in which the U.S. enjoys its current extraordinary sway in the world in terms of asymmetrical military might and economic prosperity for another hundred years. That future simply does not exist; rather, this is a plausible story of American political, economic, and social values and models being adopted more or less ubiquitously around the world, allowing the current rules to endure even as others become increasingly adept and successful at playing by them.

Is it possible, though, that the U.S.'s influence and role in the world could actually decline over the coming decade instead, leading to a very different future? I believe that the answer is, emphatically, yes.

Regardless of one's general views on the "war on terror" and the U.S.-led invasion of Iraq, it is evident that mistakes were made in the years immediately following the horror of September 11. Poor follow-through on the capture of Osama bin Laden, dubious claims regarding Iraq's supposed weapons of mass destruction, insensitive diplomacy with critical allies, bungled policies regarding prisoner treatment, appalling management of detention facilities (especially at Abu Ghraib), simplistic and wrong-headed policies regarding the "de-Baathification" of Iraq—there is a rather depressing list of ways in which the U.S. has undermined its own authority and standing in the world. But the important question is how severely and permanently these mistakes have damaged the U.S.'s status. For now, the jury is out. Just as there are strong indicators that the American models of democracy and capitalism are being embraced in more parts of the world, there is also incontrovertible evidence from opinion polls and surveys that attitudes toward the United States are more negative (in many cases significantly so) across the Muslim world and most of Western Europe than they were at the start of this century. There is also some evidence that these more negative perceptions are adversely influencing the global reputation of major American brands.

The economic strength of the U.S. is also uncertain over the coming decade, with consumer debt at record levels, unprecedented budget deficits forecast to grow for years to come, and very significant trade deficits that show no signs of closing. If markets lose faith in the U.S., we could see a major redeployment away from holding American assets, including the dollar—igniting inflation, sending interest rates higher, and further eroding business and consumer confidence. Adding to this fragility, increasing focus upon security considerations could prove to be a drag on the U.S. economy. Direct security costs are clearly set to increase significantly in the U.S. in the decade ahead, and security concerns could also act as a source of real friction in U.S. interaction with the rest of the global economy, slowing clearance of containers and shipments and causing other delays and transactional complexities.

The U.S. may also be suffering some reversals in the global war for talent—an arena in which it has been supremely dominant for decades. Its ability to attract the best, brightest, and most entrepreneurial young people from around the world in science, technology, academia, and the arts has contributed to U.S. economic and cultural dynamism for decades. There are signs that this could now be waning, as visa restrictions and increasing scrutiny make the U.S. less attractive to many high-quality foreign students. Add in the emergence of exciting global cities with great lifestyle potential and exploding cultural industries (including Wellington, Sydney, Amsterdam, London, Helsinki, and Prague) and we could also witness a continued and growing increase in the outward flow of American talent to new places. Top this off with further restrictions on biotechnology research and investment, in stark contrast to its enthusiastic endorsement by many other governments, and we could experience a "brain drain" from the U.S.—a damaging reversal of the historical trend.

Most importantly, in recent years other powerful parts of the world have started to imagine, and even design for, a future that is not determined by U.S. leadership. With the cooling of the transatlantic relationship and the dawning realization that in a post-Cold War world Europe is no longer at the center of America's global geopolitical concerns, many Europeans now openly speculate about how much they should depend upon American leadership in shaping a new global order. Russia is smarting from its failure to retain meaningful influence in Ukraine and is considering how it can reassert itself among its other neighbors in the region. China is clearly creating alliances to position itself as more than simply an economic powerhouse but also a heavyweight geopolitical influence; it is bulking up its strategic military muscle, most likely with help from Europe. China has significantly increased its military budget every year of the twenty-first century, and is now spending between $30 billion and $40 billion annually. It has developed a mobile launch system capable of delivering nuclear missiles from trucks to the Northwestern United States. And China is investing in submarines and developing a sophisticated in-flight refueling capacity to further extend its military reach. Latin America is working to strengthen its own coherence and weight as a powerful region, and is actively creating collaborative linkages elsewhere—especially with Asia—that make it less reliant on its neighbor to the north.

Meanwhile, the United States has demonstrated a willingness to go against the grain of mainstream global opinion: by being the only developed nation except Australia to refuse to sign the Kyoto Protocol limiting greenhouse gas emissions, by its outspoken criticism of the United Nations, by its greater willingness to deploy hard power than soft power, by its clear reluctance to be constrained by the rules-based multilateral system that it was so instrumental in creating 60 years ago. The U.S. may well be gambling with its future influence. If the gamble fails, and other parts of the world step up to greater levels of leadership and influence, we will witness the third scenario, *Patchwork Powers,* a mosaic of powers and alliances that eventually cohere to forge a new order.

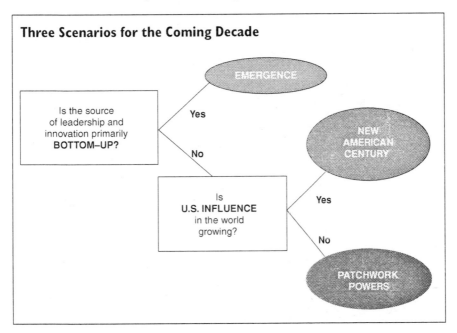

Three Scenarios for the Coming Decade

Before looking further at the core characteristics of each scenario—and their profound and different long-term consequences—two points are worth stressing. First, each of these scenarios contains elements of the other two. In fact, all three will be in play to some extent; the critical uncertainty is which one will *dominate*—none will have exclusive rights to the future. This means that we should endeavor to be fully prepared for each of them. Second, each scenario represents a genuinely radical departure from the world we have known. Even *New American Century,* which is superficially the most familiar and least discontinuous storyline, actually represents a transformation of the global order every bit as dramatic as *Emergence* and *Patchwork Powers.*

Chapter 11

Three Snapshots
of the Future

These three scenarios—*New American Century, Patchwork Powers,* and *Emergence*—cannot, of course, encompass the entire range of possibilities regarding the future world order. But they are plausible and important possibilities, and worth considering in turn. What might each of these worlds look like? Here are three snapshots that summarize each (accompanied by short vignettes that provide a glimpse of one person's life in that world), beginning with the scenario that some might consider the U.S.'s "official future."

New American Century

This is a future in which the United States achieves unparalleled leadership in world affairs, reasserting and strengthening its influence, and essentially establishing the core values and rules—economic, political, and cultural—by which the entire world will play for generations. It comes about as the second George W. Bush and the subsequent U.S. administrations recognize that they enjoy a temporary window of opportunity to cast the world in America's own image and are driven by the deep conviction that this not only serves the longer-term interests of the U.S. but is the right thing for the world. The U.S., therefore, employs a combination of diplomacy, military power, and market-driven incentives to transform the global order. American notions of democracy and freedom are attractive and increasingly valued in a world anxious about geopolitical stability and security, and especially by a new generation that has come of age amidst ubiquitous communications and great transparency and is acutely aware of the promise of the Western model.

Bold, risky moves pay off. Faltering steps toward democracy in Afghanistan and Iraq become more surefooted as both countries are able largely to leave their pasts—and their internal differences—behind them while they reap the benefits of American investment and greatly improved governance. In the Middle East, popular progressive movements gather strength and voice in many nations, leading to waves of radical political change. Wherever this is resisted by incumbent regimes, the U.S. applies new principles of "transformative diplomacy" (informed by enhanced intelligence operations and backed by the threat of U.S. military muscle) to encourage faster steps toward democracy. Besides the stick there are also carrots, as strategic trade and investment opportunities are used not only to reward change, but more importantly to enable many stagnating economies to spring into life. Perhaps most important of all, the U.S. recognizes that resolution of the Palestinian-Israeli stalemate is a necessary condition for peace and positive transformation in the region, and mobilizes international support to strongly pressure both parties to compromise, finally achieving a successful two-state solution.

As its confidence in this approach grows, and as it enjoys more support around the world, the U.S. leads military and economic "coalitions of the willing"—and there are many more willing—to work with an increasingly reactive and subservient United Nations to tackle the problems of "failed" and "recalcitrant" states. Meanwhile, Europe is struggling to achieve internal coherence following its ambitious expansion of the European Union. Recognizing the winds of change, it sets aside qualms about the dangers of a "new type of imperialism" and seeks to reestablish closer alliances with the U.S., reducing the "transatlantic drift" so evident in the tense early years of the century. China, concerned that its allies are increasingly warming to the U.S. again and recognizing the dangers of standing too firmly against a fast-rising tide of democracy and openness, adapts by slowly relaxing some internal social and political controls. It also accelerates policies that encourage entrepreneurship and innovation to keep the economy growing and moving into higher value sectors, concluding that it may be best to drive toward long-term economic supremacy rather than political or military supremacy.

Chinese and Indian businesses continue to prosper, gaining scale and influence, and it is obvious that they will, indeed, succeed playing by the economic rules of the U.S.-led Western model. In particular, as these companies start to develop and commercialize their own leading-edge intellectual property, they become more motivated to protect it and encourage their governments to support new global efforts to recognize and respect agreed-upon intellectual property rights. Meanwhile, as U.S.-influenced Western values remain ascendant in business life, large American, European, and Japanese companies also remain competitive, taking advantage of the stronger markets generated by the spread of prosperity to more parts of the world. Cities in Europe and on both U.S. coasts remain important, though not exclusive, drivers of world trade, innovation, and education, and develop links with the major hubs of innovation in Asia and Latin America as globalization enters its next, quite promising phase.

By 2015, many characteristics of the new global order have come into focus. New democratic governments in previously authoritarian states have struggled successfully to establish freedom and the rule of law; very few parts of the world remain disorderly or gravely threaten the peace and security of others. Competitive capitalism has prevailed, and the global economy is operating by a clear and shared set of rules based on the Western model. Market-based economic policies have proven valuable for billions who have moved rapidly toward middle-class comfort (mostly in increasingly prosperous parts of China and India). Powerful new businesses have emerged around the world, especially in Asia. Many countries have adopted new and creative mechanisms for formalizing the informally held property of their poorest people, unlocking value and releasing powerful entrepreneurial energy.

Yet this is far from a trouble-free Utopia. The world has been preoccupied with issues of security, political freedom, economic growth, and opportunity, and great progress has been made in these areas. But these priorities have achieved little for the more remote, poverty-stricken parts of Asia, Latin America, and especially sub-Saharan Africa. The world's poorest people have barely improved their lot, trade policies still punish the poor regions, and there is little shared urgency about addressing any of this. Meanwhile, although popular perceptions of the U.S. are quite positive across most of the world, its unabashed use of its influence and power to enforce its will has, inevitably, generated pockets of deep hostility and resentment that constantly threaten to erupt into violence. And other deep challenges remain inadequately addressed; indeed, it appears that any fundamental problem that cannot be resolved by the "two Ms" of this world—Military and Markets—is ignored, or tackled only at the level of symptoms. In particular, there has been very little coherence, and less progress, on addressing the challenges of climate change and other environmental problems (though an entire global industry is emerging to deal with weather-related disasters). Problems of equity, health, water access, and environmental sustainability are mounting; they now pose the greatest threats to the world as 2020 approaches.

New American Century

Name: Elizabeth Sterling

Age: 47

Occupation and location: Founder, Quantum Research Group, Charlotte, North Carolina

To: Board
From: esterling
Subject: Project update [CONFIDENTIAL]

Dear friends,

This last week has been pretty crazy here. Martin's breakthrough has energized everyone; I think that at least half the research team has started sleeping on cots in the labs instead of going home. It's like the startup days again—I just hope we don't see any divorces down the road!

This time a year ago we would have been happy to have a 100Q array working. Now we have two working 500Q systems, and we're looking at completing a functional 1,000Q system before the year's out. Moreover, Martin's team projects the multislice model should scale up to at least 10,000Q, if we need to go that far. God knows what we'd need that much computational ability for, but I'm sure we'll think of something. Who needs more than 640K of memory, right? :)

As per the Board's direction, I've given one of the 500Q systems to Commercial Services Development, and the other 500Q to Classified Applications. CA fought hard to get both, but as much as the government is ecstatic at our progress, the media apps will have a faster ROI. NSA is "asking" that we limit the commercial apps to 500Q, even when we scale up past 1,000Q on the CA side. Legal says that our contract obliges us to agree to this request, and we're all good citizens here.

Commercial thinks that the first immediate application will be in image and structure analysis. They've taken an image-mapping app they worked on for the *Qubit 50x* and reworked it; they say that the preliminary results are amazing. Faster, more accurate, and with a better "eye" for detail than even trained experts. The NASA/VirginGalactic team will love it for doing Mars landing site planning. They also expect it to be useful for protein folding analysis and real-time traffic models. I'm getting an email from Commercial pretty much every hour with a new application idea.

But it's the CA side that's really excited about this.

Image analysis will be enormously valuable, of course. Peacekeeping and nation-building operations still underway in North Korea, Iran, and the Philippines will be greatly aided by better monitoring tools, and CA says that their system was able to spot the telltales of the Iranian program without a problem when they fed it the image sets from before the, um, transformational diplomacy event.

CA also expects the system to be useful for doing behavioral anomaly maps. For those of you unfamiliar with the concept, BAMs look for individuals behaving in unusual ways in public settings in order to catch criminals and terrorists before they act—not just the obvious stuff, but little things, the way they look at other people, how they walk. There's been some research showing that the concept has merit. Simon, I know you've invested in some BAM projects in the past, and they haven't worked all that well. From my understanding—and correct me if I'm wrong, please—the biggest issue has been grappling with the level of detail required to avoid too-high false positives and false negatives. CA thinks that a big multislice array system, maybe a 5,000Q or so, should be able to handle that easily. I'd like you to speak with Raj, the technical lead in CA, when you have a chance; this could be a great opportunity.

I want to thank all of you for your support over the last few years. We met a lot of skepticism early on about our work, with lots of people in the technical and investment press calling it just another grid computing fantasy. The 50x series convinced many of them that we were on to something, but getting past the 50 qubit barrier was a real challenge.

I think we're all excited about the opportunities arising from this technology. The world still has some big problems to solve, and tools like these will let the best minds at the best organizations come up with the best solutions. We're all proud to be part of that effort.

Cheers,

Liz

Patchwork Powers

This is a future in which geopolitical and economic power and influence are distributed and shared between many different international bodies, geographical regions, and nation-states, and where influence is projected through a complex and sometimes confusing patchwork of alliances and treaties. It is a spaghetti-like world—messy and tangled, comprising multiple actors pursuing a variety of agendas that are not always perfectly aligned—but somehow it more or less works. China has emerged as a far more powerful strategic player in the world, leading (along with India) the Asian region as it becomes a dominant source of global innovation and economic growth. Indeed, economically, things are looking very bright for Asia. China in particular—thanks partly to government funding for basic research—is the center of new breakthroughs in biotechnology, nanotechnology, and space research, strengthening further its claim to be "the world's most important economy." But China has not settled for economic might alone; it has also developed considerable political sway, owing in part to the growth of its military muscle during a period when the U.S. military has found itself stretched much too thin. When China speaks, the world listens—though it feels under no particular obligation to agree.

Europe, meanwhile, has experienced some economic challenges as the center of gravity has moved east. But it has adapted well to the new reality and has resumed steady if unspectacular growth, in part through greatly increased trade with a booming Asia. Faced with the tricky question of which way to face—toward the U.S. (its trade partner, ally, and defender in the past) or China (its most promising partner for the future)—Europe decided to do both, and has pulled it off. However, Europe's real success lies in the political coherence and clout achieved by the expanded European Union, despite some false starts and setbacks along the way. Confounding the skeptics, the EU has become a cogent and strategically vital presence in the world, and its well-balanced approach to justice, freedom, equity, and national collaboration is the aspiration of regions across the globe, especially in Latin America, Africa, and Southeast Asia.

In contrast, the U.S. finds itself in a much weakened, and somewhat chastened, situation, and is in no position to offer the robust (and typically unilateral) world leadership that it set out to provide during the second administration of George W. Bush. In part its weakness is a consequence of a prolonged period of economic fragility caused by many factors but exacerbated by the huge capital withdrawals by the Chinese central banks that sent an already weak dollar into a tailspin. The result: high U.S. interest rates for several years. Economic weakness contributed to another critical element of declining U.S. influence—the growing unwillingness of its citizens to meet the surging costs of a "Pax Americana." Military expenditures soared as the U.S. attempted to fulfill its bold missions for democracy in the Middle East and beyond. Given the "one step forward, two steps back" nature of the progress being achieved, it is hardly surprising that the common wisdom became, "Why should we endure cuts in domestic programs in order to export democracy and freedom to places that obviously don't want it?" U.S. political leaders eventually had no option but to reduce and then reverse their ambitious course. The damage to the U.S.'s reputation was predictable. Across the globe the popular perception was that the U.S. had dangerously and irresponsibly destabilized many parts of the world, fomenting unfulfilled discontent with existing regimes on the one hand, while on the other hand provoking great resentment and increasing incidents of terrorism. Stung, the U.S. has adopted a more and more insular perspective, concentrating largely on economic recovery and homeland security; its global interests are increasingly concentrated on trade and commerce in a rapidly rebalancing economy.

The U.S. failed to provide unilateral leadership and reshape the world to its liking, but it has reluctantly joined the new world of interlocking alliances and agreements. Global corporations are also becoming increasingly involved in matters of governance, in part to help shape the new agenda, but also because it is clear that their expertise and resources are required. With no single authority designing and imposing a new global order, a rather piecemeal multilateralism is evolving, largely constructed around the "two Is" of global governance—Institutions and Initiatives. There is widespread acceptance that global problems are best addressed through collaboration and joint effort. The resulting multilateral approaches are often bureaucratic and don't always allow for rapid progress or radical breakthroughs, but they do seem to provide a robust platform for sometimes difficult decisions and changes.

By 2015, it is clear that the new global order is truly multipolar, with China, Europe, and the U.S. collaborating, competing, and aligning in many different domains, and Latin America and Africa more fully included and represented in a plethora of new institutions and initiatives aimed at the world's "priority problems." Real traction is being achieved against the top five of these priorities—poverty, climate change, disease epidemics, scientific ethics, and migration management—largely because all parties are acknowledging the need for both action and compromise. The U.S. is becoming more willing to sign off on global regulations and has bowed to Chinese pressure to amend the rules of the global economic system—including a significant softening of intellectual property rights. Europe has accepted the need to develop its military capabilities and join forces with the U.S. in applying hard power in the world's growing number of trouble spots. China has conceded that global ethical standards are required to moderate the pursuit of new scientific and technological breakthroughs.

On the surface, the world appears to be moving gradually toward greater stability. Yet there are some fundamental tensions and periodic standoffs between regions, and so many interlocking relationships can lead to ambiguity, gamesmanship, and a lack of deep trust between players. Moreover, the world seems to be increasingly vulnerable to terrorism and crime, and problems associated with "failing states" are on the rise. As the third decade of the century approaches, there are growing concerns about the rather ad hoc nature of the new order and calls for the current arrangements to be designed into a more coherent and systemic multilateral framework—one that is also capable of addressing the growing challenges of global security.

Patchwork Powers

Name: Sanjay Dasgupta

Age: 58

Occupation and location: Vice president, Ecosystems Design; Bangalore, India

Dasgupta's secretary ushers in the writer from the *Straits Times*. The old newspapers still prefer face-to-face, he muses. Good. Dasgupta stands and offers his hand. "Please, have a seat."

They spend nearly a quarter of an hour chatting informally. English is their mutual language and they slip easily into its rhythms. Dasgupta's secretary brings in tea. Finally, the reporter shifts the conversation to the topic at hand, pointing to a printout on the vice president's desk. "I see you have the new UN Carbon Remediation Goals report. Any surprises in it for you?"

The executive nods slightly. "We're doing better than I had feared, although we're still not where we should be. Carbon dioxide levels are at nearly 390 parts per million; global temperatures are up by nearly a degree and a half in the last decade, far faster than expected; glaciers are disappearing; the snows of Kilimanjaro are now nothing but an image in history books."

Dasgupta sighs, and shakes his head. "We started so very late."

The reporter presses. "Some may have been shocked at the speed of these changes, but none of them came as a surprise. We've known about the severity of global warming for nearly two decades now. Why did it take so long to act?"

"This was not a problem a single nation could solve. Individual efforts to reduce emissions, to move past the petroleum era, were important, but could not alone change the planet. In the past, we would have expected the United States to step forward and lead, to help the rest of the world take the necessary steps to avert disaster." Dasgupta pauses, frowns. "But we had come to rely on the United States too much, for when American leadership faltered, none of us was ready to step forward in its stead."

The writer takes notes, his pen recording the conversation. "Surely the United Nations was ready to do so, wasn't it?"

"Eventually, yes. It needed reforms, and it needed to be moved—unfortunately so, as New York is a wonderful city. But a strengthened UN was only part of this new reality. We soon realized that we needed greater institutional strength across the board. We had all gone too far with deregulation, with making free markets our only goal."

The *Straits Times* writer looks a bit uncomfortable. "Many critics call this simply a return to massive government spending and sclerotic bureaucracies. One economist referred to this as 'just-in-time Keynesianism.'"

Dasgupta smiles. "I think that sums up the mix of steady innovation and hard-won wisdom quite nicely, actually. The world today requires a combination of big-picture strategic thinking and carefully focused efforts. Fortunately, modern institutions handle that particular combination rather nicely."

"Does that mean that you believe we are on the right path?"

The executive gently shrugs. "Although we are sometimes reluctant to admit it, we do have good reasons for hope. As worrisome as the carbon report is, for example, it also has bright spots. In a scant 10 years, we have shifted global power generation to nearly 30 percent from renewable sources, and could hit 50 percent by 2020. The ongoing work to rebuild urban centers to deal with climate disasters and masses of refugees continues to pay growing economic dividends." Dasgupta smiles broadly. "Even the United States is looking better, as it begins to recognize again that it has much to learn from the rest of the world."

"What do you think it has learned?"

Dasgupta leans forward, focusing on the reporter. "The American Century is over, but so is the Chinese Century, the European Century, or even the Indian Century. Ultimately, the problems we face today are far too challenging and complex for one nation, no matter how mighty, to handle on its own."

Emergence

This is a future in which the established, traditional models of power and leadership prove to be largely unsuited to the challenges of a world of greatly increased interdependence, complexity, uncertainty, and diversity. Instead, change and coherence (of a sort) come from the bottom up, as centralized and hierarchical governments, international institutions, and many large corporations prove slow to adapt to new challenges and opportunities. Influence moves gradually but unmistakably toward highly interconnected and nimble networks of focused, smaller-scale players. Increasingly powerful and cohesive city regions vie for influence with national governments, and the very concept of the nation-state as the dominant level and form of governance comes into question. Entrepreneurs, small businesses, and "open-source" production networks prove more flexible—and often more effective—than larger, conventionally structured corporations. Focused nongovernmental organizations pursue their goals more nimbly and with greater global alignment than lumbering international institutions. The world is increasingly being reshaped by the power of the "two Ps": People and Passion.

This occurs in part because the old order starts to fracture under the stress of rapid change (top down just doesn't get traction) and in part for a more positive reason: the bottom up begins, for the first time, to really *add* up as a serious alternative for governance and coherence. No single nation, region, or institution is able to maintain control of a chaotic world in which insecurity, economic pressures, and worries over new looming problems are increasing. The major multilateral institutions—starting with the United Nations—are perceived as too bureaucratic and reactive, and also prone to inadvertently supporting (even occasionally indulging in) corrupt practices. Meanwhile, the U.S.'s attempts to create a new order based on its own values and beliefs falls flat; while there is certainly some spread of enthusiasm for democratic elections and the ideals of freedom, opportunity, and justice, this is not accompanied by trust and respect for the U.S., nor any real passion for its economic and political models. Fast-developing China falls victim to its own growth and success: it cannot put its new genies—of prosperity, innovation, change, and the accompanying high and growing expectations of its citizens—back in the bottle. It suffers successive waves of internal political and cultural strife as the establishment is challenged by a rebellious new generation of aspiring entrepreneurs and globally aware citizens who seek and demand greater freedom. In particular, the great cities of China achieve growing autonomy from the machinery of the state, forming innovation and trade networks with other cities all over the world.

The European Union is probably the best illustration of the failure of the old impulse toward centralization. Tensions between the original members and the new accession countries—over voting rights, policy directions, resource allocations, and future members—prove to be insurmountable, and the great European experiment slowly unravels. In Latin America, amidst discouragement at these trends, attempts to develop a coherent, new, regional power axis peter out, while across the continent of Africa, bold dreams of a grand collective renaissance give way to more localized efforts to generate meaningful change and improvement. But this increasing focus on more local solutions helps generate powerful and effective innovations in governance. Drawing especially from the principles of "deliberative democracy," which enable greater and more continuous involvement of citizens in local decision-making and leadership, parts of Latin America and Africa lead the way in developing important decentralized and flexible models for engaging citizens and greatly improving local governance.

This is only one element of a powerful and constructive trend toward bottom-up solutions and decentralized, networked entities. The voices and actions of billions of people and communities worldwide are connected into new, reconfigured networks, and innovation flourishes as local, low-cost solutions to issues such as water shortages and rural energy requirements are prioritized over grand schemes for dams and grids. The "blogosphere" is at least as legitimate a source of news and commentary as any mainstream media outlet. Several potentially devastating disease outbreaks are minimized by networks of scientists openly collaborating to share information and create vaccines. Some major corporations (having already begun to "virtualize" through outsourcing, alliances, and decentralization) more readily embrace the new order than political institutions, transforming themselves into radically networked and empowered entities with multiple, strong, local identities and decision rights.

By 2015, it is clear (even to those still walking the corridors of traditional power in governments and global institutions) that a new and rather bewildering order has emerged. It is an uncomfortable, turbulent, but, for many, energizing world. Individuals and communities are assuming greater responsibility and finding that they have more influence over their own destiny than they might once have thought. Kids who grew up playing multiplayer online games with others all over the world become adults entirely accustomed to remote but meaningful relationships and communities. Entrepreneurs and small businesses are thriving, especially those belonging to creative networks of likeminded people. A new breed of "venture altruists" has sprung up—people whose mission is to support and spread the development of breakthrough solutions to commonly repeated social and environmental problems. Their work is helping catalyze more and more intriguing innovations in more and more surprising places, and an increasingly "can-do" confidence pervades many previously impoverished and seemingly helpless parts of the world. In particular, the challenges of sustainability are being recast as opportunities, as new technologies plus new mindsets plus multiple experiments add up to bright and better solutions to many human needs around the world.

By 2015, the decentralized, bottom-up model has proved its extraordinary potential, and many of the major challenges of the twenty-first century are being addressed in promising and unexpected new ways. But this phenomenon appears ripe for some important rebalancing. Many of the large global institutions that have survived are starting to understand the new rules of the game and are scaling down, decentralizing, forging constructive alliances across multiple networks, and preparing to adopt new roles as coordinators and enablers rather than leaders and doers. Yet this bottom-up world is also fraught with mounting danger. International lawlessness has reached unprecedented levels. Small-scale but too-frequent terrorist attacks mar civic peace in many countries—and open source biotechnology carries a growing threat of synthetic viruses fabricated in garage laboratories. There are more failing states and ugly regimes than there were at the turn of the century—and there is no powerful international community to help or cajole them. For every corner of the world promising to become the next Singapore, another is threatening to become the next Somalia. All around the world, questions are being asked about what mechanisms, alliances, and accords might be required to ensure global security, and what compromises might be necessary and justified.

Emergence

Name: Ken Sakai

Age: 22

Occupation and location: Open source biotech consultant, Auckland, New Zealand

The 10-year-old Honda hybrid runs well enough, but Ken is beginning to think he may need to finally break down and buy a new car, one of those hydrogen ones (a "HindenCar," his mom said, before she bought one last year) since everyone says it's the wave of the future and the future is now and all those other clichés that creep up on you until you realize they're true. Yesterday he saw a gas station that only sold hydrogen, and hydrogen is a gas, so he can keep calling them "gas stations," right?

He has his mobile stuck on the dashboard with one of those sticky pads that doesn't leave residue so that it can project on his windshield and he can see the messages that pop up and scroll by and the random snaps of images and video his phone pulls from the web as idle entertainment. Just, you know, to let him keep an eye on things, even though he's never really been into that whole "sousveillance" thing, but he figures that a million little brothers are better than one big brother. Besides, they caught that guy spreading avian flu because of people sighting him with their mobiles a few years ago, it couldn't have been too many years ago, because that whole everybody-watches-everybody's back thing wasn't a big deal when he was a kid so it probably hasn't been around for *too* long.

Ken is late again for a meeting with the genetic design team and he's more than a little annoyed that they want to do these things in person. He could just as easily view the simulations over video, and he has to have his mobile to copy their changes to his proposals anyway, so why don't they just do it over the web like civilized people? Yeah, well, they're all older and probably like the whole "personal touch" thing, though that seems more like an excuse to waste time talking and eating bagels. Don't they realize that he's a busy guy with a ton of work to do for a dozen other clients, and damn it, was that the exit?

He runs in, five minutes past 10, glad that the gate cameras already ID'd him so that he didn't have to stop to explain himself because he always hates talking to people carrying guns, that's always where the crazies blow themselves up, and he suppresses a shudder. Changing the subject in his head, hoping that the meeting hasn't started yet, he turns the corner to the glassed-in room and sees everyone standing around the coffee and bagel cart and he says hi to the group and relaxes, just a bit.

They all sit down to start the meeting and Ken notices, immediately, who is actually there and who is simply warming a seat, including the guy next to him who seems to be taking careful notes of the conversation but is actually playing some game, *Darwin's Kingdom*, looks like, he could never really get into it because it wasn't violent enough but it's probably perfect for meetings like this. Ken wonders if he'd start playing games in meetings if he only worked at one place and always saw the same people every day, even though Jina, across the table with the Apple HedZup wearable who seems to really like his designs, is great to talk to and he could actually imagine working in the same place as her for a while.

It's Ken's turn to talk, to tell them about his own improvements to the project, adding in some genes from a cactus to provide stomatic strengthening and increase water absorption, and he hopes the coffee kicks in soon because he really needs to wake up.

Any of these three scenarios is plausible, and while elements of each are certain to unfold, the real question is which world will dominate, setting the stage for decades to come. Will the center hold, and if so, will U.S. power, influence, and values prevail, continuing to spread democracy and market economics globally? Or will the U.S. lose influence and status, becoming one of many players that collaborate through a tangled web of alliances and agreements to address rising global challenges? What if the center does not hold and leadership, power, and innovation emerge from the bottom-up, creating a creative, chaotic, networked future? How might the priorities and activities of business, government, and civic organizations change in these different worlds? And how will we know if and when the events we are seeing around us signal deeper structural shifts toward one scenario or another, so that we can get a head start on adjusting and adapting effectively? Ultimately the test of a good scenario is whether it helps you see the world differently, to read the morning paper with a new eye, and to connect the dots and find the patterns that really matter to our future.

How the Three Scenarios Compare

	New American Century	Patchwork Powers	Emergence
Global society & culture	• Ambitious, progressive, and identities • Toward U.S.-centered homogeneity • "Ownership" not "entitlement" • Numerous pushback movements (mostly environmental)	• Powerful national and regional • Ambitious, individualistic, and • Asian cultures more influential around the world • Society more inter-dependent, • Mature and risk averse • Belief in the collective, in checks and balances	• Rebellious, youthful, and risk-loving meritocratic • Localized • Connected by issues, not nationalities • Highly transparent and very confusing • Increasingly spiritual
Global economy & business environment	• Global corporations run mostly by Western rules • Further liberalization of Chinese, Indian markets • Outsourcing popular • Political pressure to "protect" vulnerable domestic industries • Lighter regulation • Bilateral trade negotiations	• Tighter regulation • Solid but sluggish economic growth • Numerous international alliances and joint ventures • Importance of cultural competence • Regional blocs retain influence over trade negotiations	• Highly turbulent ("booms" and "busts") • Networked; big organizations as enablers and small as operators • Coexistence of different models of capitalism • Emergent, open standards • Open source and other radical business models
Global politics & relationships	• China remains strategically quiet • Powerful global moral majority, with a dominant sacred worldview • EU gives more power to Eastern European nations; plans for accession of Turkey • Liberalization in Middle East states • Underlying, simmering resentment of U.S. power	• Multipolar; lots of summits and handshakes • Asian nations more powerful in global agreements • Middle East, Russia become strategic battlegrounds • Relative harmony over global problems • Ambiguity, gamesmanship, and issues of trust	• Crises of confidence for national governments • Issue-driven political alliances • City-states win power over nation-states • Darwinian approaches create real successes and failures; Singapores and Somalias • Civil society and NGOs more influential • Governments less controlling, more enabling

Section 4

So What?: Acting in an Era of Transformation

A thought which does not result in an action is nothing much,
and an action which does not proceed from a thought is
nothing at all.
—Georges Bernanos

None of us—no matter who we are or what position and power we hold—can choose the future. It will be forged by the individual and collective decisions and actions of thousands of organizations and millions of engaged citizens around the world. Yet the wiser our choices, informed by thoughtful appreciation of the drivers of change and the new challenges and opportunities that may await us, the better.

Chapter 12
_____

Creating Our
New Future

Everyone in every sector and walk of life will have much to learn about how to survive, thrive, and contribute in the future that unfolds. However the world develops, one thing is absolutely certain—we are living through an era of transformation, and we will have to learn to adapt to radically different realities. This will be particularly true for three key actors that will both shape and be shaped by the changes ahead: businesses, leaders across all sectors, and global citizens.

The New Realities for Business

No group in society will be untouched by the transformations underway and the need to change and adapt. However, business is likely to be most affected because of the immense power it wields in the world and the relatively little accountability that has been imposed to date on how that power is exercised. Indeed, in two of the scenarios—*Patchwork Powers* and *Emergence*—we can expect significant changes in the social contract that will alter the expectations and role of corporations. Even in *New American Century*, the sheer reach of market power will change what it means to be in business over the next few decades. This will, in turn, require big shifts in business logic, particularly in two areas: balancing market wisdom and moral wisdom, and moving from a narrow focus on competitiveness to embrace adaptiveness as well.

BALANCING MARKET WISDOM AND MORAL WISDOM

Market-based business activity now possesses such scale and reach that it has become a fundamental part of life on the planet. But there is accumulating and incontrovertible evidence of its economic, environmental, social, and cultural consequences. Because of this, increased business transparency and scrutiny is inevitable, and it will put greater pressure on corporations to demonstrate responsiveness to—and real willingness to accept responsibility for—social and moral concerns and expectations. Competitive pressures have tended to push businesses in the opposite direction. They assume accountability for shareholder value (a practice that is reinforced by "incentivizing" executives with stock) rather than broader stakeholder expectations. They have adopted a global perspective that often serves to dislocate or at least weaken any sense of connection and belonging to their communities of origin. They have aggressively reduced costs regardless of the human consequences. They have complied with environmental and other regulatory restrictions but have rarely gone further to reduce the negative effects of their activity. Ironically, as the footprint and impact of businesses have broadened and deepened all over the world, their ability to take full and thoughtful account of the consequences of their activity in a fast and furious competitive environment has declined just as rapidly. In a few now notorious cases (think Enron, WorldCom, Ahold, and Parmalat) they have crossed the line from moral neutrality to immorality. As a consequence, despite the fact that the vast majority of business executives are good, intelligent, and energetic people, they are less trusted and respected than previous generations of business leaders.

But many businesses are beginning to conclude that their "character" and perceived trustworthiness are among their most critical assets. This leads them to acknowledge the "both/and" imperative of sustaining market wisdom (doing the profitable thing) and achieving greater moral wisdom (doing the right thing). Increasingly, the safest strategy will be to strive for impeccable behavior that over time becomes embedded in the business brand. This means that business leaders will have to instill a deep ethical consciousness throughout their organization, not as an adjunct to business strategy but as a core organizing principle. In the next decade, anything less will produce a level of risk unacceptable to shareholders and other stakeholders. In a transparent world, we will have to presume that anything we do or are responsible for that would be embarrassing if it became public knowledge *will* become public knowledge—and we should correct our actions now. This growing imperative for business is not simply a defensive measure. A clear, shared ethical compass will be essential to navigating through the complex terrain of the future business environment. The ability of people at all levels of an organization to develop appropriate options, make rapid decisions, and act swiftly will require a common set of ethical imperatives.

Instilling such an ethical consciousness will take more than putting a statement of values beside the corporate logo on computer mouse pads; the commitment must become truly embedded in the DNA of the organization. Fortunately, promoting ethical behavior does not run counter to the personal instincts of employees and stakeholders. Most people want to act ethically and do so in their personal lives. The vast majority of businesses simply have to articulate their ethical commitment explicitly and design their systems to support the personal values of their people. By working with the grain of existing values and ethics and consistently encouraging and rewarding everyone to meet the same ethical standards in their professional and their private lives, ethical consciousness may prove surprisingly easy to achieve. One company that is taking this challenge seriously is Altria—formerly known as Philip Morris, and a holding company for that firm and several well-known food brands. No stranger to controversy and ethical dilemmas, Altria encourages its employees to ask themselves four simple questions before making a decision: Is it legal? Is it consistent with company policy? What will other people think? Is it the right thing to do? These and similar questions will underpin corporate behavior in the decade ahead.

EMBRACING COMPETITIVENESS AND ADAPTIVENESS

Over the last 20 years, most businesses around the world have undergone massive changes as they have confronted an era of near total competitiveness—driven largely by economic globalization, widespread deregulation, sectoral convergence, technological connectivity, and the extremely demanding expectations of shareholders and financial markets. Responding to these increased pressures, they have reengineered, cut costs, merged, flattened, aggressively managed their supply chains, become multinational and then truly global, virtualized and outsourced, formed complex alliances, innovated faster and faster, and reinvented their business models. For the most part, they have been astonishingly creative and nimble, acted legally and with integrity, and helped spread prosperity and well-being around the world. But these lean, fast, focused entities are ill-equipped to deal with imminent transformations in the world order. In the coming decade, they will face adaptive strains as profound as those they have endured already.

It is surely axiomatic that uncertainty will continue to rise as the world becomes more interconnected and interdependent, as transparency and scrutiny increase, as technologies and economies become more complex, and as change occurs at an accelerating pace. Mastering uncertainty will become an increasingly important business priority. It will require corporations to scan the world more broadly—to learn about critical external drivers of change, to consider multiple possibilities, to connect diverse perspectives, to develop greater systematic understanding of their business and social context, to rehearse contingencies, and to take a longer view of business prospects. Yet the systems, incentives, and structures of most businesses—designed optimally for purposes of short-term competitiveness—mitigate against such behaviors. Business leaders are typically discouraged from acknowledging that there are important factors that they do not, and often cannot, know—as Theodore Hesburgh, former president of Notre Dame University, put it, "You cannot blow an uncertain trumpet." While the concept of "organizational learning" has been proclaimed a priority for more than a decade, there seems to be less time and opportunity in most of our slimmed-down and speeded-up organizations for real learning to occur and spread. In the coming decade, we should expect to see greater emphasis on managing the dilemmas associated with remaining competitive and adapting amid uncertainty.

It won't be easy. Today's business agenda conforms to many conventional wisdoms and commonsense beliefs about business priorities that are so embedded in society that they are taken as self-evident. The most significant of these include globalization, productivity, winning, growth, focus, and technology. Together, these priorities have influenced the shape and character of most businesses today. They are based on certain assumptions about liberalization, broad acceptance of market mechanisms, and steady globalization. They are also based on the need to increase shareholder value by securing competitive advantage over organizations playing by the same rules within growing, welcoming markets. But in the coming era of transformation, these priorities may prove inadequate for the challenges ahead. Businesses will have to start thinking about radical shifts—not *away* from these priorities but, in keeping with our paradoxical times, toward including their opposites in a new "both/and" mindset that will better equip us to prosper.

GLOBALIZATION AND LOCALIZATION

Most major businesses have invested in addressing the challenges of globalization. Today, it might also make sense to consider how to more effectively "localize" our activities. For example, one can imagine a greater emphasis on localizing the work experience for executives who spend half their waking hours in airplanes or airports. Mounting pressure on travel infrastructures, continued security threats, and changing lifestyle priorities and expectations could easily combine to make this a core business issue. An obvious solution is more investment in virtual meetings, and the supporting technology for this is improving steadily. The biggest challenge may be learning new competencies and social behaviors that enable natural conversation and effective decision-making in virtual environments.

Similarly, we can anticipate the possibility that cultural pushback against large global brands might increase the importance of evolving more micro, locally positioned brands. Successful brands will need excellent close-to-market information and a heightened sensitivity to local cultures. Global businesses will also need to forge stronger links to local communities than in the past.

Even greater shifts and innovations might be required if environmental and security concerns combine with new technological possibilities to catalyze a move away from today's global industrial production and distribution system. Faced with terrorist threats, overcapacity, and new energy breakthroughs, corporations may find it necessary—and profitable—to manufacture products in thousands of different locations much closer to the end user and the point of consumption. Globalization would still continue, but it would be focused far more on the transfer of knowledge and far less on the movement of products. John Maynard Keynes envisaged this scenario many decades ago: "Ideas, knowledge, art, hospitality, travel—these are the things which should of their nature be international. But may goods be homespun." A challenging economy renders it critical to concentrate energy and imagination on the notion of business localization.

PRODUCTIVITY AND RESILIENCE

Major improvements in productivity—the efficiency of value creation—lie at the heart of economic growth and social development. An excessive focus on productivity, however, can result in critical vulnerabilities, several of which may be rising in significance.

First, the drive to productivity, if not tempered by broader concerns about the impact on stakeholders (employees, partners, communities), can lead to actions that erode the trust, reputation, and credibility that underpin every organization's legitimacy and endurance. Second, the remarkable progress made in finessing and integrating distribution, logistics, and production systems has achieved enormously efficient just-in-time capacities that boost productivity. These tend, however, to be designed for "normal" operating conditions that can be easily undermined by geopolitical and environmental events that cause severe downtime and losses. Unpredictable and extraordinary circumstances require businesses to build more flexibility, more resilience, and more options into all of their systems, which means operating with a certain level of redundancy.

Finally, many of the important productivity gains of the past 20 years have been achieved by replacing and streamlining human resources. Automation, reengineering, and "rightsizing" have driven this process in countless organizations, yet all of them fail to account for the crucial role of "slack space." Slack in the system permits social interaction, which in turn drives knowledge creation, and its absence diminishes the capacity for organizational learning. We may have to reconsider the idea of "redundancy" as potentially constructive, a condition that, with careful design, might enable corporations to retain civic confidence, acquire flexibility in difficult times, and boost their capacity for continuous learning—all likely to be business imperatives in the decade ahead.

WINNING AND COLLABORATION

Competing to "win" at all costs has been a ubiquitous goal for business in the past two decades, driving an extraordinary level of commercial creativity, innovation, and growth. But it is incomplete and imprecise. Businesses not only compete against one another in a zero-sum game, but they also collaborate within a complex value-creation system and are required to adapt to an ever-changing global context. Taken too literally and adopted too exclusively, "winning" could become a destructive rather than a constructive organizing principle.

Perhaps, then, we should also emphasize the role of collaboration and co-creation in securing long-term adaptive advantage. Along with "supply chain management," we should think in terms of "value web creation." In the aftermath of dotcom hysteria, perhaps we can adopt a calmer, more reasoned approach to working imaginatively with our customer base in the co-creation of value. Many companies already actively encourage product modifications by their leading-edge customers. Risk-sharing and partnerships could offer constructive alternatives to our conventional default: mergers and acquisitions. We may need to acquire new mindsets and approaches to support collaboration with new partners in the public and NGO sectors. And given the heightened importance of faster and more effective learning about the changing global context within which all businesses operate, we need to consider more, and more productive, learning collaborations. We would be well served by coming to understand the world from the multiple perspectives of different industries, regions, and markets.

GROWTH AND SURVIVAL

Most senior executives face enormous scrutiny and pressure from capital markets, driven by the imperative of shareholder value and motivated by the (quite deliberate) design of their incentive systems. As a result, they have felt obliged to place enormous emphasis on achieving high, often double-digit levels of growth each year. Yet few have questioned, at least in public, the level of growth that can be achieved and sustained even by the most successful business. Given compounding effects, is continuous, double-digit growth even a reasonable aspiration?

Perhaps the focus on growth should be augmented by the idea of long-term survival—sustainability of success as well as immediacy of success. Doing so would require us to ask some different and challenging questions. What, for example, would we start doing differently now if we knew that we were personally going to live another 150 years, and would be working for this company for the next 100? If we knew that within 10 years every negative effect of our commercial activity that is currently an externality must be internalized and accounted for as a transparent cost, what would we change, and how? Given the potential for mounting push-back against corporate power, we might also ask ourselves, "What must be true about our organization to make it safe to assume that, 50 years from now, most people will be happy we exist and wish us well?" Finally, we come to the simplest and toughest question of all: What are the fundamental features of our strategy, capacity, and personality that augur well for long-term success, and why do we believe this?

FOCUS AND AMBIGUITY

In a world of almost limitless possibility, we have been expected to focus keenly on what matters most, set priorities, make decisions, and simplify our thinking and activities. However, focus also implies a narrowing, an exclusion of alternatives, and can be as much a weakness as a strength when adopted as a ubiquitous principle. As Einstein once famously advised, "Everything should be made as simple as possible, but not simpler." Have we lost sight of this qualifier? Perhaps we should explicitly embrace the notion of ambiguity and consider those areas where acknowledging, rather than denying, will make us more effective.

The first candidate for this relates to the metrics by which we increasingly manage our organizations. These tightly focused and limited measurements require both expansion and balance. Moreover, they should be systematically augmented by more qualitative factors and the exercise of managerial judgment. This is admittedly more ambiguous than quantified evidence, but critical for managing complicated situations where dilemmas and tradeoffs are inevitable.

Second, we might question the adequacy of current approaches to risk management that focus mainly on known variables and are constructed around the internal dimensions of business projects. Risk is changing and becoming more ambiguous—because of the new and unknown powers of our technologies, because we can no longer take our climate or our environment for granted, and because we live in an era of heightened geopolitical tensions and the empowerment of "outlier" groups and individuals. It is essential, then, that our approaches to risk also become more complex and sophisticated, and that we actively seek out a diversity of perspectives and insights in order to contextualize risk and better inform our decision-making.

The opportunities we face are equally ambiguous and subject to change. In the future, conventional means of evaluating investments (discounted cash flow, in particular) may be less useful and appropriate than more flexible methodologies, such as real option analysis.

Next, we tend to focus so exclusively on the intentions behind our actions that we often fail to imagine the potential unintended consequences of our choices. We could start to redress this with a simple question: If we proceed as planned, what might we—or others—come to regret that we have not yet even considered? Such questions are easy to frame but difficult to deal with. They require executives to challenge their own preconceptions, stretch their imaginations, and envisage the things that could go wrong with a strategy that, at the time, feels right. Taking the "What ifs?" to a much deeper level and incorporating a more diverse set of perspectives will enrich our understanding and anticipation of risks.

Excessive focus may also be inhibiting innovation. Businesses tend to pursue changes and innovations through large-scale, tightly focused projects. These initiatives are typically based on a single approach, consume considerable resources over a long period of time, and allow little room for course corrections if things start to go wrong. Amid increasing ambiguity, business could learn a great deal from the world of science about how to design frequent, numerous, small-scale experiments that often fail but cost little and yield significant learning. This shift will require us to develop new competencies: the ability to imagine, design, and execute small-scale experiments in new, often risky, opportunity spaces; to systematically extract the learning from both success and failure; and to move swiftly to the next iteration.

TECHNOLOGY AND PEOPLE

In the last decade, every major corporation has transformed critical aspects of its technology to support virtually every function: from computing to communications, from production to distribution, from customer interaction to international activities. Yet it is difficult to think of any businesses that have made similar investments in innovations that support the attraction, retention, and development of their people. Despite the growing focus on talent and rhetoric about people as the core asset, we repeatedly witness significant cutbacks in this area during hard times.

Although innovation has been sluggish, the field of human resources has evolved over the last 20 years and is poised to do so again. The development of people once focused primarily on training them in the skills required to perform only the specific jobs with which they were directly charged. More recently, we have seen a broader scope of business education emerge that enables executives to play an evolving and fuller role in their organizations. In the coming decade, as we experience mounting complexity and risk, our emphasis will probably stretch again to promote a much wider and deeper understanding of the global context for business that translates into better and more informed judgment. This will be even more important as we face challenges for which our past experience does not equip us well, where what we have learned may no longer apply, and where our new "legacy problems" are ourselves.

The development of new, effective, and creative approaches to attracting and instructing our people must move up the business agenda from "nice to have" to "critical success factor." But a renewed focus on people and on developing them in new ways and for new purposes is only part of the challenge. Corporations will also be required to acknowledge a growing human hunger for meaning and deeper levels of fulfillment, among customers as well as among employees and other stakeholders. Understanding and respecting the human dimensions of work, the human aspirations of civic communities, and the human desire for integrity will be essential for all organizations seeking to develop and retain trust—an increasingly crucial resource for the future.

THE NEW PARADOXES OF LEADERSHIP

In an era in which uncertainty and complexity are rife and radical changes will be required to address the new challenges and opportunities laid out previously in this chapter, it is axiomatic to suggest that leadership will become more important than ever. In business—as well as in government and the civil sector—we will require many more manifestations of leadership, distributed across more people and networks, making more connections and securing commitment to action and coherence across more spheres of endeavor than ever before.

How are we to understand the nature of leadership in this messy and ambiguous world? One general tendency of followers is to seek leaders who will reduce uncertainty for us by providing clarity, acting consistently, and being decisive. But can authentic leadership really address this need in times of turbulent transformation? This dilemma highlights the increasingly paradoxical nature of leadership in the future, which will require us to adopt a different understanding of the concept and require those who lead us to think and behave in different ways.

Working with executives in business, government, and nonprofits, I have observed several paradoxes of leadership—again framed as "both/ands"—that are likely to become clearer and more important in the decade ahead. These can be thought of in terms of leaders' relationships to the external world, to others whom they wish to influence, and to themselves.

We typically think of leaders as requiring a strong and keen focus, even a rather blinkered view of the world, in order to stay connected with their mission and avoid distraction. Yet leadership in an increasingly uncertain world will also require an ability to be holistic—taking a systemic, "helicopter" view of the world, sensing new and changing patterns as they unfold, and yet having the skill to zoom in rapidly on specific issues and anomalies. Leadership will also require of us the hunger and capacity to stay well informed about the external context, both as generalists (for context) and specialists (for substance), while never denying that, even as we develop and nurture our knowledge and comprehension, we remain in a state of uncertainty.

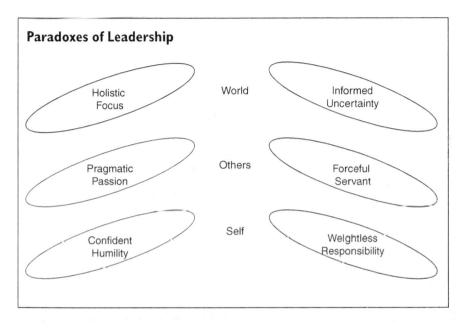

Paradoxes of Leadership

Holistic Focus — World — Informed Uncertainty

Pragmatic Passion — Others — Forceful Servant

Confident Humility — Self — Weightless Responsibility

In their relationships with others, leaders will have to learn to walk a tightrope. They must be pragmatic, level-headed, and concentrated on how to catalyze, enable, and facilitate meaningful change, all while retaining and communicating a level of passion and conviction that owes less to reason and strategy than to belief and values and personal energy. Leadership also requires forceful servants—strong-minded, thick-skinned, determined leaders willing to stand strong in defense of their principles and convictions. At the same time, they must be acutely aware of the need to serve their followers and ever mindful that their role, and the role of their organizations, is ultimately to be of service. As General Colin Powell has put it, "The day soldiers stop bringing you their problems is the day you have stopped leading them. They have either lost confidence that you can help them or concluded that you do not care. Either case is a failure of leadership."

Leadership will also require a new relationship to self, featuring a deep willingness to rise to the challenges of our era and persevere through inevitable adversity, as well as a profound humility and ability to acknowledge confusion, ask for help, and pass the baton to others. We will also need leaders to assume a weightless responsibility, an ability to be accountable and effective while also maintaining a light touch and a low-stress approach to work. In Rudyard Kipling's words, they will need the ability to "meet with triumph and disaster and treat those two impostors just the same."

Reframing our thinking about leadership to acknowledge its increasingly paradoxical nature may help us create new approaches to liberating the talents of a new and much-needed generation of leaders, well suited to their time and well worthy of being followed.

THE NEW POWER OF ENGAGED GLOBAL CITIZENS

While leadership will matter more in the decade ahead, it will also be more widely distributed than at any time in human history. It will be far more fluid, and often very temporary, as networks of engaged global citizens exercise growing power and influence in the shaping of our future. Even if the *Emergence* scenario does not prevail, the role of an increasingly connected and concerned citizenry is on the rise. Just as the "invisible hand" of human nature has shaped and organized global markets for goods and services, so the same force can now find expression in a shared marketplace of ideas, values, beliefs, possibilities, and actions.

Two of the most interesting corporations of our time have chosen prescient and revealing taglines to describe their own animating forces, and by extension they provide us with a hint of the changing role and contribution of individuals everywhere. Microsoft's tagline is "Your Potential. Our Passion," while eBay has selected "The power of all of us." Together, these phrases hit on four of the six "Ps" that will matter most in the decade ahead: People, Potential, Power, and Passion. The fifth is Participation, which is increasing in myriad ways and at a staggering pace. The sixth is Purpose.

Participating together, passionate people will continue to discover and fulfill their potential and exercise their individual and collective power in pursuit of a shared moral purpose. This may be revolutionary—that is the essence of the *Emergence* scenario—or it may be evolutionary, but either way, it will be a growing and rather disruptive force, a force that has never before existed on our planet. This is an imminent empowerment of masses of humanity who will be sometimes quite united, often quite divided, and always keenly alert, aware, inquiring, and challenging. These masses will aggregate into a new, powerful, and unpredictable actor in world affairs.

With increased power comes increased responsibility. Can we global citizens really learn enough, about enough, fast enough, and well enough for our voices to have not only weight but wisdom? I believe that the impulse to learn will increase enormously—and there is good news in this regard. Not only are our technologies making information far more available (and helping us absorb and connect it) but we are also discovering that the human brain has a vital characteristic we have greatly underestimated until now. Technically, it is known as "plasticity." The brain is far more flexible than previously thought, and it remains that way throughout adulthood. It does not "cement," as researchers used to believe, but rather continues to be capable of adapting and adjusting, learning and relearning.

These are qualities we will need in the decades ahead, and we can happily anticipate significant breakthroughs in learning processes and approaches that will benefit all, making us better at fulfilling our strong impulses as sense-makers, pattern-seekers, and, above all, meaning-makers. We must, and we will, become more adept at scanning, better at listening deeply to others, faster at connecting the dots and discovering the new patterns. This, in turn, requires some concrete changes in how we perceive and understand the world around us. We must place more emphasis on divergent thinking, drill deeper into causes and systems, and adopt a larger and more inclusive definition of "we."

DIVERGENT THINKING

Most of us tend to be rather good at convergent thinking—quickly deciding upon our point of view and setting aside the other alternatives. Being decisive is also an important and essential attribute. But it might be wise to remember that the verb "decide" derives from the Latin "to kill": it means murdering our other options. Sometimes we should at least know what they are before we kill them. Too often we simply do not because we have not first engaged in divergent thinking. If there is a single recurrent and common theme running throughout this book, it is the power of a "both/and" thought process: the deliberate search for different, and even competing, perspectives, and the realization that both might hold important truths. But we routinely default to our certainties and biases and ignore the other possibilities and interpretations, along with the inconvenient data that does not fit our worldview.

In our organizations, this tendency is strongly compounded by many norms and procedures that encourage singularity of focus and discourage the acknowledgement of uncertainty and ambiguity. Indeed, even that most crucial of organizational requirements, a clear vision, can have drawbacks if it results, as it often does, in "getting all the wood behind the same arrow," which then misses the target. Versatility is perhaps just as important as vision, and it comes largely from the ability and willingness to think beyond the obvious, beyond the comfortable.

In our societies too, there appears to be less and less tolerance for the idea that, as David Hume put it, "truth springs from argument among friends"—if they are actively listening to one another and synthesizing their points of view. This hardly describes the growing global media and political cultures that are characterized by harsh and simplistic sound bites and the theatrical exchange of polarized and mutually exclusive certainties. Yet one of the most important features of divergent thinking lies in actively trying to understand the perspectives with which we most strongly disagree.

There is a paradoxical danger that in an increasingly connected world we end up with less diversity of perspective rather than more. Networks, which often have a strong self-selecting quality, may be far-reaching and heterogeneous, but they often attract people with very similar values and worldviews. Achieving true divergence of thought therefore requires active intention and changes in our behavior. Happily, this can be achieved. Engaging in genuine dialogue at the water cooler with the colleague who sees and interprets the world differently is more likely to provoke a new insight than a dozen conversations with someone who shares most of our opinions. Reading, with an open mind, the newspaper whose editorial line sets our teeth on edge is likely to push, challenge, and stretch our thinking far more than getting all our news from publications we already love. Dancing through the blogosphere with an eye for those blogs that demonstrate high quality and originality of thought, analysis, and synthesis—and there are a great many—rather than those that conform to certain ideological preferences will reveal extraordinary new resources for information and ideas. We can all give ourselves the gift of new learning from divergent thinking if we are willing to accept the discomfort and challenge it entails.

THE FIVE WHYS

As change accelerates, it is inevitable that important, new, and pressing issues will keep arising. It is equally predictable that the immediate tendency of the media, policy makers, and concerned citizens will be to observe and analyze tangible events and other manifestations of discontinuity and turbulence. But these events—the stuff of headlines and editorials, political pronouncements and media punditry—are often just the symptoms of much deeper patterns of change. In order to separate these dynamic manifestations of our volatile times from the more fundamental causes—and to understand the linkages between them—it is useful to borrow a simple tool from the discipline of systems thinking, often referred to as the "five whys." This involves framing an issue into a crisp question beginning with "why," answering that question, and then repeating the process until we have arrived at a deep structural understanding of the issue. This generally takes several iterations—not always precisely five, but five is a reasonable rule of thumb.

The "five whys" process can take us from high-level symptoms to deeper and more consequential causes; it forces us to think harder and more systemically than we would otherwise. It is an extremely effective way of making greater sense and meaning of events and issues, and it also feels intuitive and natural. In fact, most parents are already familiar with how the process works: a young child asks an apparently simple question, hears the first answer, and replies with, "But why?" The child then repeats the question until her urge to understand begins to be satisfied.

Using the "five whys" approach to enhance our understanding of major issues of our times is an effective way of drilling down into structural causes that are often not obvious when these issues are treated superficially. The process also helps reveal to us our own biases and assumptions. It can be extremely instructive to ask people or groups with a different sense of a problem or opportunity to explore their thoughts on the "whys" separately and then share them. Often this results in quite different ideas regarding the greater system within which the issue is playing out. Used in this way, the habit of "why, why, why" can both deepen our understanding and help inform divergent, "both/and" thinking.

A BIGGER "WE"

Some years ago I was asked a rather startling question: "If you could dictate one single and simple change in the world, to be made tomorrow, that would of itself lead to a better future, what would it be?" I don't recall my answer, but I do recall asking my questioner what his would be. "Solid scientific proof that we are all randomly reincarnated immediately after our death," he said. "If the 10 percent of us who happen to live in Europe or the U.S. knew that we and our loved ones were going to be reborn one day in a much poorer continent, I think we would see the world very differently." I can't imagine his wish will ever come true, but I do think his sentiment is spot on: we must expand our sense of "we" in our new global civilization.

Of all the changes that we are experiencing during this turbulent era, one of the most significant is certainly the interconnectedness and interdependence of every part of the world. Whatever domain we look at—the political, economic, financial, social, cultural, or environmental—the pattern is the same: no place, no country, no person, and no organization stands entirely alone in any sphere, and most of the world is tightly linked in all of them. This requires more global and more inclusive thinking about our challenges and opportunities, for we have truly arrived at that period in history in which we live together, as predicted in 1960 by Marshall McLuhan, in one large "global village." An important feature of the traditional village is the "commons"—land owned, used, and cared for collectively. The global commons today comprises tightly intertwined systems upon which we all depend. Can we aspire to both a more profound understanding of and a shared commitment to sustain and nurture this shared global commons? I believe we can. But it would be naïve to think that this will prove straightforward. For we will have to recognize and overcome the tendency toward the "tragedy of the commons."

This basic principle is often explained by reference to land that is in common ownership and that can be used by all—say, for purposes of grazing cattle. The incentive for each cattle owner is to overgraze the land but to take little or no responsibility for improving or maintaining it. Such an approach appears to serve each individual well in the short term. But in the longer term, the land becomes quite useless for everyone.

Could this principle apply at the global level as well? I think it already does. Looked at through the lens of rational self-interest, why should the U.S. radically reduce its energy consumption even as China and India increase theirs? Why should France invest its blood and treasure in keeping the peace in failing nations that other countries appear to deliberately destabilize? Why should Turkey care about the water requirements of Syria and Iraq as it dams the Euphrates River? Why should China respect

Western intellectual property rights? Why should any nation pay much more than lip service (and a small fraction of one paltry percent of their GDP) on partnering with Africa as it pursues its future renaissance? In every one of these cases and countless more, the unit of analysis has to be greater than the single nation-state; it has to be global, because the ultimate consequences of failing states, terrorism, desperate poverty, famine, water shortages, and climate change will be experienced everywhere.

This is a critical paradox of our powerful times—and it is absolutely essential that we dream and imagine better ways to resolve it. It is not melodramatic to state that our future depends on doing so. Our potential and capacity to craft an enduring global civilization is not in question. But our willingness and ability to collaborate and trust the "other" is not yet established. And without the latter, the former is meaningless. The tragedy of the commons can be solved—and throughout history has often been solved—but only with a combination of communication, commitment to collaborate, and trust that the other parties will stick to the agreement. And there is an additional complication not experienced in the village commons. Our looming global dilemmas are much more complex than anything we have ever previously encountered: the available information is ambiguous, the choices unclear, and the consequences are unknown and likely to remain so until they are upon us.

Given this, there are two important shifts that must take place. The first shift is simple: it is a willingness to believe in the scale of the issues confronting us while the evidence is mounting but before it is conclusive—in other words, before it is too late. Here I think we will come to the same conclusion as the famous French philosopher Blaise Pascal. Posing the question, "Should I believe in God?" Pascal reasoned that he should. God either exists, or he doesn't. Pascal can choose to believe, or not. If God does not exist, and Pascal does not believe, Pascal is smart—but otherwise there is no great upside. If God does not exist and Pascal believes, Pascal is foolish, and may have denied himself some earthly pleasures—unfortunate, but not dreadful. If God exists and Pascal believes, Pascal is saved—a fantastic outcome. If God exists and Pascal does not believe, Pascal is doomed—a terrible outcome. Weighing these up, it clearly makes sense for Pascal to choose to believe in God because the prize of being right is much greater and the cost of being wrong is much more appalling. As evidence mounts of our shared global challenges, I think we will make the same wager as Pascal and choose to take these challenges seriously and address them collaboratively. The prizes awaiting us if we succeed are glittering indeed, and the costs of failure are frightening to contemplate.

The second shift is less straightforward: we must match our new global reality with a new global empathy, based on an acknowledgment that we have never been more interdependent and our interests have never been more inseparable. We cannot negotiate our way through the complexity and challenges of our times alone, for we are all ultimately on the same side. Rather, we must begin to expand our circle of empathy, our sense of "we," and start taking into account the interests of all those who are immediately affected by every significant issue. Because in the end, "their" interests will inevitably overlap with "ours." In a radically globalized economy and civilization, there is less room for the "us versus them" mindset of previous generations. It would be foolish to imagine that we could or should ever abandon self-interest and natural closer affiliation with family, neighbors, and fellow citizens; these are powerful and essential impulses and the foundations of our collective growth and strength. But we can and we must become a "bigger we." We have globalized the economy and culture, but we have not yet globalized our sense of ourselves; that lies in our better future.

This will not be driven by national governments; it is not how they perceive their role. Neither will it be a priority of businesses small or large, even as they embrace the concept of moral wisdom; it is not their business. In fact, there is only one actor we can expect to promote the growing consciousness of a global self, and that is us: individuals, people, citizens. We have voice, we have passion, we have information, we have unprecedented latent power, and we have an incredible common stake— only the future of our emergent yet fragile civilization. If "the times are more powerful than our brains," we must continue to increase the power of our brains by increasingly aligning and connecting them. As we increase our wisdom, harmonize our aspirations and energies, and deploy our amazing human creativity, global citizens can and will make all the difference in the world, to the world. In the elegant words of the late U.S. President Ronald Reagan, "If not us, who? If not now, when?"

Endnotes

Chapter 1: History Unleashed

The opening quote is from "Little Gidding," one of the *Four Quartets* published by T.S. Eliot in 1943. Niccolo Machiavelli relates his exchange with Pandolfo Petrucci in *Legations*, a collection of diplomatic dispatches that he wrote while serving as an envoy following France's invasion of the peninsula in 1494. Machiavelli wrote about Petrucci again in *The Prince*, calling him "a very able man."

The "gobbledygook" paragraph was a popular meme back in September 2003, when it began to circulate on the Internet and through email circles. The effect demonstrated by the paragraph—that randomizing the letters in the middle of a word does not affect a person's ability to read and understand it—was first noted by G.E. Rawlinson in 1976 ("The Significance of Letter Positioning in Word Recognition," unpublished PhD thesis, psychology department, University of Nottingham, Nottingham, UK). In May 1999, Rawlinson wrote a letter to *New Scientist* demonstrating this effect; it is unclear how and why, four years later, it made the Internet rounds. For more on the back story of this meme and its origins, see www.mrc-cbu.cam.ac.uk/personal/matt.davis/Cambridge/.

The historical human population and GDP per capita data come from a chart created by J. Bradford DeLong, a professor of economics at the University of California at Berkeley and a research associate of the National Bureau of Economic Research. The chart can be viewed at http://www.j-bradford-delong.net/ macro_online/lec_notes/LN_ch5.pdf.

The "gorilla video" was created by Daniel J. Simons and Christopher F. Chabris, both part of the department of psychology at Harvard University, as part of a study on "selective looking" ("Gorillas in Our

Midst: Sustained Inattentional Blindness for Dynamic Events," *Perception*, 1999, volume 28, pages 1059-1074). The results of their study strongly suggest that "we perceive and remember only those objects and details that receive focused attention." The original report on this study can be found at http://www.wjh.harvard.edu/~cfc/Simons1999.pdf.

A list of nearly 100 kinds of known bias can be found at http://en.wikipedia.org/wiki/List_of_cognitive_biases. There are several websites that give an account of the story of the 1701 Dutch map of North America depicting California as an island, including http://www.philaprintshop.com/calis.html.

The global adult literacy statistic (74 percent) was calculated from by-country estimates produced by UNESCO Institute for Statistics in July 2002; "adult" refers to people 15 and older. The statistics about average life span and infant mortality come from the United Nations Development Programme's Human Development Report 2004.

The statistic about half of the world's population living on fewer dollars per day than European cows comes from James Wolfensohn, former president of the World Bank and author of *The Other Crisis*. As Wolfensohn told *Life*, a television program on TVE, a station supported by the World Wildlife Foundation and the United Nations Environment Programme: "We live in a world of 6 billion people, 3 billion people that live under $2 a day. European cows get subsidized to the extent of $2.50 a day (Japanese cows get subsidized to the extent of $7.50 a day) so there's something disproportionate in terms of the way that we're attending to the question of poverty."

Section 1: What's Happening?: Predicting the Present

The opening quote by physicist Niels Bohr embodies a fundamental principle of physics known as the principle of complementarity, which states that there may be more than one way to accurately view natural phenomena. If one's observations of an object or event are in conflict, the principle holds, a full understanding of that object or event can only be achieved by considering both viewpoints.

For years, I have been attributing the conception that driving our cars like we live our lives would result in wrecks on every corner to Marshall McLuhan, but I have been unable to verify him as its source. However, I did manage to uncover another McLuhan classic, which is close: "We drive into the future using only our rearview mirror." The F. Scott Fitzgerald quote is from "The Crack-Up," a story published in *Esquire* in February 1936. Hans Eysenck, the famed temperament theorist, was a vocal critic of Sigmund Freud and the psychoanalytic method; he argued vociferously that a person's personality was largely determined by genetics. Benjamin Spock, the pediatrician who coached generations of parents how to rear their children, argued that parents are a prime determinant in shaping the personalities of their children. Thus, these influential figures fell on opposite sides of the nature/nurture debate.

Chapter 2: Clarity and Craziness

CLARITY

The opening quote from Bodhidharma comes from *The Zen Teachings of Bodhidharma*, translated by Red Pine (North Point Press, 1987). The larger passage in which it occurs seems itself to embody both clarity and craziness: "That which doesn't exist doesn't exist in relation to that which exists. This is true vision. By means of such vision nothing is seen and nothing is not seen.... The mind and the world are opposites, and vision arises where they meet. When your mind doesn't stir inside, the world doesn't arise outside. When the world and the mind are both transparent, this is true vision. And such understanding is true understanding."

The statistics on the amount of stored information produced globally and the amount of recorded information produced per person per year come from the University of California at Berkeley's School of Information Management and Systems, *How Much Information 2003*, as reported in *Looking Out for the Future*, a small book about the future of philanthropy written by my colleagues Katherine Fulton and Andrew Blau (http://www.future of philanthropy.org).

The launch of online video search capabilities by Yahoo! and Google was reported, among other places, by ClickZ ("Yahoo!, Google Thrust Video Search into Spotlight," by Pamela Parker and Zachary Rogers, January 25, 2005). Yahoo! launched the beta site for its service in December 2004; Google launched its beta site in January 2005.

In 2002, *BBC News Online* reported that there were 2.5 million closed circuit television cameras operating in Great Britain ("Watching Your Every Move," by Jane Wakefield, February 7, 2002), and that analysts forecasted a tenfold increase in that number within five years. In 2004, *The Independent* reported that more than 4 million surveillance cameras were operating in Britain, "making it the most-watched nation in the world" ("Big Brother Britain 2004," by Maxine Frith, January 12, 2004).

China's plans to launch more than 100 surveillance satellites by 2020 was reported by Reuters ("China Plans to Have Over 100 Eyes in the Sky by 2020," November 16, 2004). Information on the U.S.'s GPS satellite constellation can be found on the homepage of the U.S. Naval Observatory (http://tycho.usno.navy.mil/gpscurr.html). The European Space Agency announced the final design of its proposed satellite navigation system, Galileo, which called for the placement of 30 satellites in medium Earth orbit, in September 2000.

In April 2005, the UK's Human Genetics Commission concluded that the UK should not pursue a national databank that would profile the DNA of every newborn. Their full report can be found online at http://www.hgc.gov.uk/UploadDocs/Contents/Documents/Final%20Draft %20of%20Profiling%20Newborn%20Report%2003%2005.pdf.

Information on Poseidon, the drowning-detection system, can be found at http://www.poseidon-tech.com.us.system.html. To read more about the RFID device VeriChip, visit http://www.4verichip.com. The story about VeriChip devices being implanted in employees of Mexico's attorney general was reported by TechWeb News ("RFID Chips Implanted in Mexican Law-Enforcement Workers," by W. David Gardner, July 15, 2004).

In April 2002, Japan's Earth Simulator Center announced that its "Earth Simulator" computer, manufactured by NEC, had been verified as the fastest-performing computer in the world. It did not hold that title for long. In September 2004, IBM announced that its Blue Gene/L super-computer had performed even faster; it was able to turn in a sustained performance of 36.01 teraflops. More information on the Earth Simulator can be found on the Earth Simulator Center website (http://www.es.jamstec.go.jp/esc/eng/). The announcement of the Blue Gene/L supercomputer's speed record can be found at http://www.ibm. com/news/us/2004/09/301.html.

The global IT spending forecast by Gartner Group comes from a CNN.com story on IT spending in Asia ("Asian Companies Lead IT Spending," December 7, 2004). The IDC analyst estimate of the global data mining tools market in 2006 was reported in "Data Mining Comes of Age," by Jack Vaughan, *Application Development Trends*, May 2002. The story on Wal-Mart's interpretation and anticipation of customer buying patterns, including said customers' penchant for Pop-Tarts after a storm, is a fascinating read: "What They Know About You," by Constance L. Hays, *The New York Times*, November 14, 2004.

The "congestion tax" was introduced to central London on February 17, 2003, in an attempt to reduce traffic flow through the city's roads. For more on this taxing system, see the BBC's guide at http://www.bbc.co.uk/london/congestion/intro.shtml. The 9/11 Commission's final report can be downloaded at http://www.gpoaccess.gov/911/.

A PDF of the Report to Congress Regarding the Information Awareness Program (109 pages) can be downloaded from the website of the Electronic Frontier Foundation at http://www.eff.org/Privacy/TIA/TIA-report.pdf. Creating a "virtually" centralized database was one of TIA's many ambitious goals; the quote describing that effort, which was a component of a TIA program called Genisys, can be found in this report. The Dianne Feinstein quote is from "Massive Database Dragnet Explored," by Jim Puzzanghera, *The San Jose Mercury News*, November 21, 2002.

For more on the "second Internet," see "Pentagon Envisioning a Costly Internet for War," by Tim Weiner, *The New York Times*, November 13, 2004. For more on smart dust, see "Dust Keeping the Lights Off," by Farhad Manjoo, *Wired* News, May 28, 2001.

One of many stories about the pushback campaign against targeted advertising in Google's Gmail service is "Will Gmail Read Your Mail," by Sebastian Rupley, *PC Magazine*, April 13, 2004. The story of JetBlue Airways giving away its passenger records ran in *Wired* magazine's newswire ("JetBlue 'Fesses Up, Quietly," by Ryan Singel, September 19, 2003).

The *Washington Times* editorial mentioned in the discussion about the future of individual privacy is "Biometrics Are Coming," June 30, 2003. Scott McNealy issued his now infamous "You have zero privacy anyway" statement to a group of reporters and analysts at an event for the launch of Sun's Jini technology in January 1999.

The full reference for the Michel Foucault book that describes Jeremy Bentham's Panoptican prison is *Discipline & Punish: The Birth of the Prison* (New York: Vintage Books, 1995). The book was originally published in 1995, in France, as *Surveiller et Punir, Naissance de la Prison.* The facts about the Bush Administration's efforts to protect millions of documents from declassification and about Freedom of Information Act requests come from "Wartime Environment: Government By, For, and Secret From the People," by Eric Lichtblau, *The New York Times,* September 5, 2004.

The U.S. nationwide survey that found that 14 percent of Americans would pay to watch their home through Net-connected cameras was reported in "Forget to Turn Off the Stove? Turn to the Net," by Peter J. Howe, *The International Herald Tribune,* November 3, 2004. The example of Japanese pupils wearing RFID tags to school comes from an Associated Press story that ran in many newspapers around the world, including *The Japan Times,* where I found it ("Students Tagged in Bid to Keep Them Safe," by Kenji Hall, October 14, 2004). For an interesting story about Cincinnati's efforts to prevent crime with well-placed surveillance cameras, see "Here's Looking at You," by Pete Shuler, *Cincinnati CityBeat,* volume 5, issue 34, July 15-21, 1999 (http://www.citybeat.com/1999-07-15/cover.shtml).

For more on WITNESS, the nonprofit that uses "video and technology to fight for human rights," visit http://www.witness.org/. For more on the lascivious uses of cellphone cameras in Japan, see "Camera-Equipped Cellphones Spread New Brands of Mischief," by AP business writer Yuri Kageyama, *The Detroit News,* July 10, 2003. For more on South Korea's law requiring that cellphones beep before taking a photo, see "Camera Phones Fire a Warning Shot," by Alicia Ferrari, Forbes.com, December 10, 2003.

CRAZINESS

The full reference on the *Houston Chronicle* article about moon landing conspiracy theories is "Apollo Shrugged; Hoax Theories About Moon Landings Persist," by Patty Reinert, November 17, 2002. The results of the March 2002 Gallup Poll that found that large percentages of people in nine Islamic countries did not believe Arabs were responsible for the September 11 attacks were reported in several places, including in the story "Viewing 9/11 as the Big Lie," by Scott Shane, *The Baltimore Sun,* September 12, 2002.

The URL for the BBC's mentioning of the Diego Garcia conspiracy theory is http://news.bbc.co.uk/1/hi/programmes/newsnight/4149637 .stm. For some interesting stories on the theory that RFID tags are the work of Satan, Google "Satan and RFID." For more on the allegations that Coca-Cola supports right-wing death squads in Colombia, see "Brands Can Find the Going Tough," by Alison Maitland, *The Financial Times*, November 29, 2004. For more on the accusation that Caribou Coffee funds Islamic terrorists, see "Caribou Grinds Away at Rumor," by John Schmeltzer, *Chicago Tribune*, May 20, 2004.

Information about the power of negative advertising comes from "Going Negative: When It Works," Jim Rutenberg and Kate Zernike, *The New York Times*, August 22, 2004. Two stories on the elaboration of the Jessica Lynch story are "Unmaking the Myth of Jessica Lynch," by Anna Cock, *Sunday Mail*, November 30, 2003, and "Saving Private England," by Frank Rich, *The New York Times*, May 16, 2004.

The estimate of the size of the Astroturf industry comes from "Grassroots: The Chemical Industry's Astroturf Agenda," *The Chemical Industry Archives*, March 23, 2001.

For more on the Citigroup campaign and the counter-campaign by the Rainforest Action Network, see "Jamming Citigroup's PR Message: An Interview with Ilyse Hogue of Rainforest Action Network," by Jennifer Bauduy, TomPaine.com, May 9, 2002. The IDC data on phishing comes from "The Web: Expect More Swindles in 2005," by Gene J. Koprowski, *The Washington Times*, December 22, 2004. The Gartner data on identity theft, gathered in a February 2002 customer survey, was reported in a Gartner press release in July 2003.

The Paul Krugman quote comes from his *New York Times* column "Saving the Vote," which ran on August 17, 2004.

Chapter 3: Secular and Sacred

SECULAR

The definition of *saeculum* comes from the Merriam-Webster Dictionary. It is sometimes translated "of the era" or "of the generation."

George Jacob Holyoake coined the term "secularism" after a six-month imprisonment for blasphemy committed during a public lecture, in the early 1840s. According to Wikipedia, he was also "the last person indicted

for publishing an unstamped newspaper." Holyoake's definition of secularism can be found in the online edition of The Catholic Encyclopedia,
under "secularism" (http://www.newadvent.org/cathen/13676a.htm).

The patent statistics reported by Thomas Friedman ran in "War of
Ideas," Part 6, *The New York Times*, January 25, 2004. Friedman got those
statistics from the United Nations Development Programme's 2003 Arab
Human Development Report.

The quote from Anthony Wallace—"the evolutionary future of religion is extinction"—comes from his book *Religion: An Anthropological
View* (New York: Random House, 1966). The sentences immediately following his pronouncement read: "Belief in supernatural beings and in
supernatural forces that affect nature without obeying nature's laws will
erode and become only an interesting historical memory. ...The process
is inevitable" (pp. 264-265).

The full reference on Steve Bruce's book is *God Is Dead: Secularization
in the West* (Oxford: Blackwell Publishers, 2002). The quote beginning
"Christian ideas are not taught in schools" can be found in Bruce's journal
article "Christianity in Britain, R.I.P.," *Sociology of Religion*, Summer 2001.

The quote "not everything that counts can be counted, and not everything that can be counted counts" allegedly hung on the wall of Albert
Einstein's office at Princeton.

Depression statistics come from "Help for Depression Lacking, Studies
Find 14 Million Americans Suffer Major Episode Annually, Doctors Say,"
by Katherine Siligman, *The San Francisco Chronicle*, June 18, 2003. For
more on the World Health Organization's study of depression, suicide,
and other mental health issues, see "The World Health Report 2001:
Mental Health: New Understanding, New Hope."

SACRED

The statistic that 67 percent of Americans say religious beliefs play a role
in their lives comes from the PEW Research Center survey "Among
Wealthy Nations...U.S. Stands Alone in Its Embrace of Religion,"
December 19, 2002. The survey looked at the personal importance of
religion among citizens of 44 nations.

The *New York Times* survey on the discussion of the expression of personal religious views in political campaigns was reported in the *Times* on
July 4, 2004 ("Politicians Talk More About Religion, and People Expect

Them To"). George W. Bush met with Pope John Paul II on June 4, 2004. For a good article on Bush's efforts to win more of the Catholic vote, see "Bush's Catholic Courtship Strategy," by Deborah Caldwell, Beliefnet.com, June 2004 (http://www.beliefnet.com/story/146/story_14691_1.html).

The full reference for the quoted Pew survey is "Views of a Changing World 2003: War with Iraq Further Divides Global Publics," Pew Global Attitudes Project, June 3, 2003. Statistics on the growth of Pentecostalism come from *Operation World* by Peter Johnstone and Jason Mandryk (2000), as cited in Wikipedia. The full reference on Phillip Longman's book is *The Empty Cradle: How Falling Birthrates Threaten World Prosperity and What to Do About It* (New York: Basic Books, 2004). The quote on fundamentalism by Karen Armstrong comes from her book *Islam: A Short History* (New York: Random House, 2000).

For an excellent discussion of the philosophy of Sayyid Qutb, see "The Philosopher of Islamic Terror," by Paul Berman, *The New York Times Magazine*, March 23, 2003.

Philip Jenkins's article is "The Next Christianity," *Atlantic Monthly*, October 2002. Statistics on the *Left Behind* series come from the book series' website, http://www.leftbehind.com. Steve Bruce's quote is from his book *God Is Dead: Secularization in the West* (Oxford: Blackwell Publishers, 2002).

The full reference on William Bloom's book is *Holistic Revolution: The Essential New Age Reader* (London: Allen Lane, 2000). The statistic on the ranks of "nones" comes from "Number of 'Nones,' Those Who Claim No Religion, Swells in U.S.," by Mark O'Keefe, Newhouse News Service, November 26, 2003. For more on the work of Paul Ray and Sherry Ruth Anderson, see *The Cultural Creatives: How 50 Million People Are Changing the World* (New York: Harmony Books, 2000). "Soul of Britain" was a BBC TV series that considered the role of spirituality in Britain 2,000 years after the birth of Christ. The series ran in 2000. David Hay and Kate Hunt created a spirituality survey for the show.

In its special report "Americans Embrace Ancient Practice of Yoga" (March 26, 2005), ABC.com included this quote: "There are currently 16.5 million people who practice yoga [in the United States]," said Lynn Lehmkuhl, an editor at *Yoga Journal* magazine. "And since 2002, that's been literally an increase of 43 percent, which is phenomenal."

Information on the adoption of planet-saving principles by the Christian right is from "The Greening of Evangelicals," by Blaine Harden, *The Washington Post*, February 6, 2005. Results of a four-year longitudinal study of New Agers are reported in *The Index of Leading Spiritual*, by George Barna (Dallas: Word Publishing, 1996). The James Lovelock quote is from his well-distributed essay, "What Is Gaia?"

Chapter 4: Power and Vulnerability

POWER

Francis Fukuyama's ideas about the triumph of liberal governments over authoritarian regimes are well outlined and argued in *The End of History and the Last Man* (New York: The Free Press, January 1992).

The statistics on overall military spending for Europe and the U.S. in 1990 and 2000 as percentage of GDP come from figures reported by the U.S. Congressional Budget Office in Chapter II of "Integrating New Allies into NATO," October 2000, available online at http://www.cbo.gov/showdoc.cfm?index=2665&sequence=3. The full text of Adam Smith's *The Wealth of Nations* is also available online, at http://www.bibliomania.com/2/1/65/112/frameset.html.

The Niall Ferguson quote is from his article "An Empire in Denial: The Limits of U.S. Imperialism," *Harvard International Review*, September 22, 2003. For more on Thomas Barnett's summary of U.S. security priorities, see Chapter 8, "Hope Without Guarantees," in *The Pentagon's New Map* (New York: Putnam Publishing Group, April 2004). To read the 9-11 Commission Report online, visit http://www.gpoaccess.gov/911/.

The paragraph in which the U.S.'s military expenditures are compared and contrasted with those of other nations and regions contains statistics compiled from a number of sources: "High Military Expenditure in Some Places," by Anup Shah, Globalissues.org, June 16, 2004; the Center for Defense Information; Worldwide Military Expenditures chart, GlobalSecurity.org; "Priorities in Public Spending," the United Nations Development Programme's Human Development Report 2004; "World Military Spending," Center for Arms Control and Non-Proliferation, February 2004.

Lieutenant General Michael V. Hayden's characterization of intelligence versus mass on the battlefield ran in "Unrivaled Military Feels Strains of Unending War," by Thomas E. Ricks and Vernon Loeb, *The Washington Post*, February 16, 2003.

The full citation for Dan Baum's provocative article on innovative learning styles among junior officers in the U.S. military is "Battle Lessons: What the Generals Don't Know," *The New Yorker*, January 17, 2005.

Robert Kagan's book is *Of Paradise and Power: America and Europe in the New World Order* (New York: Alfred A. Knopf, January 2003). The hard versus soft power distinction drawn by Joseph Nye is explored in several of Joseph Nye's books, including *Bound to Lead: The Changing Nature of American Power* (New York: Basic Books, 1990); *The Paradox of American Power: Why the World's Only Superpower Can't Go It Alone* (New York: Oxford University Press, 2002); and, most recently, *Soft Power: The Means to Success in World Politics* (New York: Public Affairs Press, March 2004).

The Gallup International "Voice of the People" survey involved more than 28,000 interviews conducted during July and August 2002. Gallup published the results on September 7, 2002, in a press release titled "Global Survey Results Give a Thumbs Down to U.S. Foreign Policy."

VULNERABILITY

Barry Glasner's book is *The Culture of Fear: Why Americans Are Afraid of the Wrong Things* (New York: Basic Books, April 1999). The British media reporting study, "Health in the News: Risk, Reporting, and Media Influence," was authored by Roger Harrabin, Anna Coote, and Jessica Allen and published by the King's Fund in September 2003. Statistics on global terrorism deaths and auto vehicle deaths come from "Do We Fear the Right Things?" by David G. Myers, *American Psychological Society Observer*, December 2001. The murder statistic comes from data compiled by the FBI. The total number of people murdered in the U.S. in 2000 (15,590) was the lowest in two decades.

The full quote from Robert Cooper, a diplomat and senior advisor to Tony Blair, can be found in his book, *The Breaking of Nations* (New York: Atlantic Monthly Press, January 2004): "What kind of world would we find ourselves in if the United States were both the only military power that counted and at the same time subject to continuous terrorist attacks?

All-powerful and all-vulnerable? How long would the values that Europe and America share survive?"

The full reference on Graham Allison's book is *Nuclear Terrorism: The Ultimate Preventable Catastrophe* (New York: Times Books, August 2004). Allison is the founding dean of Harvard's John F. Kennedy School of Government. Philip Bobbitt wrote about the differences between informing, alerting, and warning in the Op-Ed piece "Being Clear About Present Dangers," *The New York Times*, August 11, 2004.

Moises Naim, editor and publisher of *Foreign Policy* magazine, outlined his ideas on crime in an interconnected world in "The Five Wars of Globalization, *Foreign Policy*, January/February 2003.

The statistics about human trafficking come from several sources: "Boost for Battle Against People Smuggling, People Trafficking and Transnational Crime," press release, Office of the Minister of Foreign Affairs, Australia, June 8, 2004; "People Smuggling, Trafficking Generate Nearly $10 Billion Annually as Core Businesses of International Criminal Networks, Third Committee Told," United Nations Information Service, October 14, 2003; "People Smuggling: Challenge and Response," Interpol fact sheet, available online at http://www.interpol.com/Public/ICPO/FactSheets/FS15.asp; "U.S. Aims to End People Trafficking," BBC News, February 17, 2004.

The "time to China" fact comes from Andrew Zolli, in a presentation at a Global Business Network meeting on the future of brands in May 2004. The Interpol statistics on counterfeit goods come from the First Global Congress on Combating Counterfeiting, co-sponsored by Interpol and the World Customs Organization and held in Brussels in May 2004. The pirated software in China statistic comes from "Manufakteture," by Ted C. Fishman, *The New York Times*, January 9, 2005.

The World Health Organization's 2001 report on drug-resistant viruses is "Antibiotic Resistance: Synthesis of Recommendations by Expert Policy Groups." For more on the renewed threat of TB, see the Harvard Medical School report "The Global Impact of Drug-Resistant Tuberculosis," which describes multidrug resistant TB as "Ebola with wings." Statistics on drug-resistant staph infections come from "When Microbes Attack," by Stuart Luman, *Wired* magazine, July 2003, and "Nurses Call for Clean Uniforms to Beat MRSA," by Celia Hall, *The Daily Telegraph*, April 28, 2004.

The computer virus statistics reported in this chapter come from several sources: "Crippling Computer Viruses and Spam Attacks Threaten the Information Economy: Can They Be Stopped?" by Steve Hamm, *BusinessWeek*, September 8, 2003; "Viruses That Cost You," Symantec website; "SoBig.f Windows Virus Damages Hit U.S. $5.59 Billion," by Bryan Chaffin, *The Mac Observer*, August 27, 2003; "Proof of Concept," by Simson Garfinkel, *Technology Review*, May 2003.

For more on plans to develop a U.S. traveler database, see "U.S. to Push Airlines for Passenger Records," by Sara Kehaulani Goo, *The Washington Post*, January 12, 2004.

Chapter 5: Technology Acceleration and Pushback

TECHNOLOGY ACCELERATION
A good, clear source on the future of biocomputing is "Biologically Inspired Computing," by Nancy Forbes, available online at the Computing in Science & Engineering Portal. The quote from Stan Williams comes from "Quantum Computing," by Kevin Maney, *USA Today*, July 29, 2000.

The Paul Saffo quote is from *What's Next?: Exploring the New Terrain for Business*, by Eamonn Kelly, Peter Leyden, and members of Global Business Network (Cambridge, MA: Perseus Publishing, 2002). Information on Harvard's Personal Genome Project comes from "The Personal Genome Project," by Jamais Cascio, Worldchanging.org, August 27, 2004.

The quote regarding the Neuro-Chip comes from "Biosensor Chip Expands Neuroscience Horizons," by Christina Nickolas, Editorial Products (a Hearst Electronics Group website), April 2003.

For much more detail on thought-power experiments with monkeys and DARPA's human enhancement projects, see Joel Garreau's book, *Radical Evolution: The Promise and Peril of Enhancing Our Minds, Our Bodies—and What It Means to Be Human* (New York: Doubleday, May 2005). Information on MIT's nanotechnology research comes from "Tiny Tech to Help Big Soldiers," by Ian Hardy, August 17, 2003.

Information on the cognitive enhancement drug modafinil is from "Eleven Steps to a Better Brain," *New Scientist*, May 28, 2005. *The Economist* article stating that Americans spend more on beauty than education is "Pots of Promise," May 22, 2003. Cosmetic surgery statistics come from the American Society for Aesthetic Plastic Surgery.

PUSHBACK

South Korean's scientist Hwang Woo-suk's views on human cloning were reported in "Korea Stem Cell Expert: No Human Clones in 100 Years," Reuters, June 7, 2005. George Bush's denouncement of Hwang's research was reported in "Washington Criticizes South Korea Cloning Research," by Terence Hunt, Associated Press, May 20, 2005. The Vatican condemned Hwang's research in a public statement issued on May 24, 2005. The *Korea Times* reported the story of Hwang's meeting with Catholic leaders in "Hwang Woo-suk to Meet Archbishop on Wednesday," June 14, 2005.

The new U.S. federal guidelines for human-animal chimeras were issued by the National Academies of Sciences in April 2005. The Kevin Kelly quote comes from his conversations with Global Business Network. The *New Scientist* quote comes from "Ebola Virus Could Be Synthesized," by Sylvia Pagan Westphal, July 17, 2002.

George Bush's speech to the Biotechnology Industry Organization was widely reported, including in "Bush Stumps for BioShield Bill," by Kristen Philipkoski, *Wired* News, June 23, 2003.

Chapter 6: Intangible and Physical Economies

INTANGIBLE

Alan Greenspan's quote comes from a speech he gave in Minneapolis on September 30, 1999. His full remarks can be found in the "speeches" section of the Federal Reserve Board's website. For more on the physiocrats, see "The History of Physiocracy in 18th Century France," by Gene Dallaire, available online at http://genedallaire.tripod.com/physiocracy.html.

Data on the size and shape of the U.S. services sector come from several sources: "Why Are the Service Sectors Important" on the TESS (Trade Enhancement for the Services Sector) website of the United States Agency for International Development; "Productivity in the Services Sector: New Sources of Economic Growth," by Jack E. Triplett and Barry

P. Bosworth, Brookings Institute Press, 2004; "U.S. Services Growth Hits Record in April, Jobs Gain," by Chris Reese, Reuters, May 5, 2004; "Liberalizing Services: Key to Faster Global Growth and the Sustainability of the U.S. Trade Deficit," testimony by the Institute for International Economics' Catherine L. Mann before the Subcommittee on International Trade, Senate Finance Committee, October 21, 1999; and "Deepening Reform and Opening Wider to Ensure Sustainable Economic Growth," presentation by Li Ruogu, deputy governor of the People's Bank of China, Trujillo, Peru, October 23, 2004.

Data on the knowledge-based percentage of the OECD's GDP comes from "The Competitiveness of Nations in a Global Knowledge-Based Economy," by Harry Hillman Chartrand, April 2002.

The computing power comparison between a modern car and Apollo 11 comes from a speech by Toyota COO Jim Press on November 10, 2004, available in Toyota's online pressroom.

The source of the statistic about tourism as the world's largest employer comes from the World Travel and Tourism Council. All other global tourism statistics come from the World Tourism Organization's "Tourism Highlights" (2004 edition), available on its website. Statistics about the size of the global spectator sports market come from PriceWaterhouseCoopers' "Global Entertainment and Media Outlook: 2004–2008."

The full reference on Pine and Gilmore's book is *The Experience Economy: Work Is Theatre and Every Business a Stage*, by B. Joseph Pine II and James H. Gilmore (Boston, MA: Harvard Business School Press, April 1999).

Statistics on the creative sector in the UK come from a 2004 call for papers by the *International Journal of Entrepreneurship and Innovation* for a special issue titled "Entrepreneurship in the Creative Industries: An International Perspective." London-specific creative sector statistics come from "London's Creative Sector: 2004 Update," Greater London Authority, April 2004.

The Progressive Corp. story comes from "Companies that Really Get It," by Heather Green, *BusinessWeek*, August 25, 2003.

A human kidney was put up for auction on eBay in August 1999. Bids reached more than $5.7 million before the company blocked the sale. The grilled cheese sandwich featuring the image of the Virgin Mary went for $28,000, according to ABC News.

Google's revenue statistic comes from "Google Reports Record Q1 Revenues," *Finfacts Business News*, April 22, 2005.

The statistic on worldwide broadband subscribers comes from an IMS Research press release, "Broadband Subscribers Surge Past 150 Million," March 3, 2005, as well as IMS data reported by IT Facts. Statistics on broadband use in U.S. households comes from the September 2004 issue of the technology analysis newsletter *The Next Big Thing*.

The quote from Andrew Blau comes from his report "The Future of Independent Media," published by Global Business Network in 2004.

The statistic on Internet users in China comes from the website Internet World Stats: Usage and Population Statistics; original comes from the China Internet Network Information Centre. Global mobile phone statistics also come from Internet World Statistics, as well as the International Telecommunications Union.

Data on blogging in the U.S. is from "The State of Blogging," Pew Internet & American Life Project, January 2, 2005. Steve Weber's book, *The Success of Open Source*, was published by Harvard University Press in April 2004. Howard Rheingold's book is *Smart Mobs: The Next Social Revolution* (Cambridge, MA: Perseus Books, October 2002).

Global online gaming market statistics come from "The Online Game Market Heats Up," June 20, 3004, a summary of a FDC Intelligence research report on the industry. Projections about China's dominance of the online gaming market come from "China Online Gaming Report," by Margaret Chen, published by Game Trust and distributed by The Diffusion Group. The *Financial Times* article about online gaming is "Realities of a Virtual Economy," by Paul Tyrrell, December 29, 2003.

PHYSICAL

Data on the U.S.'s port security upgrade budget comes from "Homeland Security: Spending More, Getting Less," by James Carafano, The Heritage Foundation, March 3, 2005. Data on the state of the U.S.'s wastewater systems, and on the required U.S. infrastructure spending, comes from the American Society of Civil Engineers' 2003 Progress Report, an update to its Report Card for America's Infrastructure, published in 2001.

Statistics about the size and scope of the 2003 North American electricity blackout, as well as George Bush's statement about the event, come from "Bush Urges U.S. Grid Upgrade," BBC News, August 15, 2003. Bruce Germano's quote about a "self-healing" grid comes from "Electricity Innovation Institute and EPRI Unveil Architecture for Upgrade of the Power Grid," by Ed Krasnow, LivePowerNews, October 15, 2004.

For the story of Los Angeles's bus sensor project, see "No Best Way: L.A. Transit Saves Commuters Money, But Takes Too Much Time," by Howard Fine, *Los Angeles Business Journal*, April 19, 2004. For more on "hot lanes" in San Diego and elsewhere, see "Solo in Carpool Lane: That's HOT," by Larry Copeland, *USA Today*, May 9, 2005.

World Bank estimates of the developing world's infrastructure investment needs were reported in the World Bank Policy Research Working Paper "Investing in Infrastructure: What Is Needed From 2000 to 2010?" by Marianne Fay and Tito Yepes, July 2003.

The statistic about migrant workers in Beijing comes from "Injury Insurance for Construction Workers," *China Daily*, May 9, 2005. Statistics on China's water and air-quality problems, as well as its energy consumption relative to the U.S. and its projected energy shortfall, comes from "China's Boom Brings Fear of an Electricity Breakdown," by Howard French, *The New York Times*, July 5, 2004. China's dominant cement and steel consumption has been widely reported.

The comparison between water consumption and population growth over time comes from "Water Scarcity: A Looming Crisis?" by Alex Kirby, BBC News, October 19, 2004. The fact about the amount of freshwater used for irrigation comes from "Water: More Nutrition per Drop," a report of the Stockholm International Water Institute, August 2004. WHO statistics on water and sanitation come from "Clean Water Advocacy Motivates Partnership," *BusinessWorld*, August 19, 2003.

The quote from the World Resources Institute comes from "World's Water Resources in Swift Decline," by Carmen Revenga, World Resources Institute commentary, March 2005. The statements of UNESCO's director-general come from "UNESCO Director-General Warns of Looming Water Crisis," UNESCO press release, March 22, 2002.

Chapter 7: Prosperity and Decline

PROSPERITY

The wealth gap ratios between rich and poor were reported in the United Nations Development Programme's 2000 Human Development Report. Bradford DeLong's data on the relative GDP of various communist and non-communist nations comes from table 5.4 in Chapter 5, "The Reality of Economy Growth: History and Prospect," in the textbook *Macroeconomics*, by Bradford DeLong, Arman Mansoorian, and Leo Michelis (New York: McGraw-Hill, 2004).

The GDP per capita data per region from 1950 to 1992 comes from Angus Maddison's Monitoring the World Economy, 1820–1992 (Organization for Economic Cooperation and Development, 1995). The Goldman Sachs study of the growing power of the BRICs is "Dreaming With BRICs: The Path to 2050," by Dominic Wilson and Roopa Purushothaman, October 1, 2003.

The size of India's English-speaking population was reported in "Subcontinent Raises Its Voice," by David Crystal, *Guardian Weekly*, November 19, 2004. Information on India's efforts to become a center for foreign patient care comes from "India: First Software, Now Surgery," by Abhay Singh and Mrinalini Datta, *Bloomberg Markets*, March 2005.

The number of Chinese students who have studied abroad since 1978 is not consistently reported. The statistic used in this chapter comes from "China's Diaspora Show the Benefits of Free Movement," by David Zweig, *The Asian Wall Street Journal*, September 2, 2004. Information about China's high-tech parks comes from "Exhibition Showcases Achievement of Overseas Returnees," by Liang Chao, *China Daily*, March 2, 2004, and AnnaLee Saxenian's working paper on "Brain Circulation and Capitalist Dynamics: The Silicon Valley-Hsinchu-Shanghai Triangle," The Center for Economy and Society, Cornell University, August 2003. Overseas Chinese students' desire to return to China was reported in "Chinese Seeking Knowledge Abroad," *China Daily*, July 4, 2003.

Information about Brazil's AIDS drug strategy is from "The Right Prescription," by Francesco Neves, *Brazzil*, April 2001, and "Brazil to Break AIDS Drug Patents," BBC News, December 1, 2004.

Statistics on India and its telecom market can be found in "India Country Commercial Guide FY 2004," produced by the U.S. Commercial Service, October 31, 2002. For more on Tata's $2,200 car, see "Getting the Best to the Masses," by Manjeet Kripalani, *Business Week,* October 11, 2004.

C.K. Prahalad's book is *The Fortune at the Bottom of the Pyramid: Eradicating Poverty Through Profits* (Upper Saddle River, NJ: Wharton School Publishing, 2004).

Information about Whirlpool's low-cost washing machine is from "Whirlpool Launches Affordable Washer in Brazil and China," by Miriam Jordan and Jonathan Karp, *The Wall Street Journal Europe,* December 9, 2003. For more about Adaptive Eyecare, visit http://www.adaptive-eyecare.com/index.htm.

Hernando de Soto's book is *The Mystery of Capital: Why Capitalism Triumphs in the West But Fails Everywhere Else* (New York: Basic Books, 2000). The statistic about rich-nation agricultural subsidies comes from "The Unkept Promise," a "harvesting poverty" editorial in *The New York Times,* December 30, 2003.

Data about U.S. tariffs comes from several sources, primarily two works by Edward Gresser ("America's Hidden Tax on the Poor," Progressive Policy Institute policy report, March 2002, and "It's Expensive Being Poor," *The Far Eastern Economic Review,* June 10, 2004). Another article based on Gresser's work, "The Truth About Industrial Country Tariffs," was published in the International Monetary Fund's *Finance & Development,* September 2002, volume 39, number 3. For more on the World Bank's position on trade protection, see "World Bank Urges Rich Countries to Cut Trade Barriers, Boost Aid," World Bank press release, May 22, 2003.

DECLINE

For a quick but useful list of facts and figures on global poverty, see the United Nations Development Programme's website at http://www.undp.org/teams/english/facts.htm; another useful summary of United Nations Development Programme data can be found at http://www.gateway.hr/index.php?folder=127&article=214.

The Joseph Stiglitz quote is from his October 2002 article in the *Atlantic Monthly,* "The Roaring Nineties."

UNAid's AIDS death projections to 2020 were widely reported, including in "AIDS Epidemic 'Still in Early Stages,'" BBC News, July 2, 2002. Data on the resurgence of polio comes from "WHO Official Is Optimistic of Halting Polio," by Jonathan Bor, *The Baltimore Sun*, May 9, 2005.

The World Bank Institute's research on corruption and explanation of the "400 percent governance dividend" can be found in "Growth Without Governance," by D. Kaufmann and A. Kraay, *Economia*, Fall 2002, Volume 3, Number 1. The WBI's calculation of cumulative global bribes comes from "The Cost of Corruption," the World Bank Group, April 8, 2004. Corruption "scores" were reported in "West Urged to Crack Down on Company Bribes in Poor Nations," by David White, *Financial Times*, October 8, 2003.

Statistics on the number of armed conflicts experienced by nations according to their Human Development Index rankings come from the UN Development Programme's *Human Development Report* 2003 and Ploughshares' *Armed Conflicts Report*. Statistics about volume of global conflicts and Africa's civil wars come from GlobalSecurity.org and "The World at War," by Col. Daniel Smith, *The Defense Monitor*, January 1, 2003.

The statistics on income growth for the world's rich versus poor have been widely reported, including in "Can Globalization Be Tamed?" by Steve Schifferes, BBC, February 24, 2004. The CIA's latest rankings of the wealthiest nations (by GDP per capita) are published in its online-accessible CIA World Factbook. Russian billionaire statistics come from Forbes data reported in *The Moscow Times* in "Russia No. 4 on Forbes' Billionaires List," by Natalia Yefimova, March 3, 2003.

Data on the income gap between urban and rural workers in China comes from "Farmers' Income Up; Urban-Rural Gap Widens," by Fu Jing, *China Daily*, April 14, 2005. Statistics on Russia's income gap come from "A Modest Bourgeoisie Buds in Russia," by Margaret Mary Henry, *The Christian Science Monitor*, February 4, 2002. The Congressional Budget Office released updated statistics on after-tax income in the U.S. from 1979 to 2000 in 2003.

The projection of the German worker-pensioner ratio in 2020 comes from "Nightmare of Social Europe," by Martin Walker, *The Washington Times*, April 24, 2005. Information on Germany's aging population is from "Survey: The Near Future (Part I)," by Peter Drucker, *CFO Magazine*, November 2, 2001.

Statistics on the U.S. account deficit come from "The Overstretch Myth," by David H. Levey and Stuart S. Brown, *Foreign Affairs*, March/April 2005. The CBO's budget deficit forecast was widely reported, including in "$2.4 Trillion U.S. Deficit Is Forecast," by Peter Gosselin, *The Los Angeles Times*, January 27, 2005. The chapter's closing quote is by British diplomat and foreign policy analyst Robert Cooper, from his article "Europe: The Post-Modern State and World Order," *New Perspectives Quarterly*, Summer 1997 v14 n3.

Chapter 8: People and Planet

PEOPLE

The full reference on Daniel Quinn's book is *Ismael: An Adventure of the Mind and Spirit* (New York: Bantam/Turner Books, 1992).

Most population estimates in this chapter are from Joseph Chamie, until recently the head of the United Nations population division. Chamie is also the founder of Population Associates, Inc., and now writes a monthly population column for Global Business Network. For a good one-page summary of global population trends, visit the "issue" page of the Population Institute website.

The Thomas Malthus quote is from "Essay on the Principle of Population" (London, printed for J. Johnson, in St. Paul's Church-yard, 1798). For details of Ehrlich's lost bet with Julian Simon, see http://www.overpopulation.com/faq/People/julian_simon.html.

The data on Italy's birth rate, which is the lowest in Europe, as well as global birth rates in 1970 and today, comes from the United Nations Development Programme's 2004 Human Development Report. Phillip Longman's book is *The Empty Cradle: How Falling Birthrates Threaten World Prosperity and What to Do About It* (New York: Basic Books, April 2004).

The distribution of population between developed and developing world in 1960 and today comes from the United Nations Population Fund's "State of the World Population 1999," available on the UNFPA website. Statistics on the aging developed-world population come from a United Nations population division report on "World Population Ageing 1950–2050." Statistics on the proportion of pensioners to workers in Europe now and in 2050 come from "Europe's Population Implosion," *The Economist*, July 17, 2003. Over-65 population projections for the United States come from U.S. Census Bureau calculations.

Statistics regarding energy consumption by the world's richest people versus that by the world's poorest come from "Facts and Trends to 2050: Energy and Climate Change," published by the World Business Council for Sustainable Development. The statistic calling out the disparity in overall consumption between rich and poor is from the 1998 UN Human Development Report. You can read (and hear) the quote by Dr. Mathis Wachernagel, director of the sustainability program for the public policy group Redefining Progress, on Pulse of the Planet's website, under the title "Ecological Footprint: Only One Planet" (program #2634), recorded in 2002.

Statistics on the number of barrels of oil used per capita in various nations are from an interview with "contrarian" investment expert Marc Faber: "Dr. Marc Faber: We Are Never Prepared By What We Expect," by Tim Wood, *Resource Investor*, December 1, 2004.

The size and distribution of the current international migrant population was reported in the UN population division's "International Migration Report 2002." The statistic regarding the total migrant population in more than 50 countries was reported in "Global Threats Against U.S. Will Rise, Report Predicts," by Vernon Loeb, *The Washington Post*, December 18, 2000.

Information on dominant migrant populations in the U.S. is from the U.S. Census Bureau's "How the Nation Has Changed Since the 1930 Census" fact sheet, viewable online at http://www.census.gov/pubinfo/www/1930_factsheet.html.

Results of the Pew Global Attitudes Project survey on national attitudes toward immigrants can be found in its report, "What the World Thinks: How Global Publics View Their Lives, Their Countries, The

World, America," December 4, 2002. Publication of the Mexican government's pamphlet for border-crossers and the reactions it evoked were reported in "Word for Word/Border Crossing: A Guide for the Illegal Migrant," by James C. McKinley Jr., *The New York Times*, January 9, 2005.

The urban/rural distribution in the U.S. over time was calculated by the U.S. Census Bureau. Information on the number of million-plus cities and urban population projections to 2015 is from "Cities," by Erla Zwingle, *National Geographic*, November 2002. Other city data comes from the United Nations Division's "World Urbanization Prospects: The 2001 Revision." The fact about China boasting more than 160 cities with 1 million inhabitants comes from *The World Is Flat: A Brief History of the Twenty-first Century*, by Thomas Friedman (New York: Farrar, Straus and Giroux, 2005). Statistics on China's "floating population" come from "China's Floating Population Exceeded 10% of Total," Chinanews.com, January 6, 2005.

Sources for the running list of examples of the depletion of global natural resources: Martin Gorke's *The Death of Our Planet's Species*; CNN (2003); UNESCO; Food and Agriculture Organization; Green Women; Earth Policy Institute; CNN (1997) and *The New York Times* (1990); *National Post* (2003); World Bank; Clean Up Australia; Mother Earth News.

McDonough and Braungart's book is *Cradle to Cradle: Remaking the Way We Make Things* (New York: North Point Press, 2002). William Strauss's book, coauthored with Neil Howe, is *Millennials Rising: The Next Great Generation* (New York: Vintage Books, 2000). Paul Ray and Sherry Anderson's book is *The Cultural Creatives: How 50 Million People Are Changing the World* (New York: Harmony Books, 2000).

Information on the energy efficiency of fluorescent light bulbs comes from ebuild.com; information about refrigerator energy-efficiency comes from the American Council for an Energy-Efficient Economy. Amory Lovins's book is *Winning the Oil Endgame: Innovation for Profits, Jobs, and Security* (Snowmass, CO: Rocky Mountain Institute, September 2004).

Peter Schwartz's *Wired* article is "How Hydrogen Can Save America," April 2003. For more on the CO_2 Capture Project, see its website at http://www.co2captureproject.org.

Information on Germany's 30-acre solar energy plant is from "Germany Shines a Beam on the Future of Energy," by Robert Collier, *The San Francisco Chronicle*, December 20, 2004. For more on Scotland's wave and tidal energy efforts, see the European Marine Energy Centre's website at http://www.emec.org.uk/.

Percentages of energy derived from nuclear power, by nation, are based on data from the International Atomic Energy Association. Janine Benyus is the author of *Biomimicry: Innovation Inspired by Nature* (New York: William Morrow & Co., 1997).

PLANET

The CO_2 concentration figures reported in this chapter (pre-industrial, present, and projected future if our energy patterns continue as expected) are widely known and accepted. While their effects and meanings are the subject of considerable debate, the figures themselves are not. David King's quote is from his article "Climate Change Science: Adapt, Mitigate, or Ignore?" *Science*, January 2004.

Findings from the team of scientists who drilled the 3,623-meter Vostok ice core were reported in "Climate and Atmospheric History of the Past 420,000 Years from the Vostok Ice Core, Antarctica," by J.R. Petit, J. Jouzel, D. Raynaud, et al, *Nature*, June 3, 1999. The findings of the 2004 ice core extraction were also reported in the journal *Nature* ("Eight Glacial Cycles from an Antarctic Ice Core," June 10, 2004).

For more on the Gulf Stream slow down, see "Britain Faces Big Chill as Ocean Current Slows," by Jonathan Leake, *The Sunday Times* (UK), May 8, 2005. Information on the warming of the northern hemisphere is from "Global Warming May Be Speeding Up, Fears Scientist," by John Vidal, *The Guardian* (UK), August 6, 2003.

Neuroscientist Bill Calvin is the author of *A Brain for All Seasons: Human Evolution and Abrupt Climate Change* (Chicago: University of Chicago Press, 2002). Some of his thoughts on climate change were captured at a presentation he made ("When Climate Staggers") at a May 2003 GBN meeting.

The National Research Council's report is "Abrupt Climate Change: Inevitable Surprises," 2002. Paul Hawken's quote if from *What's Next?: Exploring the New Terrain for Business*, by Eamonn Kelly, Peter Leyden, and members of Global Business Network (Cambridge, MA: Perseus Publishing, 2002).

The increase in extreme weather events since the 1950s was reported in "Climate Change Beyond Kyoto," by Ian Johnson, *New Perspectives Quarterly*, December 13, 2004. Data on economic losses due to extreme weather in 2004 is from "Extreme Weather Losses Soar to Record High," by UN Environment Programme, Environmental News Network, December 16, 2004.

The Vladimir Putin quote was reported by *New Scientist* in "Climate Change in Quotes: World Leaders, Scientists, and Campaigners in Their Own Words."

The James Lovelock quote comes from *Gaia: The Practical Science of Planetary Medicine* (London: Gaia Books Limited, 1991). Brian Fagan's quote is from his book, *The Long Summer: How Climate Changes Civilization* (New York: Basic Books, 2004).

The Gwynne Dyer quote (and the statistic about U.S. carbon emissions) is from his column "Kyoto Comes into Effect," February 9, 2004; Dyer's columns run in more than 40 newspapers worldwide.

More on the Maldives island-building project can be found in "Maldives: Islands Get Preview of Future with Unfriendly Sea," by Benjamin Joffe-Walt, *The San Francisco Chronicle*, January 2, 2005.

Section 2: What If?: Changing for the Challenges Ahead

The apocryphal tale of the British Army's arcane artillery ritual comes from Elting E. Morison's *Men, Machines, and Modern Times* (Cambridge, MA: MIT Press, 1966).

Chapter 9: Governance

A nice, short summary of John Williamson's notion of "Washington Consensus" can be found on the Center for International Development at Harvard University website: http://www.cid.harvard.edu/cidtrade/issues/washington.html.

The figure for the number of nations that hold multi-party elections comes from "World Civilisation: Barking Up the Wrong Tree?" by Sergio Vieira de Mello (former United Nations High Commissioner for Human Rights), *New Academy Review*, Winter 2003.

Eliot A. Cohen's essay, "History and Hyperpower," appeared in the July/August 2004 issue of *Foreign Affairs*. His quote is used by permission of Foreign Affairs. Copyright © 2004 by the Council on Foreign Relations Inc. The Jean Monnet quote comes from *Memoirs*, translated by Richard Mayne (London: William Collins and Son Ltd., 1976).

Pete Hamill's column on the citizen assembly brought together by the Civic Alliance to Rebuild Downtown New York is "Thrilling Show of People Power," *The New York Daily News*, July 21, 2002. Information on British Columbia's Citizens' Assembly on Electoral Reform can be found on its website, http://www.citizensassembly.bc.ca/public. The Zeguo story is from "China's New Frontiers: Tests of Democracy and Dissent," by Howard W. French, *The New York Times*, June 19, 2005. Andrew Selee's article can be read online at http://www.deliberative-democracy.net/cart3_pfv.html. His words are used by permission of Canada's International Development Research Centre (www.idrc.ca).

The source for Howard W. French's column on the experiments in democracy all over China is "China's New Frontiers: Tests of Democracy and Dissent," *The New York Times*, June 19, 2005.

Reinicke and Deng's book, *Critical Choices,* was published by the International Development Research Centre in 2000. Jean-François Rischard's book, *High Noon: 20 Global Problems, 20 Years to Solve Them,* was published by Perseus Press in October 2002. Martin Albrow's book, *The Global Age: State and Society Beyond Modernity,* was published by Stanford University Press in 1996.

James Moore's essay, "The Second Superpower Rears Its Beautiful Head" (March 31, 2003), is available on the website of Harvard Law School's Berkman Center for Internet & Society, where he is a senior fellow: http://cyber.law.harvard.edu/people/jmoore/secondsuperpower.html. His quote is included in this chapter by his kind permission.

Chapter 10: Innovation

C.K. Prahalad's book, referenced earlier in the endnotes, is *The Fortune at the Bottom of the Pyramid: Eradicating Poverty Through Profits* (Upper Saddle River, NJ: Wharton School Publishing, August 2004).

For more on Ralf Hotchkiss's organization Whirlwind Wheelchair International, see its website: http://www.whirlwindwheelchair.org/index.htm. For more on NEPAD's African Biosciences Initiative, see its website: http://www.nepadst.org/index.html.

Data on India's climbing R&D-to-sales ratios and its solar energy usage come from "India: A Champion of New Technologies," by Ashok Parthasarathi, *Nature*, March 6, 2003.

For the latest information on Brian Sager's company Nanosolar, see its website: http://www.nanosolar.com/.

More information on large-scale tidal power projects in South Korea and China can be found in "South Korea to Build World's Largest Tidal Power Plant" (May 25, 2005) and "China Endorses 300 MW Ocean Energy Project" (November 2, 2004), both in *Renewable Energy Access*.

Information on China's efforts to train African and Latin American solar power and irrigation technicians comes from "China to Train Developing Nations in Solar Technologies," by Jia Hepeng, SciDev.Net, August 20, 2004.

James Lovelock's quote is from his May 24, 2004 article in *The Independent* (UK), "Nuclear Power Is the Only Green Solution." Spencer Reiss's article on China's nuclear efforts, "Let a Thousand Reactors Bloom," ran in the September 2004 edition of *Wired*.

The OECD study referenced in this chapter is "Understanding the Brain: Towards a New Learning Science," published in 2002. Information on the short half-life of engineering knowledge is from "Lifelong Learning for Engineers: Riding the Whirlwind," by Ernest T. Smerdon, *The Bridge* (a publication of the National Academy of Engineering), volume 26, number 1/2, Spring/Summer 1996.

Howard Gardner is the author of *Intelligence Reframed: Multiple Intelligences for the 21st Century* (New York: Basic Books, September 1999) and *Changing Minds: The Art and Science of Changing Our Own and Other People's Minds* (Cambridge, MA: Harvard Business School Press, March 2004), among others. Daniel Goleman's groundbreaking book is *Emotional Intelligence: Why It Can Matter More Than IQ* (New York: Bantam Books, September 1995).

For more on Singapore's "Thinking Schools, Learning Nation" program, see "Implementation of the 'Thinking Schools, Learning Nation' Initiative in Singapore," by Agnes Chang Shook Cheong, *Journal of Southeast Asian Education*, Volume 2, Number 1, 2001. Robert Brown made his statement about education in Singapore during a visit by the International Academic Advisory Panel (of which he was a member) to Singapore in 2003.

For more on Nelly Ribot's work in Argentina, written in her own words, see "My Experiences Using Multiple Intelligences," available on the website of New Horizons for Learning: http://www.newhorizons.org/trans/international/ribot.htm.

For information on free education efforts in Africa, see "In Africa, Free Schools Feed a Different Hunger," by Celia W. Dugger, *The New York Times*, October 24, 2004. SciDev.Net reported on India's education satellite in "India's 'Teacher in the Sky,'" by K. S. Jayaraman, November 29, 2004. Information on India's Barefoot College comes from "Barefoot College Provides Model of Self-Development at Village Level," *Global Village News and Resources*, Issue 57, March 10, 2003, and from the Barefoot College website (http://www.barefootcollege.org). For more on the UNESCO Task Force for Education in the Twenty-first Century and its "four pillars" of education, visit its website: http://www.unesco.org/delors/. More information on Kerala's Akshaya Project can be found on its website at http://www.akshaya.net/.

Jonathon Levy's quote comes from his article "The Next China Revolution," *Training and Development Magazine*, May 2003.

Section 3: What's Next?: Scenarios for the Next Decade

More information about the role that text messaging may have played in the early demise of would-be blockbusters like *The Hulk* can be found in "Texting Blamed for Summer Movie Flops," by Andrew Gumbel, *The Independent* (UK), August 18, 2003.

The statistics about U.S. percentages of global population and consumption come from data reported by the Foreign Policy Research Institute and the Economic Research Service. The United States' share of global R&D spending comes from figures published by the OECD in the 2003 edition of its Research and Development Statistics report.

China's annual military spending is a matter of some debate. While China has said that it spent $25 billion in 2003, the U.S. Defense Department's estimates of China's military spending for that year topped $65 billion. The RAND Corporation puts the figure at $31 billion to $38 billion. For more on this discrepancy, see "U.S. Overstated China's Military Spending," by Jim Wolf, Reuters, May 20, 2005.

Section 4: So What?: Acting in an Era of Transformation

For more detail on Altria's "four simple questions" approach to decision-making, see "The Altria Family of Companies: Learning to Change," a speech delivered by Altria's director of government affairs policy and out-reach, Marcia Sullivan, April 11, 2003. The speech is available on Altria's website: http://www.altria.com/media/executive_speech/03_09_02 _sullivanKilleenspeech.asp.

Theodore Hesburgh's full quote is even better: "The very essence of leadership is that you have to have a vision. It's got to be a vision you artic-ulate clearly and forcefully on every occasion. You can't blow an uncertain trumpet." The John Maynard Keynes quote comes from his essay "National Self-Sufficiency," *The Yale Review*, vol. 22, no. 4 (June 1933).

The Colin Powell quote about leadership and confidence is No. 2 on a list of 18 leadership secrets included in the book, *The Leadership Secrets of Colin Powell*, by Oren Harari (New York: McGraw-Hill, January 2002). The words of Rudyard Kipling are from his poem "If," from his collec-tion *Rewards and Fairies* (1909).

Ronald Reagan's parting words come from a famous saying by the influential Jewish scholar Rabbi Hillel: "If I am not for myself, then who will be for me? And if I am only for myself, than what am I? And if not now, when?"

Afterword: Using This Book in Your Life and Work

In *Powerful Times*, I have set out some frameworks that have proved extremely useful for my own thinking and learning about our volatile world, and have populated these frameworks with information and ideas that I consider highly important. But learning only becomes embedded and useful when it is made immediately relevant and specific to your own context.

Therefore, I hope that you will find it helpful to reflect on how the content of this book relates to you and your organization. To facilitate your thinking, I have posed a series of questions about each of the main chapters that might help structure your ideas and insights. You can turn to these pages as you read *Powerful Times* to make notes, or simply review the questions after you have finished reading the book. I hope that you might also be interested in using this book and the questions as a catalyst for strategic conversation within your team or organization. And I hope that many of you will share your ideas on the *Powerful Times* website—**http://www.powerfultimes.net**—a place where we can explore the future together over time. I look forward to meeting you there.

What's Happening?: Predicting the Present

CLARITY AND CRAZINESS

We enjoy unprecedented **clarity**, driven by abundant information, powerful analysis, ubiquitous connectivity, and remarkable transparency—yet these same forces also empower **craziness**, as every storyline and conspiracy theory, no matter how bizarre, can be supported by some distortion of real data and spread like a virus.

What have you seen in your life and work that illustrates either or both sides of this dynamic tension?

What else is happening in the world today that is better understood through this dynamic tension?

In what ways has it mattered already to you and/or your organization?

How might it matter more and differently in the future?

Name one key risk and one key opportunity that this tension poses for you and/or your organization.

What should you be tracking/monitoring that is not currently on
your radar?

Who in the world at large and within your own organization do you
wish would understand this dynamic tension better, and why?

SECULAR AND SACRED

Secular ideals continue to drive much of modern civilization, especially with regards to governance and commerce—yet these have to coexist and co-evolve with powerful (and powerfully different) **sacred** worldviews.

What have you seen in your life and work that illustrates either or both sides of this dynamic tension?

What is happening in the world today that is better understood through this dynamic tension?

In what ways has it mattered already to you and/or your organization?

How might it matter more and differently in the future?

Name one key risk and one key opportunity that this tension poses for you and/or your organization.

What should you be tracking/monitoring that is not currently on your radar?

Who in the world at large and within your own organization do you wish would understand this dynamic tension better, and why?

POWER AND VULNERABILITY

The U.S. seems set to call upon its unmatchable military **power**, yet may face challenges that hard power alone cannot meet even as its soft power weakens—contributing to a growing sense of **vulnerability** in the Western world as a variety of looming threats come into sharper focus.

What have you seen in your life and work that illustrates either or both sides of this dynamic tension?

What is happening in the world today that is better understood through this dynamic tension?

In what ways has it mattered already to you and/or your organization?

How might it matter more and differently in the future?

Name one key risk and one key opportunity that this tension poses for you and/or your organization.

What should you be tracking/monitoring that is not currently on your radar?

Who in the world at large and within your own organization do you wish would understand this dynamic tension better, and why?

TECHNOLOGY ACCELERATION AND PUSHBACK

Technology **acceleration** proceeds apace, providing us with greater power to manipulate our world and to increasingly manipulate nature and the very essence of life itself—thus triggering increased (but globally uneven) moral, ethical, and pragmatic concern and **pushback** against the untrammeled pursuit of science.

What have you seen in your life and work that illustrates either or both sides of this dynamic tension?

What is happening in the world today that is better understood through this dynamic tension?

In what ways has it mattered already to you and/or your organization?

How might it matter more and differently in the future?

Name one key risk and one key opportunity that this tension poses for you and/or your organization.

What should you be tracking/monitoring that is not currently on your radar?

Who in the world at large and within your own organization do you wish would understand this dynamic tension better, and why?

INTANGIBLE AND PHYSICAL ECONOMIES

The economy becomes increasingly **intangible** as the relationship between mass and value continues to decline in a world of services, experiences, and virtualization—yet the **physical** economy also matters more as we have to renew and create critical infrastructure everywhere.

What have you seen in your life and work that illustrates either or both sides of this dynamic tension?

What is happening in the world today that is better understood through this dynamic tension?

In what ways has it mattered already to you and/or your organization?

How might it matter more and differently in the future?

Name one key risk and one key opportunity that this tension poses for you and/or your organization.

What should you be tracking/monitoring that is not currently on your radar?

Who in the world at large and within your own organization do you wish would understand this dynamic tension better, and why?

PROSPERITY AND DECLINE

Prosperity spreads further around the globe as new players exert increasing influence on the world economy—while **decline** in some countries and regions and among certain groups leads to increased polarization between those doing well and those faring poorly.

What have you seen in your life and work that illustrates either or both sides of this dynamic tension?

What is happening in the world today that is better understood through this dynamic tension?

In what ways has it mattered already to you and/or your organization?

How might it matter more and differently in the future?

Name one key risk and one key opportunity that this tension poses for you and/or your organization.

What should you be tracking/monitoring that is not currently on your radar?

Who in the world at large and within your own organization do you wish would understand this dynamic tension better, and why?

PEOPLE AND PLANET

The needs and expectations of **people** have led to an increased mandate to pay attention to the principles of sustainability—yet the **planet** continues to exert its own clear authority and autonomy, leading to deeper and urgent concern about the robustness of our civilization's footprint.

What have you seen in your life and work that illustrates either or both sides of this dynamic tension?

What is happening in the world today that is better understood through this dynamic tension?

In what ways has it mattered already to you and/or your organization?

How might it matter more and differently in the future?

Name one key risk and one key opportunity that this tension poses for you and/or your organization.

What should you be tracking/monitoring that is not currently on
your radar?

Who in the world at large and within your own organization do you
wish would understand this dynamic tension better, and why?

CONSIDER THE SEVEN DYNAMIC TENSIONS AS A WHOLE

Clarity and Craziness...Secular and Sacred...Power and Vulnerability...Technology Acceleration and Pushback...Intangible and Physical...Prosperity and Decline...People and Planet

---

Looking across these dynamic tensions, what are the three or four most important uncertainties facing you and/or your organization?

What assumptions does your organization tend to make that you should be challenging as a consequence?

What If?: Changing for the Challenges Ahead

ORGANIZING FOR CHANGE

What are some examples of citadel characteristics in your organization? Of web characteristics?

What is one serious unresolved tension between them?

How can the power of both citadel and web approaches be better aligned in your organization?

GOVERNANCE

What are the most compelling experiments in governance that you have observed?

What types of experiments—in deliberative democracy, local governance, international collaboration—would you like to see happen?

What new risks and opportunities might these or future experiments create for you and/or your organization?

INNOVATION

What additional evidence do you see that innovation is coming from new places and from the bottom up?

What risks and opportunities might these trends create for you and/or your organization?

How might this new order help organizations, including yours, to clarify and achieve their moral purpose?

What's Next?: Scenarios for the Next Decade

NEW AMERICAN CENTURY

This is a future in which the United States achieves unparalleled leadership in world affairs, reasserting and strengthening its influence, and essentially establishing the core values and rules—economic, political, and cultural—by which the entire world will play for generations.

What evidence do you see today that makes this a credible scenario?

How well prepared are you and/or your organization for this scenario?

What new risks and opportunities would you face if this did, indeed, prove to be the future?

What could you be tracking today that would provide an early indication that this scenario is unfolding?

Patchwork Powers

This is a future in which geopolitical and economic power and influence is distributed and shared between many different international bodies, geographical regions, and nation-states. This is also a future in which influence is projected through a complex and sometimes confusing patchwork of alliances and treaties.

What evidence do you see today that makes this a credible scenario?

How well prepared are you and/or your organization for this scenario?

What new risks and opportunities would you face if this did, indeed, prove to be the future?

What could you be tracking today that would provide an early indication that this scenario is unfolding?

EMERGENCE

This is a future in which the established, traditional models of power and leadership prove to be largely unsuited to the challenges of a world of increased interdependence, complexity, uncertainty, and diversity. Instead, change and coherence come from the bottom up, as centralized and hierarchical governments, international institutions, and many large corporations prove slow to adapt to new challenges and opportunities.

What evidence do you see today that makes this a credible scenario?

How well prepared are you and/or your organization for this scenario?

What new risks and opportunities would you face if this did, indeed, prove to be the future?

What could you be tracking today that would provide an early indication that this scenario is unfolding?

CONSIDERING THE SCENARIOS AS A WHOLE
New American Century...Patchwork Powers...Emergence

Which of these scenarios seems closest to you and your organization's "official future"—how you think the world will unfold?

Which scenario do you find most appealing to live in?

Which scenario do you find least appealing to live in?

Overall, having looked at these three alternative futures, what do you think you and your organization are least prepared for? How could you become better prepared?

So What?: Acting in an Era of Transformation

How might your organization's agenda have to change in these powerful times?

How well does your organization harness and align the powers and passions of its people?

How might purpose and participation be better deployed within your organization?

What might accelerate the emergence of a global "we"?

In what ways might you personally be affected by the emergence of a bigger and more global sense of "we?" How might you contribute?

Post your answers to these questions at **http://www.powerfultimes.net**.

Index

Ideas. Action. Impact.
Wharton School Publishing

Bernard Baumohl
THE SECRETS OF ECONOMIC INDICATORS
Hidden Clues to Future Economic Trends and Investment Opportunities

Randall Billingsley
UNDERSTANDING ARBITRAGE
An Intuitive Approach to Investment Analysis

Sayan Chatterjee
FAILSAFE STRATEGIES
Profit and Grow from Risks That Others Avoid

Tony Davila, Marc Epstein, and Robert Shelton
MAKING INNOVATION WORK
How to Manage It, Measure It, and Profit from It

Sunil Gupta, Donald R. Lehmann
MANAGING CUSTOMERS AS INVESTMENTS
The Strategic Value of Customers in the Long Run

Stuart L. Hart
CAPITALISM AT THE CROSSROADS
The Unlimited Business Opportunities in Solving the World's Most Difficult Problems

Lawrence G. Hrebiniak
MAKING STRATEGY WORK
Leading Effective Execution and Change

Jon M. Huntsman
WINNERS NEVER CHEAT
Everyday Values We Learned as Children (But May Have Forgotten)

Eamonn Kelly
POWERFUL TIMES
Rising to the Challenge of Our Uncertain World

Doug Lennick, Fred Kiel
MORAL INTELLIGENCE
Enhancing Business Performance and Leadership Success

Vijay Mahajan, Kamini Banga
THE 86 PERCENT SOLUTION
How to Succeed in the Biggest Market Opportunity of the Next 50 Years

Alfred A. Marcus
BIG WINNERS AND BIG LOSERS
The 4 Secrets of Long-Term Business Success and Failure

Robert Mittelstaedt
WILL YOUR NEXT MISTAKE BE FATAL?
Avoiding the Chain of Mistakes That Can Destroy Your Organization

Peter Navarro
THE WELL-TIMED STRATEGY
Managing the Business Cycle for Competitive Advantage

Capitalism at the Crossroads
The Unlimited Business Opportunities in Solving the World's Most Difficult Problems
BY STUART L. HART

"Professor Hart is on the leading edge of making sustainability an understandable and useful framework for building business value."
—Chad Holliday, Chairman and CEO, DuPont

Capitalism is at a crossroads, facing international terrorism, worldwide environmental change, and an accelerating backlash against globalization. Your company is at a crossroads, too: finding new strategies for profitable growth is now more challenging than it has ever been. Both sets of problems are intimately linked: the best way to recharge growth is to pursue strategies that also solve today's most crucial social and environmental problems. In this book, you'll learn how to identify sustainable products and technologies that can drive new growth; how to market profitably to four billion people who have been bypassed or damaged by globalization; how to build effective new bridges with stakeholders; and much more.

ISBN 0131439871, © 2005, 288 pp., $27.95

The Next Global Stage
Challenges and Opportunities in Our Borderless World
BY KENICHI OHMAE

A radically new world is taking shape from the ashes of yesterday's nation-based economic world. To succeed, you'll need to act on a global stage-and master entirely new rules about the sources of economic power and the drivers of growth. In *The Next Global Stage*, legendary business strategist Kenichi Ohmae synthesizes today's emerging trends into the first coherent view of tomorrow's global economy, and its implications for politics, business, and personal success. Ohmae begins with a clear-eyed view of what's already happened: the triumph of globalization and the abject failure of traditional economists to make sense of it. Next, he explores the dynamics of the new regional state, rapidly emerging as tomorrow's most potent form of economic organization. He introduces the powerful concept of 'platforms' for economic progress, illuminating examples ranging from the use of English to Microsoft Windows. Next, Ohmae offers a blueprint for businesses, governments, and individuals who intend to thrive in this new environment: what they must change, and what can endure. Ohmae concludes with a detailed look at corporate strategy in an era where it's tougher to define competitors, companies, and customers than ever before. As important as Huntington's *The Clash of Civilizations,* as fascinating and relevant as Friedman's *The Lexus and the Olive Tree,* this book doesn't just explain what's happened: it prepares you for what will happen next.

ISBN 013147944X, © 2005, 312 pp., $27.95